REA's Test Prep Book

(a sample of the <u>hundreds of letters</u> REA receives each year)

(more on next page)

(continued from front page)

" I just wanted to thank you for helping me get a great score
on the AP U.S. History exam... Thank you for making great test preps! "

Student, Los Angeles, CA

" Your *Fundamentals of Engineering Exam* book was the absolute best
preparation I could have had for the exam, and it is one of the major
reasons I did so well and passed the FE on my first try. "

Student, Sweetwater, TN

" I used your book to prepare for the test and found that the advice and the
sample tests were highly relevant... Without using any other material, I earned
very high scores and will be going to the graduate school of my choice. "

Student, New Orleans, LA

" What I found in your book was a wealth of information sufficient to shore up
my basic skills in math and verbal... The section on analytical ability was
excellent. The practice tests were challenging and the answer explanations most
helpful. It certainly is the *Best Test Prep for the GRE*! "

Student, Pullman, WA

" I really appreciate the help from your excellent book. Please keep up
the great work. "

Student, Albuquerque, NM

" I am writing to thank you for your test preparation... your book helped me
immeasurably and I have nothing but praise for your *GRE* preparation. "

Student, Benton Harbor, MI

(more on back page)

THE BEST TEST PREPARATION FOR THE
SAT II: Subject Test

GERMAN

Michael Büsges
Instructor of German
Rutgers University, New Brunswick, New Jersey

Frederic Curry, Ph.D.
Associate Professor of German
Broward Community College, Fort Lauderdale, Florida

James V. McMahon, Ph.D.
Associate Professor of German
Emory University, Atlanta, Georgia

Peter Schroeck, Ph.D.
Adjunct Professor
Raritan Valley Community College, North Branch, New Jersey

Linda Thomas, Ph.D.
Associate Professor of German
Randolph–Macon Woman's College, Lynchburg, Virginia

Research & Education Association
61 Ethel Road West
Piscataway, New Jersey 08854

The Best Test Preparation for the
SAT II: SUBJECT TEST IN GERMAN

Printed in the United States of America

Library of Congress Control Number 2001088130

International Standard Book Number 0-87891-402-1

Research & Education Association
61 Ethel Road West
Piscataway, New Jersey 08854

REA supports the effort to conserve and
protect environmental resources by
printing on recycled papers.

CONTENTS

Chapter 10
ADJECTIVES A-44

Chapter 11
WORD ORDER A-48

Chapter 12
SPECIAL PROBLEMS A-53

ABOUT RESEARCH & EDUCATION ASSOCIATION

Research & Education Association (REA) is an organization of educators, scientists, and engineers specializing in various academic fields. Founded in 1959 with the purpose of disseminating the most recently developed scientific information to groups in industry, government, high schools, and universities, REA has since become a successful and highly respected publisher of study aids, test preps, handbooks, and reference works.

REA's Test Preparation series includes study guides for all academic levels in almost all disciplines. Research & Education Association publishes test preps for students who have not yet completed high school, as well as high school students preparing to enter college. Students from countries around the world seeking to attend college in the United States will find the assistance they need in REA's publications. For college students seeking advanced degrees, REA publishes test preps for many major graduate school admission examinations in a wide variety of disciplines, including engineering, law, and medicine. Students at every level, in every field, with every ambition can find what they are looking for among REA's publications.

Unlike most test preparation books—which present only a few practice tests that bear little resemblance to the actual exams—REA's series presents tests that accurately depict the official exams in both degree of difficulty and types of questions. REA's practice tests are always based upon the most recently administered exams, and include every type of question that can be expected on the actual exams.

REA's publications and educational materials are highly regarded and continually receive an unprecedented amount of praise from professionals, instructors, librarians, parents, and students. Our authors are as diverse as the subject matter represented in the books we publish. They are well-known in their respective disciplines and serve on the faculties of prestigious high schools, colleges, and universities throughout the United States and Canada.

ACKNOWLEDGMENTS

We would like to thank Dr. Max Fogiel, President, for his overall guidance, which brought this publication to completion; Larry B. Kling, Quality Control Manager of Books in Print, for his editorial direction; Melanie Seickel, Editorial Assistant, for coordinating the revision of this book; Beth Hackett and Bernadette Brick, Editorial Assistants, and Nicole Bator for their editorial contributions; and Michael C. Cote and Barbara Jacinto for typesetting the manuscript.

PASSING THE SAT II: GERMAN SUBJECT TEST

ABOUT THIS BOOK

This book provides you with an accurate and complete representation of the SAT II: German Subject Test. Inside you will find a complete course review, as well as six REA practice tests based on the actual exam. Our practice tests contain every type of question that you can expect to encounter on the actual exam. Following each test you will find an answer key with detailed explanations designed to help you master the test material.

ABOUT THE TEST

Who takes the test and what is it used for?

Students planning to attend college take the SAT II: German Subject Test for one of two reasons:

(1) Because it is an admission requirement of the college or university to which they are applying,

   OR

(2) To demonstrate proficiency in German.

The SAT II: German exam is designed for students who have taken two, three, or four years of German.

Who administers the test?

The SAT II: German Subject Test is developed by the College Board and administered by Educational Testing Service (ETS). The test development process involves the assistance of educators throughout the country, and is designed and implemented to ensure that the content and difficulty level of the test are appropriate.

When and where is the test given?

The SAT II: German Subject Test is offered once a year, in June, at many locations throughout the country.

To receive information on upcoming administrations of the exam, consult the publication *Taking the SAT II: Subject Tests,* which can be obtained from your guidance counselor or by contacting:

College Board SAT Program
P.O. Box 6200
Princeton, NJ 08541-6200
Phone: (609) 771-7600
Website: http://www.collegeboard.com

Is there a registration fee?

You must pay a registration fee to take the SAT II: German Subject Test. Consult the publication *Taking the SAT II: Subject Tests* for information on the fee structure. Financial assistance may be granted in certain situations. To find out if you qualify and to register for assistance, contact your academic advisor.

HOW TO USE THIS BOOK

What do I study first?

Remember that the SAT II: German Subject Test is designed to test knowledge that you have acquired throughout your education. Therefore, the best way to prepare for the exam is to refresh yourself by thoroughly studying our review material and taking the sample tests provided in this book. Our practice tests will familiarize you with the types of questions, directions, and format of the SAT II: German Subject Test.

To begin your studies, read over our course review and suggestions for test-taking. Then take the first practice test to determine your area(s) of weakness. When you're done, restudy the review material, focusing on your specific problem areas. The course review includes the information you need to know when taking the exam. Make sure to take the remaining practice tests to further test yourself and become familiar with the format of the SAT II: German Subject Test. Further recommendations are detailed in our study schedule in the front of this book.

When should I start studying?

It is never too early to start studying for the SAT II: German test. The earlier you begin, the more time you will have to sharpen your skills. Do not procrastinate! Cramming is *not* an effective way to study! The sooner you learn the format of the exam, the more comfortable you will be when you take it.

FORMAT OF THE SAT II: GERMAN TEST

The SAT II: German is a one-hour exam consisting of 80 to 85 multiple-choice questions that are designed to measure the gradual development of competence in the German language acquired over a period of years.

About 50% of the test measures vocabulary and structure in context or grammar. The rest measures reading comprehension. In light of Educational Testing Service's stated intention to comply with the German spelling reform (*Rechtschreibreform*), REA, too, has sought to adhere to the spelling reform throughout this book.

SCORING THE SAT II: GERMAN TEST

How do I score my practice tests?

The SAT II: German Test, like all other SAT Subject Tests, is scored on a 200–800 scale. Your exam is scored by crediting one point for each correct answer and deducting one-third of a point for each incorrect answer. There is no deduction for answers that are left blank. Use the worksheet below to calculate your raw score and to record your scores for the six practice tests. Use the Practice-Test Score Conversion Table that follows to convert your raw score to a scaled score.

PRACTICE-TEST SCORING WORKSHEET

_____ − (_____ x 1/3) = _____
Number correct   Number incorrect   Raw Score
                        (do not include   (round to nearest
                        unanswered questions)   whole point)

	Raw Score	Scaled Score
Test 1	_____	_____
Test 2	_____	_____
Test 3	_____	_____
Test 4	_____	_____
Test 5	_____	_____
Test 6	_____	_____

PRACTICE-TEST SCORE CONVERSION TABLE*

SAT II: Subject Test in German

Raw Score	Scaled Score	Raw Score	Scaled Score	Raw Score	Scaled Score
80	780	45	550	10	360
79	770	44	540	9	360
78	760	43	540	8	350
77	750	42	530	7	350
76	740	41	530	6	340
75	730	40	520	5	340
74	720	39	520	4	330
73	710	38	510	3	320
72	700	37	500	2	320
71	690	36	500	1	310
70	680	35	490	0	310
69	670	34	490	-1	300
68	670	33	480	-2	300
67	660	32	480	-3	290
66	660	31	470	-4	290
65	650	30	470	-5	280
64	650	29	460	-6	280
63	640	28	460	-7	270
62	640	27	450	-8	270
61	630	26	450	-9	260
60	630	25	440	-10	260
59	620	24	440	-11	250
58	620	23	430	-12	250
57	610	22	430	-13	240
56	610	21	420	-14	230
55	600	20	410	-15	230
54	590	19	410	-16	220
53	590	18	400	-17	220
52	580	17	400	-18	210
51	580	16	390	-19	210
50	570	15	390	-20	200
49	570	14	380	-21	200
48	560	13	380	-22	200
47	560	12	370	-23	200
46	550	11	370	-24	200
				-25	200
				-26	200
				-27	200

*Your scaled scores on REA's practice tests may be higher or lower than your score on the actual test. Bear in mind that scaled scores for different editions of the SAT II: German Test are adjusted to take into account small shifts in its level of difficulty.

When will I receive my score report and what will it look like?

You can expect to receive your score report within about five weeks after you take the test. This report will include your scores, percentile ranks, and interpretive information.

STUDYING FOR THE SAT II: GERMAN TEST

It is critical to choose the time and place for studying that works best for you. Some students may set aside a certain number of hours every morning to study, while others may choose to study at night before going to sleep. Only you can determine when and where your study time will be most effective. Be consistent and use your time wisely. Work out a study routine and stick to it!

When you take the practice tests, try to make your testing conditions as much like the actual test as possible. Turn your television and radio off, and sit down at a quiet desk or table free from distraction. Make sure to clock yourself with a timer.

As you complete each practice test, score it and thoroughly review the explanations to the questions you answered incorrectly; however, do not review too much at any one time. Concentrate on one problem area at a time by reviewing the questions and explanations, and by studying our review until you are confident you completely understand the material.

Keep track of your scores. By doing so, you will be able to gauge your progress and discover general weaknesses in particular sections. You should carefully study the reviews that cover your areas of difficulty, as this will build your skills in those areas.

TEST-TAKING TIPS

Although you may be unfamiliar with standardized tests such as the SAT II: German Subject Test, there are many ways to acquaint yourself with this type of examination and help alleviate your test-taking anxieties. Here are six specific ways you can give yourself a leg up:

Become comfortable with the format of the exam. When you are practicing, simulate the conditions under which you will be taking the actual test. Stay calm and pace yourself. This will allow you to sit down for the actual exam with much more confidence.

Read all of the possible answers. Just because you think you have found the correct response, do not automatically assume that it is the best answer. Read through each choice to be sure that you are not making a mistake by jumping to conclusions.

Use the process of elimination. Go through each answer to a question and eliminate as many of the answer choices as possible. By eliminating just two answer choices, you give yourself a better chance of getting the item correct, since there will only be two choices left from which to make your guess.

Work quickly and steadily. You will have only 1 hour, so avoid focusing on any one question too long. Taking the practice tests in this book will help you learn to budget your time.

Learn the directions and format for each section of the test. Familiarizing yourself with the directions and format of the exam will save you valuable time on the day of the actual test.

Be sure that the answer oval you are marking corresponds to the number of the question in the test booklet. Since the exam is graded by machine, marking one wrong answer can throw off your answer key and your score. Be extremely careful when filling in your answer sheet.

Before the Test

Make sure you know where your test center is well in advance of your test day so you do not get lost on the day of the test. On the night before the test, gather together the materials you will need the next day:

- Your admission ticket
- Two forms of identification (e.g., driver's license, student identification card, or current alien registration card)
- Two No. 2 pencils with erasers
- Directions to the test center
- A wristwatch (if you wish) but not one that makes noise, as it may disturb other test-takers

On the day of the test, you should wake up early (it is hoped after a decent night's rest) and have a good breakfast. Dress comfortably so that you are not distracted by being too hot or too cold while taking the test. Also, plan to arrive at the test center early. This will allow you to collect your thoughts and relax before the test, and will also spare you the stress of being late. If you arrive after the test begins, you will not be admitted and you will not receive a refund.

During the Test

When you arrive at the test center, try to find a seat where you feel you will be comfortable. Follow all the rules and instructions given by the test supervisor. If you do not, you risk being dismissed from the test and having your scores canceled.

Once all the test materials are passed out, the test instructor will give you directions for filling out your answer sheet. Fill this sheet out carefully since the information you supply will appear on your score report.

After the Test

When you have completed the SAT II: German Subject Test, you may hand in your test materials and leave. Then, go home and relax!

INDEPENDENT STUDY SCHEDULE
SAT II: GERMAN SUBJECT TEST

This study schedule is set up to thoroughly prepare you for the SAT II: German Subject Test. Although it is designed to allow you to pace yourself comfortably over an eight-week preparation period, it can be condensed into a four-week course by collapsing each two-week period into one. Be sure to set aside enough time—at least two hours each day—to study. No matter which study schedule works best for you, however, the more time you spend acquainting yourself with the subject matter and the test, the more prepared and relaxed you will feel on Test Day.

Week	Activity
1	Read the introduction to this book, which details critical aspects of the SAT II: German Subject Test for you. Then take Practice Test 1 to determine your strengths and weaknesses. Score each section by using the worksheet on page xiii. You'll now have a baseline for your study needs.
2	Carefully read and study the Course Review included in this book. Cover all the material, but highlight those areas that gave you trouble in Practice Test 1. Go through each of the items you answered incorrectly and make sure you understand how to arrive at the correct answer. Recognizing where you went wrong will boost your confidence and, as a practical matter, help you avoid making the same mistakes come Test Day.
3 and 4	Take Practice Test 2 and Practice Test 3. After scoring each exam, flag your incorrect answers. For any types of questions or particular subjects that continue to pose difficulty for you, check our detailed explanations and consult our Course Review. →

Week	Activity
5 and **6**	Take Practice Test 4 and Practice Test 5. After scoring each exam, flag your incorrect answers. For any types of questions or particular subjects that continue to pose difficulty for you, check our detailed explanations and consult our Course Review.
7	Take Practice Test 6. After scoring your exam, carefully review the explanations for all your incorrect answers. By this point, you should be nearing mastery of the subject matter. Again, consult our Course Review as often as possible to ensure that you're sufficiently at ease with our model tests.
8	This is the week you'll consolidate your gains and eliminate any continuing subject-matter weaknesses. Retake one or more of the practice tests (as you deem necessary), paying particular attention to the questions with which you had difficulty the first time around. Going through the practice tests once again will put you on completely familiar terms with the subject matter and the SAT II itself.

Good Luck on the SAT II: Subject Test in German!

Chapter 1

NOUNS

GENDER

German has three genders: masculine *(der)*, feminine *(die)*, and neuter *(das)*. Persons have natural gender, i.e., the nouns for man and brother are masculine, the nouns for sister and woman are feminine. The gender of nouns referring to objects or abstractions must be memorized, i.e., the nouns for table and ball are masculine, the nouns for ink and school are feminine, and the nouns for house and book are neuter. All nouns are capitalized.

The ending *-in* is added to the masculine form of occupations and many forms designating nationality to form feminine nouns, i.e., *der Professor, die Professorin, der Arzt, die Ärztin, der Däne, die Dänin, der Japaner, die Japanerin*, etc.

All nouns ending in *-chen* or *-lein* (diminutives) are neuter: *das Kätzchen, das Mädchen, das Fräulein, das Büchlein*, etc.

All nouns ending in *-heit*, *-keit*, *-ie*, *-ik*, *-sion*, *-tion*, *-schaft*, *-tät*, or *-ung* are feminine: *die Kindheit, die Geschwindigkeit, die Bürokratie, die Grammatik, die Nation, die Passion, die Freundschaft, die Nationalität, die Gründung*, etc.

Most nouns ending in *-e* are feminine: *die Katze, die Note, die Woche*.

The names of most countries, such as *Deutschland* and *Frankreich*, are neuter. Articles are seldom used with countries or cities, except for the feminine names of countries, i.e., *die Schweiz, die Türkei*.

PLURALS

There are five possibilities for the formation of plural nouns:

1. **no change** — nouns with more than one syllable ending in *-el*, *-en*, *-er*; all diminutives (nouns ending in *-chen* or *-lein*); no feminine nouns except for *Mütter* and *Töchter*; (i.e., *die Onkel, die Wagen, die Brüder, die Mädchen*)
2. *-e* – most one-syllable masculine nouns; some one-syllable neuter nouns (i.e., *die Söhne, die Beine*)

3. **-er** – most one-syllable neuter nouns; some one-syllable masculine nouns (i.e., *die Kinder, die Wälder*)
4. **-en** or **-n** – most feminine nouns; masculine nouns ending in **-e** (i.e., *die Wochen, die Krankheiten, die Jungen*); all feminine nouns that are formed by adding **-in** to the masculine add **-nen** (i.e., *die Lehrerinnen*)
5. **-s** – most foreign "loan words" (i.e., *die Restaurants, die Büros*)

Most nouns add an internal umlaut.

COMPOUND NOUNS

A compound noun consists of two or more joined nouns, i.e., *das Wochenende, der Handschuh, die Donauschifffahrtsgesellschaft*. A compound noun may also consist of a verb and a noun, i.e., *der Schreibtisch*; or an adjective and a noun, i.e., *das Neujahr*. The gender is determined by the final noun. Their meaning can often be guessed from the meaning of each part.

ARTICLES

German has two articles, as determined by the gender of the noun:

1. definite article (the): *der, die, das* (pl.: *die*)
2. indefinite article (a): *ein, eine, ein* (no plural)

The article and its noun are declined according to gender, number, and case (see Chapter 3).

Chapter 2

CASES

German has four cases. Without an understanding of the function of each case, it is impossible to proceed with German grammar.

In English, grammatical function often is determined by word order. The meaning of English sentences can be changed drastically by changing the word order.

The dog bit the man. The man bit the dog.

In German, however, word order does not necessarily determine meaning; the sentence can be started with any part of the sentence.

Den Mann biss der Hund.
Der Hund biss den Mann. } The dog bit the man.

Den Mann is in the accusative case (as indicated by the form of the article) and thus remains the direct object; **der Hund** is nominative and thus remains the subject. The case of the noun or pronoun determines its meaning. Generally the item that is emphasized is placed at the beginning of a sentence.

See Chapter 11 for more on word order.

THE NOMINATIVE CASE

The nominative case is the subject case. The subject of the sentence performs the action expressed by the verb. It tells us who or what performs the action.

Der Hund *hat den Mann gebissen.* **The dog** bit the man.

The verbs *heißen, sein,* and *werden* can never have an object. They are always followed by the nominative case. One should think of these verbs as an equal sign. The nouns on both sides of the equation are nominative.

Er heißt **Herr Schmidt.** His name is/He is called Mr. Schmidt.
Er ist **unser Lehrer.** He is our teacher.
Sie wird **die beste Schülerin** *der Klasse.* She is becoming the best pupil in the class.

THE ACCUSATIVE CASE

The accusative case is the direct object case. The direct object receives the action performed by the subject and expressed by the verb. It answers the question "whom?" or "what?" after the verb.

Der Hund hat **den Mann** *gebissen.* The dog bit **the man**.

The accusative case also functions as the object of the prepositions *durch*, *für*, *gegen*, *ohne*, and *um*. This will be discussed further in Chapter 9.

THE DATIVE CASE

The dative case is the indirect object case. The indirect object denotes a person to or for whom something is done. It answers the question "to whom?" after the verb. Unlike English, which signals the indirect object by a preposition or by word order, German changes the form of the article, pronoun, or noun.

Der Mann hat **dem Hund** *einen Knochen gegeben.* The man gave a bone **to the dog**./The man gave **the dog** a bone.
Der Hund hat **dem Mann** *einen Ball gegeben.* The dog gave a ball **to the man**./The dog gave **the man** a ball.

The dative case also functions as the object of the prepositions *aus*, *außer*, *bei*, *mit*, *nach*, *seit*, *von*, *zu*, and *gegenüber* (discussed in Chapter 9). In addition, the dative case is used with certain verbs. Some of the most common are *antworten, danken, gefallen, gehören, helfen*, and *zuhören*.

Er antwortet **dem Lehrer**. He is answering the teacher.
Wir danken **dir**. We thank you.
Diese Musik gefällt **mir**. I like this music. [Literally: This music is pleasing to me.]
Die Bücher gehören **meiner Schwester**. The books belong to my sister.
Kannst du **dem Kind** *helfen?* Can you help the child?

*Du hörst **mir** nie zu.* You never listen to me.

THE GENITIVE CASE

The genitive case is used to show possession or the relationship between two objects. This is often achieved in English with an apostrophe. Sometimes the equivalent English expression uses "of the," "of a," "of my," and so on.

> *Der Mann hat den Knochen **des Hundes**.* The man has the dog's bone.
> *Das ist der Wagen **meiner Mutter**.* That is my mother's car.

Proper names form the genitive by adding an *-s* with no apostrophe, unless they end in *-s*.

> *Johanns Mutter kommt heute.* Johann's mother is coming today.
> *Das ist Hans' Adresse.* That is Hans' address.

The genitive case also functions as the object of the prepositions *(an)statt, außerhalb, diesseits, innerhalb, jenseits, oberhalb, trotz, wegen,* and others. Examples will be given in Chapter 9.

Chapter 3

DECLENSION OF NOUNS

DECLENSION OF THE DEFINITE ARTICLE AND *DER*-WORDS

The following words have the same declensional endings as the definite article; hence their classification as *der*-words:

dies-	this	*manch-*	many a, several, some	*all-*	all
jed-	each, every	*solch-*	such, such a		
jen-	that	*welch-*	which		

	Masculine	**Feminine**	**Neuter**	**Plural**
Nominative	*-er Mann*	*-e Frau*	*-es Kind*	*-e Kinder*
Accusative	*-en Mann*	*-e Frau*	*-es Kind*	*-e Kinder*
Dative	*-em Mann*	*-er Frau*	*-em Kind*	*-en Kindern***
Genitive	*-es Mannes**	*-er Frau*	*-es Kindes**	*-er Kinder*

*Masculine and neuter nouns in the genitive add *-s* (*-es* if consisting of only one syllable).
**Plural nouns in the dative add *-n* if not already ending in *-n*.

Welcher Lehrer gab jedem Schüler seiner Klasses solche Note?
Which teacher gave such a grade to every pupil of his class?

DECLENSION OF THE INDEFINITE ARTICLE AND *EIN*-WORDS

Possessive adjectives and the negative pronoun (*kein-*) have the same endings as the indefinite article; hence their classification as *ein*-words.

mein-	my		*unser-*	our
dein-	your (fam., sing.)		*euer-*	your (fam., pl.)

	Masculine	Feminine	Neuter	Plural
Nominative	*-Mann*	*-e Frau*	*-Kind*	*-e Kinder*
Accusative	*-en Mann*	*-e Frau*	*-Kind*	*-e Kinder*
Dative	*-em Mann*	*-er Frau*	*-em Kind*	*-en Kindern***
Genitive	*-es Mannes**	*-er Frau*	*-es Kindes**	*-er Kinder*

*Masculine and neuter nouns in the genitive add *-s* (*-es* if consisting of only one syllable).

**Plural nouns in the dative add *-n* if not already ending in *-n*.

Mein Mann gab seiner Mutter ein Foto unseres Kindes.
My husband gave a photo of our child to his mother.

NEGATION OF NOUNS

Nouns with no article and nouns preceded by the indefinite article are negated by using **kein** (vs. *nicht*). **Kein** is declined like the indefinite article.

*Wir haben **Geld**. Wir haben **kein Geld**.*
We have **money**. We have **no money**.

*Sie bringt **einen Kuchen**. Sie bringt **keinen Kuchen**.*
She is bringing **a cake**. She is **not** bringing **cake**.

But

*Sie bringt **den** Kuchen. Sie bringt **den Kuchen nicht**.*
She is bringing **the cake**. She is **not** bringing **the cake**.

WEAK MASCULINE NOUNS

Some masculine nouns have an ending of **-n** or **-en** in all cases except the nominative. They include most masculine nouns ending in **-e**, such as *Junge, Löwe, Däne*. Some other nouns are *Herr, Nachbar, Tourist, Mensch, Student*. Some of these also add an **-s** in the genitive, i.e., *der Name* becomes *des Namens*.

Chapter 4

PRONOUNS

PERSONAL PRONOUNS

Personal pronouns stand for nouns and must agree in gender and number with the nouns to which they refer. English speakers tend to use the German pronoun *es* in all cases when it corresponds to "it"; however, *es* (or some declensional form of *es*) is correct only if the noun referred to is neuter; *er* or *sie* (in its proper case) must be used for masculine or feminine nouns, respectively.

> *Wie findest du **die Farbe**? **Sie** ist schön.* How do you like **the color**? **It** is beautiful.
> ***Den Wagen**? Ich mag **ihn** nicht.* **That car**? I don't like **it**.

PERSONAL PRONOUNS
SINGULAR

Nominative		Accusative		Dative	
ich	I	*mich*	me	*mir*	to me
du	you (fam.)	*dich*	you	*dir*	to you
Sie	you (form.)	*Sie*	you	*Ihnen*	to you
er	he, it	*ihn*	him, it	*ihm*	to him, to it
sie	she, it	*sie*	her, it	*ihr*	to her, to it
es	it	*es*	it	*ihm*	to him, to it

PLURAL

Nominative		Accusative		Dative	
wir	we	*uns*	us	*uns*	to us
ihr	you (fam.)	*euch*	you	*euch*	to you
Sie	you (form.)	*Sie*	you	*Ihnen*	to you
sie	they	*sie*	them	*ihnen*	to them

Notice that there are personal pronouns for all cases except the genitive.

REFLEXIVE PRONOUNS

A reflexive pronoun refers back to and is identical with the subject. English uses "-self" or "-selves" to form reflexive pronouns. German reflexive pronouns are identical to the personal pronouns, except in the third-person singular and plural, where it is **sich**.

*Er wäscht **sich**.* He is washing **himself.** *Sie waschen **sich**.* They are washing **themselves.**

In the case of the other reflexive pronouns, they are usually in the accusative case. However, if there is another direct object in the sentence, the reflexive pronoun must be in the dative case.

*Ich wasche **mich*** (acc.). I am washing myself. *Ich wasche **mir*** (dat.) *die Hände.* I am washing my hands.

Note: German uses the definite article when referring to parts of the body or clothing, not the possessive adjective, as in English. Nevertheless, in the spoken language, possessive adjectives are being used in this context more and more frequently.

*Ich wasche **meine** Hände.* I am washing **my** hands.

RELATIVE PRONOUNS

Relative pronouns relate a subordinate clause (relative clause) to a main clause by referring back to a noun in the main clause. In English, the relative pronouns are **who**, **which**, and **that**.

She is the woman **who** was here yesterday.

The noun to which the relative pronoun refers is known as its antecedent. In German, the relative pronoun must agree with its antecedent in gender and number. The case is determined by its use in the relative clause.

*Sie ist die Frau, **die** gestern hier war.* She is the woman **who** was here yesterday.
*Er ist der Mann, **dem** ich das Buch gab.* He is the man **to whom** I gave the book.

In the first example, the relative pronoun *die* is feminine because it refers to **die Frau,** and it is nominative because it serves as the subject of the relative clause. In the second example, the relative pronoun *dem* is masculine because it refers to **der Mann,** and it is dative because it is the dative object in the relative clause.

When the meaning of the relative pronoun is "whose," it is genitive no matter what its grammatical function in the relative clause is, but it still must agree in gender with its antecedent.

> *Sie ist die Frau, in **deren** Haus ich wohnte.* She is the woman in **whose** house I lived.

Note that in German, a relative clause is always set off by a comma.

The form of the relative pronoun is almost the same as that of the definite article. In the paradigm below, the deviations from the definite article are shown in bold type.

RELATIVE PRONOUNS

	Masculine	Feminine	Neuter	Plural
Nominative	der	die	das	die
Accusative	den	die	das	die
Dative	dem	der	dem	**denen**
Genitive	**dessen**	**deren**	**dessen**	**deren**

INDEFINITE RELATIVE PRONOUNS

When the antecedent is an unspecified person, the appropriate form of the pronoun *wer* is used.

Nominative: *wer* (who)
Accusative: *wen* (whom)
Dative: *wem* (to whom)
Genitive: *wessen* (whose)

> *Ich weiß nicht, **wem** er das Buch gab.* I don't know **to whom** he gave the book.

When the antecedent is an unspecified thing, a superlative adjective used as a noun, an indefinite pronoun, or an entire main clause, *was* is used.

> *Hast du gesehen, **was** er getan hat?* Did you see **what** he did?
> *Es war das Beste, **was** ich machen konnte.* It was the best **(that)** I could do.

*Nicht alles, **was** er sagte, war interessant.* Not everything **(that)** he said was interesting.

*Er meint, er kann nicht kommen, **was** ich nicht glauben kann.* He says he cannot come, **which** I cannot believe.

DA(R) - AND WO(R) -COMPOUNDS

A preposition + a pronoun referring to a thing is always replaced by a **da(r)**-construction. The **r** is inserted before a vowel.

*Das Buch war interessant. Sie sprechen **darüber**.* **The book** was interesting. They are talking **about** it.

$$(über + es = darüber)$$

This happens only when the pronoun refers to a thing. If it refers to a person, it remains unchanged.

*Der Professor war interessant. Sie sprechen **über ihn**.* **The professor** was interesting. They are talking **about him.**

The interrogative **was?** + a preposition is replaced by the **wo(r)**-construction.

Wovon/Worüber sprechen sie? **What** are they talking **about?**

$$(was? + von = wovon; was? + über = worüber)$$

The interrogative **was?** always refers to a thing. If the reference is to a person, the appropriate form of **wer?** is used.

Von wem sprechen sie? **Whom** are they talking **about?**

Chapter 5

VERBS

ABOUT VERBS IN GENERAL

The basic form of a verb is the infinitive. Most infinitives in German end in *-en*, but a few end in *-n*. The stem of a verb consists of the infinitive minus the *-(e)n* ending.

German has three types of verbs: regular, irregular, and mixed. Regular verbs form their tenses by adding appropriate endings to the stem. Irregular verbs have a stem vowel change in some of their forms. Mixed verbs have a stem vowel change but use the endings of regular verbs.

THE USE OF THE PRESENT TENSE *(DAS PRÄSENS)*

The present tense is used more extensively in German than in English. German has only one present tense, whereas English has several.

I **do** that.
I **am doing** that. } *Ich* **mache** *das*.
I **do do** that.

The present tense is often used, for example, where the future would be used in English. If the sentence contains an adverb indicating that the future is intended, the present tense is preferred.

Ich **fliege morgen** *nach Berlin*. I **will fly** to Berlin tomorrow.

The present tense is also used to express an event that began in the past but is still continuing.

Er **wohnt seit einem Jahr** *in Berlin*. He has been living in Berlin for a year.

The Formation of the Present Tense (Regular Verbs)

The present tense is formed by adding the following endings to the stem of the verb:

ich	*-e*	*wir*	*-en*
du	*-st*	*ihr*	*-t*
er/sie/es	*-t*	*sie/Sie*	*-en*

Ich mache.	*Wir machen.*
Du machst.	*Ihr macht.*
Er/Sie/Es macht.	*Sie/Sie machen.*

Verbs that have a stem ending in *-d* or *-t* (i.e., *arbeiten*), or verbs that have a stem ending in *-m* or *-n* with a preceding consonant (i.e., *widmen*), insert an *-e-* in the *du-*, *er/sie/es-*, and *ihr-* forms.

arbeiten:	*Du arbeitest.*	*Er/Sie/Es arbeitet.*	*Ihr arbeitet.*
reden:	*Du redest.*	*Er/Sie/Es redet.*	*Ihr redet.*
widmen:	*Du widmest.*	*Er/Sie/Es widmet.*	*Ihr widmet.*
ordnen:	*Du ordnest.*	*Er/Sie/Es ordet.*	*Ihr ordet.*

Verbs like *schließen* or *lesen* that have stems ending in *-ß* or *-s* drop the *-s* in the *du*-form:

Du schließt.   *Du liest.*

The Formation of the Present Tense (Irregular Verbs)

Irregular verbs change the stem vowel in the *du-* and *er/sie/es-* forms. The other forms keep the vowel of the stem unchanged.

The vowel *e* changes to *i* or *ie*:

Sehen (to see)

Ich sehe ihn.	*Wir sehen ihn.*
Du siehst ihn.	*Ihr seht ihn.*
Er/Sie/Es sieht ihn.	*Sie/Sie sehen ihn.*

Geben (to give)	**Essen** (to eat)
Du gibst.	*Du isst.*
Er/Sie/Es gibt.	*Er/Sie/Es isst.*

The stem vowel *a* takes an umlaut:

Schlafen (to sleep)

Ich schlafe.	*Wir schlafen.*
Du schläfst.	*Ihr schlaft.*
Er/Sie/Es schläft.	*Sie/Sie schlafen.*

Tragen (to carry, to wear)	**Laufen** (to run)
Du trägst.	*Du läufst.*
Er/Sie/Es trägt.	*Er/Sie/Es läuft.*

The verb **haben** is irregular in the *du-* and *er/sie/es-* forms.

*Du **hast** kein Geld.* You have no money.
*Er **hat** kein Geld.* He has no money.

The present tense of the verb **sein** (to be) is completely irregular.

*Ich **bin** Student.*	*Wir **sind** Studenten.*
*Du **bist** Student.*	*Ihr **seid** Studenten.*
*Er/Sie/Es **ist** Student(in).*	*Sie/Sie **sind** Student(en).*

For a list of common irregular verbs and their stem changes for the present tense, see the chart at the end of the chapter.

The Formation of the Present Tense (Modals)

Modal auxiliary verbs modify the meaning of other verbs and express ideas such as desire, obligation, ability, and permission. Modals must be used with an infinitive, either expressed or understood. In English, one can say "I can" or "I must" if something in the conversation tells us what one can or must do. The same is true for German.

*Er **kann** heute kommen.* He **can** come today.
*Er **darf** heute kommen.* He **may** come today.
***Soll** er heute kommen?* Is he **supposed** to come today?
*Ja, er **soll**.* Yes, he is **supposed** to.

Modals in German are irregular in the singular of the present tense and must be learned. Since the plural follows the regular pattern of present-tense conjugations, it will only be given in the first example below.

Dürfen (to be allowed to, to have permission to)

Ich **darf** lange schlafen.   Wir dürfen lange schlafen.
Du **darfst** lange schlafen.   Ihr dürft lange schlafen.
Er/Sie/Es **darf** lange schlafen.   Sie/Sie dürfen lange schlafen.

Können (to be able to)   **Müssen** (to have to)
Ich **kann** kommen.   Ich **muss** kommen.
Du **kannst** kommen.   Du **musst** kommen.
Er/Sie/Es **kann** kommen.   Er/Sie/Es **muss** kommen.

Sollen (to be supposed to)   **Wollen** (to want to)
Ich **soll** kommen.   Ich **will** kommen.
Du **sollst** kommen.   Du **willst** kommen.
Er/Sie/Es **soll** kommen.   Er/Sie/Es **will** kommen.

The subjunctive form of **mögen** (to like to) is used far more frequently than its present-tense form. It corresponds to the English phrase "would like."

Ich **möchte** kommen.   Wir **möchten** kommen.
Du **möchtest** kommen.   Ihr **möchtet** kommen.
Er/Sie/Es **möchte** kommen.   Sie/Sie **möchten** kommen.

THE IMPERATIVE

In English, the imperative has only two forms.

Go home early today.
Let's go home early today.

In German the imperative can be expressed in four ways.

Gehen Sie heute früh nach Hause! (formal singular and plural)
Geh heute früh nach Hause! (informal singular)
Geht heute früh nach Hause! (informal plural)
Gehen wir heute früh nach Hause! (inclusive)

The Formation of the Imperative

As the examples above illustrate, the formal imperative is simply the **infinitive + Sie.** The verb comes first.

The informal singular imperative has no pronoun. It consists of the **du** form of the verb without the ending.

(du) geh(st) = ***Geh!*** Go!

If the ***du*** form is irregular and has added an umlaut, the umlaut is dropped.

(du) läufst schnell = ***Lauf*** *schnell!* **Run** fast!

The informal plural ***ihr*** imperative is simply the verb without the pronoun. It is used when speaking to more than one person with whom you are on familiar terms.

(ihr) lauft schnell = ***Lauft*** *schnell!* **Run** fast!

The equivalent of the English **let's**-form (inclusive command) is simply the ***wir***-form with the verb first.

Laufen wir schnell! **Let's run** fast!

THE USE OF THE SIMPLE PAST TENSE *(DAS IMPERFEKT)*

Except for ***sein*** and ***haben*** and the modals, the simple past tense (also called the narrative past) in German is used primarily in written rather than in spoken language. For conversation, the present perfect tense is preferred. Just as in the present tense, in the simple past one verb form in German corresponds to several forms in English.

I **did** that.
I **was doing** that. } *Ich **machte** das.*
I **did do** that.

The Formation of the Simple Past Tense (Regular Verbs)

The simple past tense of regular verbs is formed by adding endings to the stem:

ich	-te	wir	-ten
du	-test	ihr	-tet
er/sie/es	-te	sie/Sie	-ten

Machen (to do)

Ich machte.	*Wir machten.*
Du machtest.	*Ihr machtet.*
Er/Sie/Es machte.	*Sie/Sie machten.*

Verbs whose stems end in **-d** (i.e., *reden*), **-t** (i.e., *arbeiten*), or in two consonants, insert an **-e-** before the past-tense endings to aid pronunciation.

Ich arbeitete.	*Wir arbeiteten.*
Du arbeitetest.	*Ihr arbeitetet.*
Er/Sie/Es arbeitete.	*Sie/Sie arbeiteten.*

The Formation of the Simple Past Tense (Irregular Verbs)

Irregular verbs change the stem vowel and use the same endings as the present tense, except for *ich-* and *er/sie/es-* forms, which have no endings.

ich	--	*wir*	**-en**
du	*-st*	*ihr*	*-t*
er/sie/es	--	*sie/Sie*	**-en**

Sehen (to see)

Ich sah ihn.	*Wir sahen ihn.*
Du sahst ihn.	*Ihr saht ihn.*
Er/Sie/Es sah ihn.	*Sie/Sie sahen ihn.*

For stem changes of some common verbs, see the chart at the end of the chapter.

The Formation of the Simple Past Tense (Mixed Verbs)

Mixed verbs change their stem vowel to **a** and add the past-tense endings for regular verbs to form the simple past tense (except *wissen>wusste*). *Bringen* and *denken* have **ach** in the stems.

brennen/brannte	*kennen/kannte*	*senden/sandte*
bringen/brachte	*nennen/nannte*	*wenden/wandte*
denken/dachte	*rennen/rannte*	*wissen/wusste*

*Ich **kannte** ihn gut.* I **knew** him well.
*Er **wusste** das schon.* He **knew** that already.
*Ich **dachte** oft an ihn.* I often **thought** of him.

The Formation of the Simple Past Tense (Modals)

Modals that have an umlaut in the infinitive drop the umlaut and add the past-tense endings for regular verbs.

Ich durfte nicht gehen. I **wasn't allowed** to go.
Du konntest nicht gehen. You **weren't able** to go.
Er musste nicht gehen. He **didn't have** to go.
Wir sollten nicht gehen. We **weren't supposed** to go.
Ihr wolltet nicht gehen. You **didn't want** to go.
*Sie mochten nicht gehen.** You **didn't want** to go.

*Mögen is rarely used in the simple past tense. The *g* of the stem changes to *ch*.

THE USE OF THE PRESENT PERFECT TENSE (DAS PERFEKT)

The present perfect tense is used primarily in conversation. It refers to the same past time as the simple past and has the same meaning. The major exceptions are *haben*, *sein*, *werden*, and the modals, which are usually used in the simple past, even in conversation.

The Formation of the Present Perfect Tense

The present perfect tense consists of the present tense of the auxiliaries *haben* or *sein* + the past participle.

The Formation of the Past Participle

The past participle of regular verbs adds a *ge-* prefix to the stem and the suffix *-t* (*ge* + stem + *t*).

Ich habe das gemacht. I did do that. I have done that.

The past participle of verbs whose stems end in *-d* , *-t* , or two consonants, insert an *-e-* just as in the simple past tense.

reden	*geredet* (talked)
arbeiten	*gearbeitet* (worked)
widmen	*gewidmet* (dedicated)

Er hat lange gearbeitet. He worked for a long time. He has worked
    for a long time. He did work for a long time.

The past participles of irregular verbs often have a vowel change (and in some cases, a consonant change) and end in *-en*. Their forms are not predictable and must be learned. For a list of common verbs and their past participles, see the chart at the end of the chapter.

finden	*gefunden* (found)
bleiben	*geblieben* (remained)

The past participles of mixed verbs change their vowels to *a* (except *wissen>gewusst*) and end in *-t*. *Bringen* and *denken* have **ach** in the stems.

bringen	*gebrach**t*** (brought)
kennen	*gekannt*(known)
denken	*gedach**t***(thought)
nennen	*genannt*(named)

Two groups of verbs have no **ge-** prefix. The first consists of verbs with the inseparable prefixes **be-**, **emp-**, **ent-**, **er-**, **ge-**, **ver-**, **miss-**, or **zer-**.

be*stellen*	**be***stellt* (ordered)
emp*fehlen*	**emp***folen* (recommended)
ver*brennen*	**ver***brannt* (burnt)

*Sie hat ein Bier **bestellt**.* She ordered a beer.
*Er hat mich **empfohlen**.* He recommended me.

The other group consists of verbs that end in **-ieren.**

*stud**ieren***	*studiert* (studied)
*gratul**ieren***	*gratuliert* (congratulated)

*Wie lange hast du **studiert**?* How long were you a student?
*Er hat mir **gratuliert**.* He congratulated me.

The past participle of *sein* is *gewesen*.

*Bist du da **gewesen**?* Were you there?

The Choice of the Auxiliary *haben* or *sein*

It might be easiest to learn *sein* along with the verbs requiring it. Since most verbs form the perfect tenses with **haben,** it is indicated in a dictionary when the auxiliary is *sein.* However, the choice can also be determined by asking these questions:

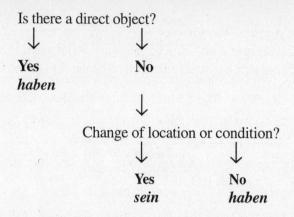

Is there a direct object?

↓   ↓

Yes   **No**
haben

              ↓

Change of location or condition?

        ↓   ↓

Yes   **No**
sein   *haben*

The present perfect of the verb *fahren* can illustrate the application of this process.

*Ich **bin** nach Hause gegangen.* I went home.

Is there an accusative object? No. Is there a change of location or condition? Yes. Therefore, ***sein*** is used as the auxiliary verb.

*Ich **hat** das Buch **gelesen**.* He read the book.

Is there an accusative object? Yes. Therefore ***haben*** is used as the auxiliary verb.

The Formation of the Present Perfect Tense (Modals)

Although it is possible to use modals in the present perfect tense, the preferred tense is the simple past.

*Ich **habe** das **gewollt**.* I wanted that.
Preferable: *Ich **wollte** das.*

When the modal is used with another verb in the present perfect tense, a double infinitive occurs.

*Ich **habe** arbeiten **wollen**.* I wanted to work.
Preferable: *Ich **wollte** arbeiten.*

THE USE OF THE PAST PERFECT TENSE (DAS PLUSQUAMPERFEKT)

Once you have mastered the present perfect tense, the past perfect tense is a simple matter. It expresses a time further in the past than the simple past and the present perfect, and occurs mostly in conjunction with the simple past. Unlike the simple past and the present perfect, there is only one possible English equivalent for the German past perfect tense.

> *Ich **hatte** das schon **getan, als er ankam.*** I **had** already **done** that when he came.
> *Nachdem er schon **abgefahren war**, änderte sich das Wetter.* After he **had left**, the weather changed.

THE USE OF THE FUTURE TENSE *(DAS FUTUR)*

The future tense is used when there is nothing else in the sentence to indicate that the future is intended.

The Formation of the Future Tense

The future tense consists of the present tense of ***werden*** + infinitive. The verb ***werden*** has some irregular forms which must be memorized.

> *Ich **werde kommen**.* *Wir **werden kommen**.*
> *Du **wirst kommen**.* *Ihr **werdet kommen**.*
> *Er/Sie/Es **wird kommen**.* *Sie/Sie **werden kommen**.*

> *Ich **werde** das **machen müssen**.* I will have to do that.

SEPARABLE-PREFIX VERBS

Many German verbs have a prefix that is separated from the verb in a main clause in the present and simple past tenses, and in the imperative. In the past participle, the separable prefix comes before the ***ge-*** and the rest of the verb. Separable-prefix verbs can be recognized in the spoken language by the stress on the prefix. In the written language, the separable prefix generally has a meaning on its own, whereas a nonseparable prefix usually does not. The most common separable prefixes are ***ab-, an-, auf-, aus-, ein-, her-, hin-, mit-, nach-, vor-, vorbei-, zu-,*** and ***zurück-***.

> ***Haben** die Studenten immer **zu** gehört?* Did the students always listen?
> *Die Familie zieht nächste Woche **am**.* The family is moving next week.
> *Er **brachte** seinen Hund **mit**.* He brought along his dog.

A-21

PRINCIPAL PARTS OF VERBS

Infinitive	Present	Imperfect	Past Participle
		Regular Verbs	
spielen		spielte	gespielt
antworten		antwortete	geantwortet
diskutieren		diskutierte	diskutiert
begegnen		begegnete	(ist) begegnet
ausmachen		machte .. aus	ausgemacht
		Irregular Verbs (grouped by vowel changes)	
beginnen		begann	begonnen
helfen	hilft	half	geholfen
nehmen	nimmt	nahm	genommen
schwimmen		schwamm	(ist)geschwommen
sprechen	spricht	sprach	gesprochen
treffen	trifft	traf	getroffen
essen	isst	aß	gegessen
vergessen	vergisst	vergaß	vergessen
geben	gibt	gab	gegeben
lesen	liest	las	gelesen
sehen	sieht	sah	gesehen
bitten		bat	gebeten
liegen		lag	gelegen
sitzen		saß	gesessen
finden		fand	gefunden
singen		sang	gesungen
sinken		sank	gesunken
stinken		stank	gestunken
trinken		trank	getrunken
fallen	fällt	fiel	(ist) gefallen
halten	hält	hielt	gehalten
lassen	lässt	ließ	gelassen
schlafen	schläft	schlief	geschlafen
laufen	läuft	lief	(ist) gelaufen
fangen	fängt	fing	gefangen

Infinitive	Present	Imperfect	Past Participle
fahren	fährt	fuhr	(ist) gefahren
schlagen	schlägt	schlug	geschlagen
tragen	trägt	trug	getragen
waschen	wäscht	wusch	gewaschen
bleiben		blieb	(ist) geblieben
scheinen		schien	geschienen
schreiben		schrieb	geschrieben
schweigen		schwieg	geschwiegen
beißen		biss	gebissen
greifen		griff	gegriffen
heißen		hieß	geheissen
pfeifen		pfiff	gepfiffen
reiten		ritt	(ist) geritten
bieten		bot	geboten
fliegen		flog	(ist) geflogen
schließen		schloss	geschlossen
verlieren		verlor	verloren
ziehen		zog	gezogen
lügen		log	gelogen
gehen		ging	(ist) gegange
hängen		hing	gehangen
stehen		stand	gestanden
tun		tat	getan
kommen		kam	(ist) gekommen
rufen		rief	gerufen
haben	hat	hatte	gehabt
sein	ist	war	(ist) gewesen
werden	wird	wurde	(ist) geworden

Unless otherwise indicated, the auxiliary verb is *haben*.

Mixed Verbs

brennen		brannte	gebrannt
bringen		brachte	gebracht
denken		dachte	gedacht
kennen		kannte	gekannt
nennen		nannte	genannt

Infinitive	Present	Imperfect	Past Participle
rennen		*rannte*	*(ist) gerannt*
senden		*sandte*	*gesandt*
wenden		*wandte*	*gewandt*
wissen	*weiß*	*wusste*	*gewusst*

Modal Verbs

Infinitive	Present			Imperfect			Past Participle
dürfen	*darf*	*--*	*-en*	*durfte*	*-te*	*-t*	*gedurft*
können	*kann*	*-st*	*-t*	*konnte*	*-test*	*-tet*	*gekonnt*
mögen	*mag*	*-*	*-en*	*mochte*	*-te*	*-ten*	*gemocht*
müssen	*muß*			*musste*			*gemußt*
sollen	*soll*			*sollte*			*gesollt*
wollen	*will*			*wollte*			*gewollt*

Chapter 6

THE SUBJUNCTIVE (DER KONJUNKTIV)

THE USE OF THE GENERAL SUBJUNCTIVE (DER KONJUNKTIV II)

The general subjunctive is used to express ideas that are unreal or unlikely. In deciding whether or not to use it, one must decide whether or not the situation is real/likely (indicative) or unreal/unlikely (subjunctive).

Likely
*Sie **wird** kommen, wenn sie **kann**.* She will come, if she can.
[indicative]

Unlikely
*Sie **käme**, wenn sie **könnte**.* She would come, if she could.
[subjunctive]

The general subjunctive is also used:

(a) When one wishes to be very polite in expressing a request.

> ***Hättest** du Lust, ins Kino zu gehen?* Do you feel like going to the movies?

(b) To express hypothetical statements and questions.

> ***Wären** Sie zufrieden, wenn Sie diesen Wagen **hätten**?* Would you be satisfied if you had this car?

(c) To express a wish.

> *Wenn ich nur mehr Geld **hätte**!* If only I **had** more money!

The Formation of the Present-Time General Subjunctive (Regular Verbs)

The general subjunctive of regular verbs is identical to the simple past tense. The subjunctive meaning is usually clear from the context.

Ich machte das. I would do that.

Ich machte das.	*Wir machten das.*
Du machtest das.	*Ihr machtet das.*
Er/Sie/Es machte das.	*Sie/Sie machten das.*

The Formation of the Present-Time General Subjunctive (Irregular Verbs)

The general subjunctive of irregular verbs is formed by adding modified endings of the present tense (*-e* ending in the third-person singular) to the stem of the simple past tense. In addition, irregular verbs with the vowels *a*, *o*, or *u* add an umlaut.

ich	*-e*	*wir*	*-en*
du	*-est*	*ihr*	*-et*
er/sie/es	*-e*	*sie/Sie*	*-en*

ich käme	*wir kämen*
du kämest	*ihr kämet*
er/sie/es käme	*sie/Sie kämen*

ich hätte	*wir hätten*
du hattest	*ihr hättet*
er/sie/es hätte	*sie/Sie hätten*

ich wäre	*wir wären*
du wärest	*ihr wäret*
er/sie/es wäre	*sie/Sie wären*

The Formation of the Present-Time General Subjunctive (Modals)

Modals with an umlaut in the infinitive (all but *sollen* and *wollen*) also have an umlaut in the subjunctive. The present-time general subjunctive of *sollen* and *wollen* is thus identical to the simple past. Only the context makes the meaning clear.

*Wir **mussten** schwer arbeiten.* (simple past) We had to work hard.
*Wir **müssten** schwer arbeiten.* (subjunctive) We would have to work hard.
*Wir **sollten** schwer arbeiten.* (simple past and subjunctive) We were supposed to work hard./We should work hard.
*Er **sollte** schwer arbeiten.* (simple past and subjunctive) He was supposed to work hard./He should work hard.

Würde + Infinitive

The subjunctive of individual verbs can often be avoided by using the *würde*-form. This form is interchangeable with the other forms.

*Ich **würde** das nicht **machen**.*   *Wir **würden** das nicht **machen**.*
*Du **würdest** das nicht **machen**.*   *Ihr **würdet** das nicht **machen**.*
*Er/Sie/Es **würde** das nicht **machen**.*   *Sie/Sie **würden** das nicht **machen**.*

*Wenn ich nur mehr Geld **hätte**!* If only I **had** more money!
*Wenn ich nur reich **wäre**!* If only I **were** rich!
*Wenn ich nur alles **wüsste**!* If only I **knew** everything!
*Wenn er wollte, **könnte** er kommen.* If he wanted to, he **could** come.

The *würde*-form is preferred in conversation, except for **haben**, **sein**, **wissen**, and the modals. Also, it must be used for polite request command forms, such as **Würden Sie bitte mitkommen!** **Would** you please **come** along!

THE USE OF THE PAST-TIME GENERAL SUBJUNCTIVE

Except for the fact that there are no polite requests in the past-time general subjunctive, the use is the same as that of the present-time general subjunctive. There is only one past tense in the subjunctive, so the past-time general subjunctive corresponds to the simple past, the present perfect, and the past perfect of the indicative.

The Formation of the Past-Time General Subjunctive

The past-time general subjunctive is derived from the past perfect tense of the indicative. It consists of the past subjunctive form of the auxiliary **haben** or **sein** + the past participle.

Ich **hätte** *das* **getan.**	*Wir* **hätten** *das* **getan.**
Du **hättest** *das* **getan.**	*Ihr* **hättet** *das* **getan.**
Er/Sie/Es **hätte** *das* **getan.**	*Sie/Sie* **hätten** *das* **getan.**

Ich **wäre gekommen.**	*Wir* **wären gekommen.**
Du **wärest gekommen.**	*Ihr* **wäret gekommen.**
Er/Sie/Es **wäre gekommen.**	*Sie/Sie* **wären gekommen.**

Wir **hätten** *das* **getan.** We would have done that.
Er **wäre gekommen.** He would have come.

The Formation of the Past-Time General Subjunctive (Modals)

As is the case with the present and past perfect tenses of the indicative, the past-time subjunctive of modals has a double infinitive.

Wir **hätten** *das* **machen sollen.** We **should have done** that.
Ich **hätte kommen können.** I **could have come.**

THE USE OF THE SPECIAL SUBJUNCTIVE (DER KONJUNKTIV I)

The special subjunctive is used primarily in newspapers and literature, and in literary and scientific writings. It is seldom used in conversation; nonetheless, one needs to be able to recognize it. The special subjunctive is used in indirect discourse to convey the thoughts and opinions of someone else. It absolves the person reporting from any responsibility by making it clear that the thoughts expressed are those of another person. It does not express contrary-to-fact conditions or wishes.

The Formation of the Special Subjunctive

Whereas the general subjunctive is based on the past tense form, the special subjunctive is based upon the present tense form of that verb, on the stem of the infinitive. It has the same endings as the general subjunctive. When the special subjunctive form is the same as the indicative form, the general subjunctive is preferred.

ich gehe	*wir gehen*
du gehest	*ihr gehet*
er/sie/es gehe	*sie/Sie gehen*

The special subjunctive of *sein* is irregular.

ich sei	*wir seien*
du seiest	*ihr seiet*
er/sie/es sei	*sie/Sie seien*

Note that in German, just as in English, the pronoun often changes in indirect discourse and that the tense of the introductory statement has no effect on the tense of the indirect statement. The forms of the third-person singular are the ones most frequently used because they differ from the indicative forms.

*Sie sagte, sie **werde kommen**, wenn sie **könne**.* She said she'll come if she can.

*Er fragte, ob ich morgen wieder **vorbeikomme***/**vorbeikäme**.* He asked if I'll come by again tomorrow.

*Ich sagte, wir **haben***/**hätten** das **gemacht**.* I said we did that.

*Er sagt, wir **müssen***/**müssten** schwer arbeiten.* He says we have to work hard.

*Sie sagte, er **solle** schwer arbeiten.* She said he should work hard.

*Sie sagte, er **habe** schwer **arbeiten sollen**.* She said he should have worked hard.

*When the special subjunctive form is the same as the indicative form, the general subjunctive is preferred.

Chapter 7

THE PASSIVE VOICE (DAS PASSIV)

THE USE OF THE PASSIVE VOICE

In German, the passive voice is used more frequently than in English. In the active voice, the subject performs an action.

ACTIVE
Der Hausmeister **schließt** *das Fenster.* The custodian **is closing** the window.

In the passive voice, the subject is passive and does not perform an action, but is acted upon.

PASSIVE
Das Fenster **wird** *vom Hausmeister geschlossen.* The window **is being closed** by the custodian.

The passive voice shifts the emphasis from the performer to the recipient of the action. As the examples above illustrate, the direct object of the active sentence *(das Fenster)* becomes the subject of the passive sentence.

It is important to remember that the passive is always used to describe an action and not a state. Do not confuse it with constructions involving the verb *sein* (to be) and a past participle used as a predicate adjective.

Das Fenster **ist geschlossen.** The window **is closed**. (not passive—describes a state)
Das Fenster **wird** *jeden Tag um 5 Uhr geschlossen.* The window is being closed every day at 5 o'clock. (passive voice—describes an action)

Notice that in the English examples above there is no difference in construction between the passive form and the form describing a state (false passive). In German, in contrast, the passive form differs from the active form; this often causes problems for English speakers learning the passive in German.

The Formation of the Present Tense of the Passive Voice

All tenses of the passive voice in German consist of an appropriate form of the verb *werden* and a past participle. The present tense of the passive consists of the present tense of *werden* + past participle.

*Ich **werde begrüßt**.*	*Wir **werden begrüßt**.*
*Du **wirst begrüßt**.*	*Ihr **werdet begrüßt**.*
*Er/sie/es **wird begrüßt**.*	*Sie/Sie **werden begrüßt**.*

In the passive, the agent (the person or thing performing the action) is often omitted, but when it is included, the preposition *von* is used when the agent is a person, and the preposition *durch* when the agent is impersonal and the meaning is "as a result of" or "by means of."

*Das Fenster **wird vom** Hausmeister **geschlossen**.* The window is closed by the custodian.
*Das Fenster **wird durch** den Wind **geschlossen**.* The window is closed by the wind.

The Formation of the Simple Past Tense of the Passive Voice

The simple past tense of the passive consists of the simple past of *werden* + past participle.

*Ich **wurde begrüßt**.*	*Wir **wurden begrüßt**.*
*Du **wurdest begrüßt**.*	*Ihr **wurdet begrüßt**.*
*Er/sie/es **wurde begrüßt**.*	*Sie/Sie **wurden begrüßt**.*

*Das Fenster **wurde** vom Hausmeister **geschlossen**.* The window **was closed** by the custodian.

The Formation of the Present Perfect Tense of the Passive Voice

The present perfect tense of the passive consists of the present tense of *sein* + past participle + *worden*.

Das Fenster ist vom Hausmeister geschlossen worden. The window **was/has been closed** by the custodian.

The Formation of the Past Perfect Tense of the Passive Voice

The past perfect tense of the passive consists of the simple past of *sein* + past participle + *worden*.

Das Fenster war vom Hausmeister geschlossen worden. The window **had been closed** by the custodian.

The Formation of the Future Tense of the Passive Voice

The future tense of the passive consists of the present tense of *werden* + **past participle** + *werden*.

Das Fenster wird vom Hausmeister geschlossen werden. The window **will be closed** by the custodian.

Modals in the Passive Voice

Modals are rarely used in the passive voice in tenses other than the present and the simple past. The present usually covers the future as well, and the simple past is used for all past tenses.

The present passive with a modal consists of the present tense of the **modal** + past participle + *werden*.

Das Fenster muss geschlossen werden. The window **must be closed**.

The simple past passive with a modal consists of the simple past of the **modal** + past participle + *werden*.

Das Fenster musste geschlossen werden. The window **had to be closed**.

PASSIVE SUBSTITUTES

Several methods are commonly used to avoid the passive altogether in German. The most common is the use of *man* (one, a person, you, they).

> *Hier spricht man Deutsch.* = *Hier wird Deutsch gesprochen.* German is spoken here.

Another possibility is the use of *sich lassen* + infinitive.

> *Das lässt sich machen.* = *Das kann gemacht werden.* That **can be done**.

Sein + *zu* + infinitive is often used in place of a passive construction with a modal.

> *Das Auto ist heute zu reparieren.* = *Das Auto muss heute repariert werden.* The car must be repaired today.

Chapter 8

INTERROGATIVES

ABOUT QUESTIONS IN GENERAL

There are three ways to form questions in German:

1. To form general questions without interrogatives, simply **invert the subject and verb**.

    Kommt er heute? Is he coming today?
    Sieht sie ihn? Does she see him?

2. Specific questions use interrogatives. Note that in these questions the subject and verb are also inverted.

    Wann kommt er? When is he coming?
    Warum kommt er? Why is he coming?
    Wie lange bleibt er? How long is he staying?
    Was hat er gesagt? What did he say?
    Wie alt ist er? How old is he?
    Wie viele Kinder hat er? How many children does he have?
    Wie viel/Was kostet das? How much does that cost?
    Was für ein Mann ist er? What kind of a man is he?
    Was für einen Wagen hat er? What kind of a car does he have?

Note that the case of the noun following *was für* is determined by its use in the sentence. In the first example with *was für* above, *ein Mann* is nominative because of the verb *sein*. In the second example, *einen Wagen* is accusative because it is the direct object of the verb *haben*.

When an interrogative is used in an indirect statement, the conjugated verb goes to the end of the clause.

> *Ich weiß nicht, **wann er kommt.*** I don't know when he is coming.
> *Hat er gesagt, **wie viel das kostet?*** Did he say how much that costs?

3. A question can also be formed by simply adding ***nicht wahr?*** to the end of a statement.

*Er kommt heute, **nicht wahr?*** He's coming today, isn't he?
*Er hat einen VW, **nicht wahr?*** He has a VW, doesn't he?

THE INTERROGATIVE *WER?* (WHO?)

The form of the German interrogative *wer?* (who) depends upon its case.

NOMINATIVE
***Wer** ist das?* **Who** is that?

ACCUSATIVE
***Wen** hast du gesehen?* **Whom** did you see?

DATIVE
***Wem** gibt er das Buch?* **To whom** is he giving the book?

GENITIVE
***Wessen** Buch ist das?* **Whose** book is that?

THE INTERROGATIVES *WO?, WOHER?,* AND *WOHIN?* (WHERE?)

German has three words that correspond to the English "where?".

1. ***Wo?*** simply asks about location.

   ***Wo** wohnt er?* **Where** does he live?
   ***Wo** liegt Essen?* **Where** is Essen situated?

2. ***Wohin?*** (literally, **where to?**) is used only with verbs of motion, and indicates motion **away from** the speaker to another location.

   ***Wohin** geht er?* **Where** is he going?

3. ***Woher?*** (**from where?**) is also used only with verbs of motion; it indicates motion from another location **toward** the speaker.

Woher kommt er? **Where** does he come **from**?

THE INTERROGATIVE *WELCHER?* (WHICH?)

The interrogative **welcher?** is declined exactly like the definite article.

Welcher Mann kommt? **Which** man is coming?
Welchen Mann siehst du? **Which** man do you see?
In welchem Haus wohnt sie? In **which** house does she live?

Chapter 9

PREPOSITIONS

ABOUT PREPOSITIONS IN GENERAL

Prepositions are problematic in any language because they can have many meanings, both literal and figurative, and are often idiomatic. When learning German prepositions and their meanings, one should also learn which case follows the preposition. Some prepositions are always followed by an accusative object, some by a dative object, and others by a genitive object. Some can have either a dative or an accusative object. In addition, certain verb and preposition combinations should be learned together.

PREPOSITIONS WITH THE ACCUSATIVE CASE

Five prepositions are always followed by the accusative case: *durch* (through), *für* (for), *gegen* (against), *ohne* (without), *um* (around, at).

> *Wir fuhren durch die Stadt*. We drove **through the city**.
> *Ich habe etwas für dich*. I have something **for you**.
> *Was hat er gegen mich?* What does he have **against me**?
> *Sie kamen ohne die Kinder*. They came **without the children**.
> *Der Hund läuft um den Wagen*. The dog is running **around the car**.
> *Sie kommen um 3 Uhr an*. They are arriving **at 3 o'clock**.

PREPOSITIONS WITH THE DATIVE CASE

The following prepositions are always followed by the dative case: *aus* (out of, from), *außer* (besides, except for), *bei* (at/for, near, at the home of), *mit* (with, by means of), *nach* (after, to [a city or country]), *seit* (since, for [with time expressions]), *von* (of, from, by), *zu* (to) and *gegenüber* (opposite, across from). *Gegenüber* often follows its object.

> *Er kommt aus dem Haus*. He is coming **out of the house**.

*Sie kommen **aus Berlin**.* They are **from Berlin**.

__Außer mir__ war niemand dort. **Except for me**, no one was there.

*Er arbeitet **bei VW**.* He works **for VW**.

*Die Drogerie ist **bei der Tankstelle**.* The drug store is **near the gas station**.

*Sie wohnt **bei uns**.* She lives **at our place**.

*Kommt er **mit uns**?* Is he coming **with us**?

*Er fährt **mit dem Zug**.* He is traveling **by train**.

*Was machst du **nach der Arbeit**?* What are you doing **after work**?

*Wir fliegen **nach Berlin**.* We are flying **to Berlin**.

*Wir arbeiten **seit dem 4. Juni** hier.* We have been working here **since the 4th of June**.

*Wir wohnen **seit drei Jahren** dort.* We have been living there **for three years**.

*Ist sie eine Freundin **von dir**?* Is she a friend **of yours**?

*Er arbeitete dort **von Januar** bis Mai.* He worked there **from January** to May.

__Von wem__ ist der Roman? **By whom** is the novel?

*Gehst du jetzt **zum Bahnhof**?* Are you going **to the train station** now?

__Der Post gegenüber__ steht das Ratbaus. **Across from the post office** stands the city hall.

PREPOSITIONS WITH THE GENITIVE CASE

Several prepositions take the genitive case, although the dative is frequently used in colloquial speech: *(an)statt* (instead of), *trotz* (in spite of), *während* (during), *wegen* (because of). Other genitive prepositions include *außerhalb* (outside of), *innerhalb* (inside of), *oberhalb* (above), *unterhalb* (below), *diesseits* (this side of), and *jenseits* (on the other side of).

__(An)statt des Buches__ lese ich eine Zeitung. **Instead of** the book I'll read a newspaper.

__Trotz des Unwetters__ gehen wir heute schwimmen. **In spite of** the bad weather we are going swimming today.

__Während der Woche__ habe ich wenig Zeit. During the week I have little time.

__Wegen__ der Krankheit ist sie zu hause geblieben. **Because of** her illness she stayed at home.

*Wir wohnen **außerhalb der Stadt**.* We live **outside the city**.

*Das Projekt ist **innerhalb eines Monats** fällig.* The project is due **within a month**.

Oberhalb der Stadt liegt ein Berg. **Above the city** there is a mountain.

Der Dom liegt diesseits des Parkes. The cathedral is **on this side of the park**.

Jenseits der Mauer ist eine kleine Wiese. **On the other side of the wall** is a small meadow.

PREPOSITIONS WITH EITHER THE DATIVE OR THE ACCUSATIVE CASE

The following prepositions can be followed either by a dative or an accusative object: *an* (on, at), *auf* (on, upon, on top of), *hinter* (behind, in back of), *in* (in, into, inside of), *neben* (next to, beside), *über* (over, above, across), *unter* (under, among), *vor* (in front of, before), *zwischen* (between). If the prepositional phrase simply describes location, that is, answers the question "where?" *(wo?)* — the **dative** is used. If it describes motion toward a destination (not just motion), that is, answers the question "where to?" *(wohin?)* — the **accusative** is used.

*Das Buch **liegt auf dem Tisch**.* The book is **on the table**.
   wo? = dative
*Er **legt** das Buch **auf den Tisch**.* He **puts** the book **on the table**.
   wohin? = accusative
*Das Bild **hängt an der Wand**.* The picture **is hanging on the wall**.
   wo? = dative
*Ich **hänge** das Bild **an die Wand**.* I **am hanging** the picture **on the wall**.
   wohin? = accusative
*Wir **arbeiten hinter dem Haus**.* We **are working behind the house**.
   wo? = dative
*Wir **gingen hinter das Haus**.* We **went behind the house**.
   wohin? = accusative
*Ich **esse** gern **in diesem Restaurant**.* I **like eating in this restaurant**.
   wo? = dative
*Ich **gehe** gern **in dieses Restaurant**.* I **like going to this restaurant**.
   wohin? = accusative
*Sie **saß neben mir** gestern abend.* She **sat next to me** last night.
   wo? = dative
*Sie **setzte sich neben mich**.* She **sat down next to me**.
   wohin? = accusative

*Die Lampe **hängt über dem Tisch***. The lamp **is hanging over the table**.
wo? = dative
*Sie **hängte** die Lampe **über den Tisch***. She **hung** the lamp **over the table**.
wohin? = accusative
*Wir **gingen über die Straße***. We **went across the street**.
wohin? = accusative
*Der Hund **liegt unter dem Tisch***. The dog **is lying under the table**.
wo? = dative
*Der Ball **rollt unter den Tisch***. The ball **rolled under the table**.
wohin? = accusative
*Das Auto **steht vor der Garage***. The car **is in front of the garage**.
wo? = dative
*Er **fuhr** das Auto **vor die Garage***. He drove the car to the **front of the garage**.
wohin? = accusative
*Mein Wagen **steht zwischen dem grünen und dem blauen Auto***. My car is **between the green and the blue car**.
wo? = dative
*Ich **fuhr** meinen Wagen **zwischen das grüne und das blaue Auto***. I **drove** my car **between the green and the blue car**.
wohin? = accusative

SOME IDIOMATIC AND OTHER USES OF PREPOSITIONS

an (at)

> *Wie lange studiert er **an der Universität?*** How long has he been studying **at the university**?

auf (in, to)

> *Sie wohnen **auf dem Land***. They live **in the country**.
> *Wir fahren oft **auf das Land***. We often drive **to the country**.

aus (out of, of, for, made out of)

> *Sie tat es **aus Angst***. She did it **out of fear**.
> *Sein Haus ist **aus Holz***. His house is **made of wood**.

außer (out of, beside [himself, etc.])

> *Die Maschine ist **außer Betrieb***. The machine is **out of order**.
> *Wir waren alle **außer Atem***. We were all **out of breath**.
> *Er war **außer sich***. He was **beside himself**.

bei (with, by/in the process of, whenever/in the case of)

> *Du hast nie Geld **bei dir**.* You never have money **with you**.
>
> ***Beim Sprechen*** *macht er viele Fehler.* **In the process of speaking**, he makes lots of mistakes.
>
> ***Bei schönem Wetter*** *machen wir einen Spaziergang.* **Whenever the weather is nice**, we take a walk.

bis in (into) ***bis an*** (right up to)

> *Wir feierten **bis in die Nacht**.* We celebrated **into the night**.
>
> *Wir fuhren **bis an seine Tür**.* We drove **right up to his door**.

durch (by means of, through)

> *Wir haben uns **durch Zufall** kennengelernt.* We met **by chance**.
>
> *Er hat seine Frau **durch Freunde** kennengelernt.* He met his wife **through friends**.

für (for, by)

> *Er kennt das Gedicht **Wort für Wort**.* He knows the poem **word for word**.
>
> *Man muss das **Schritt für Schritt** machen.* One must do that **step by step**.

gegen (around, about)

> *Wir waren **gegen 6 Uhr** zu Hause.* We were home **around 6 o'clock**.

in (to, at, on)

> *Wann geht sie **in die Schule**?* When does she go **to school**?
>
> *Sie ist schon **in der Schule**.* She is already **at school**.
>
> *Ich gehe gern **ins Konzert**.* I like going **to a concert**.
>
> *Wir wohnen **im dritten Stock**.* We live **on the third floor**.

nach (in, according to)

> ***Meiner Meinung nach*** *soll er länger daran arbeiten.* **In my opinion**, he should work on that longer.
>
> ***Diesem Buch nach*** *war er jahrelang Lehrer.* **According to this book**, he was a teacher for years.

Note that ***nach*** follows its object when it corresponds to English "according to."

unter (beneath, between, under the influence of)

*Das ist **unter seiner Würde***. That is **beneath his dignity**.

***Unter uns** gesagt, versteht er das nicht*. **Just between us**, he doesn't understand that.

***Unter dem Einfluß von** Alkohol darf man nicht Auto fahren*. One is not allowed to drive a car **under the influence** of alcohol.

zu (at, by, for)

*Wo seid ihr **zu Weihnachten?** Where will you be **at Christmas**?

*Ich bin heute abend **zu Hause***. I will be **at home** this evening.

*Gehst du oft **zu Fuß?** Do you often go **by foot**?

*Er ist jetzt **zum dritten Mal** in Frankreich*. He is now in France **for the third time**.

*Was hast du **zum Geburtstag** bekommen?* What did you receive **for your birthday**?

CONTRACTIONS

The following contractions of prepositions and the definite article are possible:

*an das = **ans***	*bei dem = **beim***	*von dem = **vom***	*zu dem = **zum***
*an dem = **am***	*in das = **ins***	*vor das = **vors***	*zu der = **zur***
*auf das = **aufs***	*in dem = **im***	*vor dem = **vorm***	

COMMON VERB-PREPOSITION COMBINATIONS

In verb-preposition combinations, the preposition must be followed by an object in the appropriate case. Prepositions that can be followed by either the dative or the accusative usually take the accusative.

denken an [+ acc.] to think of
*Ich **denke** oft **an** dich*. I often **think of** you.

schreiben an [+ acc.] to write to
*Du musst **an** deine Eltern **schreiben***. You must **write to** your parents.

sich freuen auf [+ acc.] to look forward to
*Er **freut sich auf** seine Reise*. He **is looking forward** to his trip.

warten auf [+ acc.] to wait for
Wartest du auf mich? **Are** you **waiting for** me?

sich interessieren für [+ acc.] to be interested in
Sie interessiert sich für moderne Musik. She **is interested in** modern music.

sich ärgern über [+ acc.] to be annoyed at
Wir ärgern uns über sein Benehmen. We **are annoyed at** his behavior.

erzählen von [+ dat.] to tell about
Ich erzählte ihr von meiner Reise. I **told** her **about my trip**.

halten von [+ dat.] to think about
Was hältst du von dem Roman? What do you **think about** the novel?

sprechen von [+ dat.] to talk of
Wir haben gerade von Ihnen gesprochen. We were just **talking of** you.

sprechen über [+ acc.] to talk about
Wir haben über den Film gesprochen. We **talked about** the movie.

bitten um [+acc.] to ask for
Er bat mich um Geld. He **asked** me **for** money.

hoffen auf [+ acc.] to hope for
Wir hoffen auf besseres Wetter. We **hope for** better weather.

Chapter 10

ADJECTIVES

ABOUT ADJECTIVES IN GENERAL

There are two basic kinds of adjectives: predicate and attributive adjectives. **Predicate adjectives** follow the verb:

Er ist interessant. He is **interesting**.

Attributive adjectives precede a noun:

Er ist ein interessanter Mann. He is an **interesting** man.

As these examples illustrate, there is no difference in English in the form of predicate and attributive adjectives, whereas there is in German. In German, predicate adjectives have no ending *(interessant)*, but attributive adjectives do *(interessanter)*.

ADJECTIVE ENDINGS

The endings of adjectives can best be learned by thinking in terms of first and second endings, not separate determiner and adjective endings. The first word that requires an ending receives its ending from the first column (see chart below) in its gender and case. If it is followed by another word requiring an ending, that word receives the ending from the second column.

	Masculine	**Feminine**	**Neuter**	**Plural**
Nominative	*-*/-er -e*	*-e -e*	*-*/-es -e*	*-e -en*
Accusative	*-en -en*	*-e -e*	*-*/-es -e*	*-e -en*
Dative	*-em -en*	*-er -en*	*-em -en*	*-en -en*
Genitive	*-es -en*	*-er -en*	*-es -en*	*-er -en*

Notes: **Ein-* words, ***kein***, and possessive adjectives have no endings in this slot.

For all cities used as adjective, add ***-er*** (i.e., ***Berliner***, ***Wiener***).

A-44

Adjectives in a series take the same endings.
Adjectives following indicators of indefinite quantity keep the ending from the first column (**ander-**, **einig-**, **manch-**, **mehrer-**, **viel-**, **wenig-**).
All **adjectives** genitive masculine and neuter add *-en* (not *-es*).

Meine kleine Familie besteht aus meinem Vater, meiner Mutter, mehreren netten Geschwistern und mir. Ich habe meiner lieben kleinen Schwester ein- schönes buntes Buch zu ihrem zwölften Geburtstag gekauft. Auch habe ich einen großen Bruder. Mein- großer Bruder möchte gern einen roten BMW ein- schönes Münchner Auto.

COMPARISON OF ADJECTIVES AND ADVERBS

In both English and German, adjectives can have three forms.

Positive	Comparative	Superlative
nett	*netter*	*nettest-*
(nice)	*(nicer)*	*(nicest)*
intelligent	*intelligenter*	*intelligentest-*
(intelligent)	*(more intelligent)*	*(most intelligent)*

Formation of the Comparative and Superlative

In the comparative, adjectives add an *-er*. In the superlative, they add an *-(e)st*. The *-e-* is inserted for most adjectives ending in *-d*, *-t*, or an *s-* sound. In addition, most one-syllable adjectives with the vowels *a, o,* or *u* add an umlaut.

Positive	Comparative	Superlative
alt	*älter*	*ältest-*
jung	*jünger*	*jüngst-*
kalt	*kälter*	*kältest-*
warm	*wärmer*	*wärmst-*

Attributive Adjectives in the Comparative and Superlative

The comparative can occur as either a **predicate adjective** or an **attributive adjective**.

Predicate adjective

*Mein Auto ist neu, aber seines ist **neuer**.* My car is new, but his is **newer**.

Attributive adjective

*Er hat ein **neueres** Auto als ich.* He has a **newer** car than I.

Note that in the previous example the comparative attributive adjective ***neueres*** first adds the comparative ending ***(-er)*** and then the adjective ending ***(-es)***.

Just as in English, German superlative forms are preceded by the definite article or a possessive adjective (**the/my oldest, the/her youngest, the/our coldest, the/his warmest**). Therefore, they are attributive adjectives and must have an adjective ending, which is added after the superlative ending.

*Sein Auto ist **das neueste** Auto hier.* His car is **the newest** car here.

The Superlative Predicate Adjective/Adverb

There is an alternate form for the superlative predicate adjective or adverb. It always follows this pattern: ***am*** + (adjective or adverb) + ***-sten***.

*Mein Auto ist neu, aber sein Auto ist **am neuesten**.* My car is new, but his car is **the newest**.

IRREGULAR FORMS IN THE COMPARATIVE AND SUPERLATIVE

gern	*lieber*	*liebst-*	(see examples below)
groß	*größer*	*größt-*	(big, bigger, biggest)
gut	*besser*	*best-*	(good, better, best)
hoch	*höher*	*höchst-*	(high, higher, highest)
nah	*näher*	*nächst-*	(near, nearer, nearest)
viel	*mehr*	*meist-*	(much, more, most)

*Ich sehe **gern** fern.* I **like** watching TV.
*Ich arbeite **lieber** im Garten.* I **prefer** working in the yard.
***Am liebsten** lese ich ein Buch.* I **like** reading a book **best of all**.

A-46

EQUAL AND UNEQUAL COMPARISONS

(a) *so...wie* and *nicht so...wie* (as...as, not as...as) are used to say that one thing is, or is not, like another.

> *Sein Auto ist genau so neu wie meines.* His car is just **as** new **as** mine.
> *Sein Auto ist nicht so schön wie meines.* His car **isn't as** beautiful **as** mine.

(b) *als* is used to compare two things of different value.

> *Mein Auto ist schöner als seines.* My car is more beautiful **than** his.

SPECIAL PHRASES USED IN COMPARISONS

(a) *immer* + comparative is used to express the idea that something is continually becoming more and more so.

> *Es wird immer kälter.* It is getting **colder and colder**.

(b) *je* + comparative... *desto* + comparative (the...the) is used with two comparatives.

> *Je reicher wir werden, desto weniger arbeiten wir.* **The** richer we become, **the** less we work.

ADJECTIVAL NOUNS

Some nouns in German are derived from adjectives and have adjective endings. A few examples are *der/die Deutsche, der/die Angestellte* (employee), *der/die Bekannte* (acquaintance), *der/die Kranke* (sick person), *der/die Verwandte* (relative). These adjectival nouns are capitalized, but they follow the rules for adjective endings, according to whether they are preceded by the definite article, indefinite article, or no article.

> *Der/Die Verwandte war bei ihm.* The relative was with him.
> *Ein/Eine Verwandter war bei ihm.* A relative was with him.
> *Die Verwandten waren bei ihm.* The relatives were with him.
> *Verwandte kommen oft zu ihm.* Relatives often come to him.

Chapter 11

WORD ORDER

ABOUT WORD ORDER IN GENERAL

The most general and basic rule of German word order is that **the conjugated verb comes in second place.** The first element can be any of the following things (also see introduction of Chapter 2):

(a) the subject

*Der Hund **beißt** den Mann.* The dog bites the man.

(b) an object

*Den Mann **beißt** der Hund.* The dog bites the man.

(c) an interrogative

*Was **macht** der Hund?* What is the dog doing?

(d) an adverb

*Gestern **hat** der Hund den Mann gebissen.* The dog bit the man yesterday.

(e) or an entire phrase

*Als ich gestern vorbeiging, **hat** der Hund den Mann gebissen.* As I walked by yesterday, the dog bit the man.

In only three instances does the verb come first.

(a) in a general question

***Beißt** der Hund den Mann?* Does the dog bite the man?

(b) in a command

   ***Bleiben** Sie still!* Stay still!

(c) to express an if-clause

   ***Bliebe** der Mann still, würde der Hund ihn nicht beißen.* If the
   man would remain still, the dog wouldn't bite him.

COORDINATING CONJUNCTIONS

Coordinating conjunctions join two independent clauses. They do **not** affect word order: in both clauses, the conjugated verb remains in second place. The coordinating conjunctions are ***aber*** (but), ***denn*** (because, for), ***oder*** (or), ***sondern*** (but, but rather, on the contrary), and ***und*** (and). ***Sondern*** rather than ***aber*** is used to connect a negative clause to a correction in the following clause.

   *Der Hund beißt den Mann, **aber** es tut nicht weh.* The dog bites
   the man, **but** it doesn't hurt.
   *Der Mann muss still bleiben, **oder** der Hund wird ihn beißen.* The
   man must stay still, **or** the dog will bite him.
   *Der Hund beißt den Mann, **denn** er bleibt nicht still.* The dog bites
   the man, **because** he doesn't stay still.
   *Der Mann bleibt nicht still, **und** der Hund beißt ihn.* The man
   doesn't stay still, **and** the dog bites him.
   *Der Mann bleibt nicht still, **sondern** (er) läuft weg.* The man doesn't
   stay still, **but rather** runs away.

   Note that coordinating conjunctions in German are set off by a
   comma.

SUBORDINATING CONJUNCTIONS

Subordinating conjunctions join an independent and a dependent (subordinate) clause. A subordinate clause is a clause that cannot stand alone as a complete sentence. In a clause introduced by a subordinating conjunction, the conjugated verb is pushed to the end of the clause. A subordinate clause is always set off by a comma.

Here are the most common subordinating conjunctions.

als when	***ob*** whether, if
bevor before	***obwohl*** although
bis until	***seitdem*** since (temporal)

da since (casual)　　　　　　*sobald* as soon as
damit so that, in order that　*solange* as long as
dass that　　　　　　　　　　*während* while
ehe before　　　　　　　　　　*weil* because
falls in case　　　　　　　　　*wenn* if, when/whenever
nachdem after

Als *der Mann noch still war, hat der Hund ihn nicht gebissen.*
When the man was still quiet, the dog didn't bite him.

Bevor *der Hund ihn gebissen hat, hat der Mann sich bewegt.*
Before the dog bit him, the man moved.

Der Hund hat ihn nicht gebissen, **bis** *er sich bewegt hat.* The dog
didn't bite him **until** he moved.

Der Hund hat ihn gebissen, **weil** *er sich bewegt hat.* The dog bit
him **because** he moved.

Der Mann blieb still, **damit** *der Hund ihn nicht beißen würde.* The
man remained still **so that** the dog wouldn't bite him.

Er wusste, **dass** *der Hund ihn beißen würde.* He knew **that** the
dog would bite him.

Ehe *der Hund ihn gebissen hat, hatte der Mann sich bewegt.* **Before**
the dog bit him, the man moved.

Der Mann blieb still, **falls** *der Hund ihn beißen könnte.* The man
remained still **in case** the dog might/could bite him.

Nachdem *der Hund ihn gebissen hatte, fuhr man ihn ins*
Krankenhaus. **After** the dog had bitten him, he was driven to
the hospital.

Ich weiß nicht, **ob** *es weh tat.* I don't know **if** it hurt.

Obwohl *der Hund ihn gebissen hatte, konnte der Mann noch gehen.*
Although the dog had bitten him, the man could still walk.

Seitdem *der Hund ihn gebissen hat, hat er Angst vor Hunden.*
Since the dog bit him, he has been afraid of dogs.

Sobald *er im Krankenhaus war, ging es ihm besser.* **As soon as** he
was in the hospital, he was better.

Solange *er still blieb, hat der Hund ihn nicht gebissen.* **As long as**
he remained still, the dog didn't bite him.

Während *er im Krankenhaus war, ließ er sich untersuchen.* **While**
he was in the hospital, he had himself examined.

Da *der Hund ihn gebissen hat, hat er Hunde nicht gern.* **Since** the
dog bit him, he doesn't like dogs.

Wenn *ein Hund Sie gebissen hätte, hätten Sie Hunde auch nicht*
gern. **If** a dog had bitten you, you would not like dogs either.

Wenn *er einen Hund sieht, möchte er am liebsten weglaufen.*

When/Whenever he sees a dog, he would prefer to run away.

Interrogatives in a Subordinate Clause

Interrogatives may also be used to introduce a subordinate clause that is an indirect question.

Ich weiß nicht, **warum** *der Hund ihn gebissen hat.* I don't know **why** the dog bit him.
Er wusste nicht, **wem** *der Hund gehört.* He didn't know **to whom** the dog belongs.

Modals in a Subordinate Clause

When a modal occurs with a dependent infinitive in a subordinate clause, the modal, as the conjugated verb, goes to the end of the clause.

Der Arzt sagte, dass der Mann nach Hause **gehen dürfte**. The doctor said that the man **was allowed to go** home.

When there is a double infinitive, the auxiliary precedes the double infinitive.

Der Arzt sagte, dass der Mann **hätte weglaufen sollen**. The doctor said that the man **should have run away**.

Separable-Prefix Verbs in a Subordinate Clause

Separable-prefix verbs are reunited with their prefix at the end of a subordinate clause and are written as one word.

Als der Mann im Krankenhaus **ankam***, war seine Frau schon da.* When the man **arrived** at the hospital, his wife was already there.

TIME, MANNER, PLACE

Another basic rule of German word order is that adverbs of time come first, followed next by those of manner, and finally those of place.

TIME	MANNER	PLACE
Heute fahre ich	*mit dem Wagen*	*nach Berlin.*
Today I am going	by car	to Berlin.

If two time expressions occur together, the more general one precedes the more specific one.

*Er ist **heute um 3 Uhr** abgefahren.* He left **today at 3 o'clock**.

THE POSITION OF OBJECTS

The position of objects is somewhat complicated in the abstract. It might be easier to memorize the simple examples below than to learn the rules that follow.

Examples:

*Ich gebe **dem Mann ein Buch**.* I am giving **the man a book**.

Rule: When there are two noun objects, the **indirect object** comes **before** the **direct object**.

*Ich gebe **ihm ein Buch**.* I am giving **him a book**.
*Ich gebe **es dem Mann**.* I am giving **it to the man**.

Rule: When there is a **pronoun object** and a **noun object,** the pronoun object comes **first**.

*Ich gebe **es ihm**.* I am giving **it to him**.

Rule: When there are **two pronoun objects,** the **direct object** comes **before** the **indirect object**.

THE POSITION OF *NICHT*

Generally, *nicht* precedes the item it negates.

*Der Hund hat **nicht** den Mann gebissen, sondern seine Frau.* The dog **didn't** bite the man, but rather his wife.

If the verb or the whole sentence is negated, *nicht* comes at the end of the sentence before any infinitive or past participle.

*Der Hund wird den Mann morgen **nicht** beißen.* The dog **won't** bite the man tomorrow.

Chapter 12

SPECIAL PROBLEMS

ALS, WENN, WANN

Als, *wenn*, and *wann* all correspond to the English word "when."

Als is used in statements about one past event.

Als ich vor kurzem mit ihm sprach, war er freundlich. **When** I
 talked to him a short time ago, he was friendly.

Wenn corresponds to the English word "whenever" (recurrence)
and often implies the future.

Wenn ich mit ihm spreche, ist er freundlich. **When/Whenever** I
 talk to him, he is friendly.

Wann is used only in questions, direct and indirect.

Wann fängt die Vorstellung an? **When** does the performance
 begin?
Ich weiß nicht, wann die Vorstellung anfängt. I don't know **when**
 the performance begins.

NACHDEM, NACH, NACHHER

Nachdem (after) is a subordinating conjunction. It is used only
with the present perfect or past perfect tenses.

Nachdem ich mit ihm gesprochen hatte, war er freundlich. **After**
 I had talked to him, he was friendly.

Nach (after) is a preposition.

Nach dem Gespräch war er freundlich. **After** the conversation, he
 was friendly.

Nachher (afterwards) is an adverb of time.

*Gestern gingen wir ins Kino. **Nachher** haben wir gegessen.*
Yesterday we went to the movies. **Afterwards**, we ate.

SEITDEM, SEIT

Seitdem (since) is a subordinating conjunction.

Seitdem ich mit ihm arbeite, ist er freundlich. **Since** I have been
working with him, he has been friendly.

Seitdem is also an adverb meaning "since then."

*Ich habe neulich mit ihm gesprochen. **Seitdem** ist er nett zu mir.* I
spoke to him recently. **Since then** he has been nice to me.

Seit (for, since) is a preposition used in time expressions. It does
not express a causal relationship.

*Ich arbeite mit ihm **seit** drei Monaten.* I have been working with
him **for three months**.
*Ich arbeite mit ihm **seit** Januar.* I have been working with him
since January.

BEVOR, VOR, VORHER

Bevor (before) is a subordinating conjunction.

Bevor ich mit ihm sprach, war er unfreundlich. **Before** I spoke to
him, he was unfriendly.

Vor (before, in front of) is a preposition.

*Er stand **vor** meinem Haus.* He was standing **in front of** my house.

With time expressions, *vor* corresponds to the English word "ago."

*Das war **vor** drei Monaten.* That was three months **ago**.

Vorher (before that) is an adverb of time.

*Ich habe neulich mit ihm gesprochen und er war nett. **Vorher** war er nicht nett.* I spoke to him recently and he was nice. **Before that**, he was not nice.

NOCH EIN, EIN ANDER

Noch ein is used to ask for an additional one of something that one has.

*Herr Ober, **noch ein** Bier bitte!* Waiter, **another** beer please!

Ein ander is used to obtain a different version of something that one has.

*Ich möchte **ein anderes** Bier. Dieses holländische Bier schmeckt mir nicht.* I would like **another** beer. This Dutch beer doesn't taste good.

KENNEN, WISSEN

Kennen means "to know, be acquainted with, be familiar with."

***Kennst** du Berlin?* **Are you familiar with** Berlin?
***Kennt** ihr seine Romane?* **Are you familiar with** his novels?
***Kennt** sie seine Freundin?* Does she **know** his girl friend?

Wissen means "to know facts, answers, details."

***Weißt** du, wo Konstanz liegt?* Do you **know** where Konstanz is?
***Weißt** du, wie viele Romane er geschrieben hat?* Do you **know** how many novels he has written?
***Weiß** sie, wie seine Freundin heißt?* Does she **know** his girl friend's name?

ENDLICH, SCHLIEßLICH, ZULETZT

Endlich means "finally" in the sense of "at last."

*Er hat uns **endlich** angerufen.* He **finally** called us.

Schließlich means "finally" in the sense of "at the end of several stages."

*Er hat die anderen zuerst und **schließlich** mich angerufen.* He called the others first and **finally** me.

Zuletzt means "finally" in the sense of "last of all."

Zuletzt hat er mich angerufen, ehe er wegging. **Finally** he called me, before he went away.

EIN PAAR, ein paar

Ein Paar is equivalent to the English phrases "a couple" or "a pair."

*Sie sind **ein** glückliches **Paar.*** They are a happy couple.
*Sie hat **ein Paar** Lederhandschuhe.* She has a pair of leather gloves.

Ein paar is equivalent to the English word "several."

*Ich habe noch **ein paar** Fragen.* I have a few more questions.

TREFFEN, BEGEGNEN, KENNENLERNEN

Treffen, begegnen, and *kennenlernen* all mean "to meet."

Treffen refers to a planned meeting.

*Ich **treffe** ihn morgen um 7 Uhr.* I **am meeting** him tomorrow at 7 o'clock.

Begegnen refers to an unplanned meeting.

*Ich **bin** ihr in der Stadt **begegnet.*** I **ran into** her in town.

Kennenlernen refers to meeting someone in the sense of becoming acquainted.

*Wir **haben** uns in Deutschland **kennengelernt.*** We **met/became acquainted** in Germany.

ES GIBT, ES SIND

Es gibt (there is, there are) is followed by the accusative and indicates existence in general and in a large space.

Es gibt weiße Mäuse. **There are** white mice./White mice exist.

Es sind (there are) is more specific and refers to persons or things clearly defined and in a limited space.

Es sind zwei weiße Mäuse in diesem Zimmer. **There are** two white mice in this room.

NUR, ERST

Nur means "only" in the sense of "no more than."

Sie haben nur ein Kind. They have only one child.

Erst implies that more is to come.

Sie haben erst ein Kind. They have **only** one child (implying that they expect more).

LERNEN, STUDIEREN

Lernen is equivalent to the English phrases "to study" or "to prepare for class." It also means "to learn a particular skill."

Abends müssen die Studenten viel lernen. The students have to **study** a lot in the evenings.

Studieren expresses the act of being a student and of learning something in depth.

Sie studiert an Rutgers Universität. She **studies** at Rutgers University.
Er studiert gründlich alle Artikel zu diesem Thema. He **studies** all articles about this topic thoroughly.

WORTE, WÖRTER

Das Wort has two plurals. The plural for words in context is **Worte**.

Mit anderen Worten, ich verstehe das nicht. In other **words**, I don't understand that.

The plural for words in isolation is **Wörter**.

Viele Fremdwörter stehen in diesem Wörterbuch. Many foreign **words** are in this dictionary.

SPÄT, SICH VERSPÄTEN, VERSPÄTUNG HABEN

The adverb *spät* (late) can be used with a verb to express the idea of lateness.

> *Sie kommt immer zu **spät** in die Arbeit.* She always comes to work too **late**.
> *Es war zu spät anzufangen.* It was **too** late to begin.

The verb *sich verspäten* (to be late) can be used both for people and for public transportation.

> *Der Zug aus Hannover **verspätet sich** immer.* The train from Hannover **is** always **late**.
> *Sie wurde entlassen, weil sie **sich** immer **verspätet** hat.* She was fired, because she **was** always **late**.

Verspätung haben (to be late) refers only to public transportation.

> *Der Zug **hatte** heute zwanzig Minuten **Verspätung**.* The train **was** twenty minutes **late** today.

ÄNDERN, SICH ÄNDERN, SICH VERÄNDERN

The most general of these verbs is *ändern* (to change, alter).

> *Ich will meine Pläne nicht **ändern**.* I don't want to **change** my plans.
> *Das lässt sich leider nicht **ändern**.* Unfortunately, that can't be **changed**.

Sich ändern implies an internal change, a change in character or attitude, a change in the weather, or a change in the times.

> *Du **hast dich geändert**. Du bist jetzt viel netter.* You **have changed**. You are much nicer now.
> *Das Wetter **hat sich** in den letzten Jahren viel geändert.* The weather **has changed** much in the last few years.

Sich verändern usually expresses an external change.

> *Sie **hat sich** sehr **verändert**. Sie ist viel schöner geworden.* She **has changed** a lot. She has gotten much more beautiful.

SONDERN, ABER

Both *sondern* and *aber* correspond to the English word "but." *Sondern* is used after a negative statement when the meaning is "but rather" or "on the contrary." It contradicts the negative statement.

> *Wir waren nicht reich, **sondern** arm.* We were not rich. **On the contrary**, we were poor.

Aber can also be used after a negative statement, but no contradiction is implied.

> *Wir waren nicht reich, **aber** wir waren trotzdem glücklich.* We were not rich, **but** in spite of that we were happy.

KEIN VS. NICHT

Kein is the equivalent of *nicht + ein.* It is used to negate nouns preceded by the indefinite article or nothing—but not those preceded by the definite article, which require *nicht.*

> *Ich habe **kein** Geld.* I have **no** money.
> *Hast du **einen** Hund? Nein, ich habe **keinen** Hund.* Do you have **a** dog? No, I do **not** have a dog.
> *Hast du **den** Hund? Nein, ich habe **den** Hund **nicht**.* Do you have **the** dog? No, I **don't** have **the** dog.

Nicht is also used to negate verbs.

> *Ich will **nicht** arbeiten.* I **don't** want to work.

Chapter 13

NUMERALS

CARDINAL NUMBERS

0	*null*	10	*zehn*	20	*zwanzig*
1	*eins*	11	*elf*	21	*einundzwanzig*
2	*zwei*	12	*zwölf*	22	*zweiundzwanzig*
3	*drei*	13	*dreizehn*	30	*dreißig*
4	*vier*	14	*vierzehn*	40	*vierzig*
5	*fünf*	15	*fünfzehn*	50	*fünfzig*
6	*sechs*	16	*sechzehn*	60	*sechzig*
7	*sieben*	17	*siebzehn*	70	*siebzig*
8	*acht*	18	*achtzehn*	80	*achtzig*
9	*neun*	19	*neunzehn*	90	*neunzig*

100	*(ein) hundert*
1,000	*(ein) tausend*
1,000,000	*eine Million*

Note that the numbers from thirteen through nineteen are simply a combination of the numbers three through nine plus ten. The only exceptions are **sechzehn** which drops the **-s** and **siebzehn**, which drops the **-en**. The numbers forty through ninety add **-zig**. Again the **-s** is dropped in **sechzig** and the **-en** is dropped in **siebzig**.

Numbers in German are written as one word, no matter how long.

eintausenddreihundertvierundzwanzig (1,324)

The example above shows that whenever anything follows **eins**, the **-s** is dropped. This also happens when **ein(s)** is followed by another word.

Es ist eins. It is one.
> BUT
Es ist ein Uhr. It is one o'clock.

ORDINAL NUMBERS

Ordinal numbers (first, second, third) are formed by adding *-t-* to cardinal numbers under twenty, and *-st-* to twenty and above. Exceptions are ***erst-, dritt-, siebt-,*** and ***acht-*** (which adds no extra *-t-*).

1.	***erst-***	7.	***siebt-***
2.	*zweit-*	8.	***acht-***
3.	***dritt-***	9.	*neunt-*
4.	*viert-*	20.	*zwanzigst-*
5.	*fünft-*	21.	*einunzwanzigst-*
6.	*sechst-*	30.	*dreißigst-*

Ordinal numbers are declined like adjectives. When written as figures, ordinal numbers are always followed by a period.

*Das war unser **zweites** Gespräch.* That was our **second** conversation.

*Das ist das **vierte** Auto, das vorbeigefahren ist.* That is the **fourth** car that has driven past.

*Heute ist der **siebzehnte** Juli.* Today is the **seventeenth** of July.

*Am **12.** Januar habe ich Geburtstag.* On January **12** I have my birthday.

DAYS, MONTHS, AND SEASONS

The gender of the days of the week, the months, and the seasons is masculine.

DAYS OF THE WEEK
der Montag, der Dienstag, der Mittwoch, der Donnerstag, der Freitag, der Samstag/Sonnabend, der Sonntag

MONTHS
der Januar, der Februar, der März, der April, der Mai, der Juni, der Juli, der August, der September, der Oktober, der November, der Dezember

SEASONS
der Frühling (spring), *der Sommer* (summer), *der Herbst* (fall), *der Winter* (winter)

The German equivalent of the English word "on" before days of the week is *am.*

Wir treffen uns am Montag. We are meeting **on** Monday.

Like English, German adds an *-s* to form adverbs with days of the week. As always, adverbs are **not** capitalized.

Wir treffen uns montags. We meet on **Mondays.**

The German equivalent of the "in" before months and seasons is *im.*

Wir treffen uns im Januar. We are meeting **in** January.
Wir treffen uns im Winter. We are meeting **in** the winter.

TELLING TIME

For the most part, asking about and telling time in German is similar to English.

Wie viel Uhr ist es? **What time** is it?
Es ist sieben Uhr. It is **seven o'clock.**
Es ist sieben Uhr fünfzehn. It is **seven fifteen.**
Es ist Viertel nach sieben. It is **(a) quarter past seven.**
Es ist sieben Uhr dreißig. * It is **seven thirty.**

* It is also common to say:

Es ist halb acht. Literally: It is **half of the eight hour.**
Es ist Viertel vor acht. It is **(a) quarter to eight.**
Es ist Dreiviertel acht. It is **(a) quarter to eight.** Literally: It is **three-quarters of the eight hour.**

The preposition *um* (at) is used in expressing time of day.

Wir kommen um 5 Uhr. We're coming **at** 5 o'clock.

In public places, such as train stations and airports, the twenty-four-hour system is used to avoid confusion. It is also used on radio and television. In order to avoid confusing *zwei* and *drei, zwei* is usually pronounced *zwo.*

*Der Zug kommt **um 18.02** an.* The train arrives **at 6:02** p.m.

DATES AND AGE

The question *Welches Datum/Den Wievielten haben wir heute?* (What's the date today?) can be answered with either the verb *haben* or the verb *sein*.

*Heute **haben** wir den zwanzigsten Juli.*
OR
*Heute **ist** der zwanzigste Juli.*
} Today is the twentieth of July.

In German, the numerical version of dates follows the pattern of the spoken version, with the date coming before the month—the opposite of the American habit of putting the month first. On a letterhead, the article is in the accusative.

den 23.03.01 (3/23/01)

To give information or to inquire about place and/or date of birth, the past participle *geboren* is used with either the present tense of *sein* or the past tense of *werden*. When referring to the dead, forms of *werden* are always used.

*Ich **bin** 1954 **geboren**.* **I was born** in 1954.
*Wann **wurde** Bertolt Brecht **geboren**? Er **wurde** im Jahre 1898 **geboren**.* When **was** Bertolt Brecht **born**? He **was born** in the year 1898.
*Ich **wurde** 1954 in Berlin **geboren**.* **I was born** in 1954 in Berlin.

TIME EXPRESSIONS

Definite time expressions in German are in the accusative unless there is a preposition.

Nächsten März fliegen wir nach Deutschland. **Next March** we are flying to Germany.

The accusative noun phrase can be replaced by a prepositional phrase in the dative.

Im nächsten März fliegen wir nach Deutschland. **Next March** we are flying to Germany.

The accusative is also used to express a period of time.

*Er hat **den ganzen Tag** gearbeitet.* He **worked the whole day**.

Indefinite time is expressed with the genitive.

***Eines Tages** ist er einfach verschwunden.* **One day** he just disappeared.

Habitual time is also expressed with the genitive.

***Abends** habe ich keine Lust zu arbeiten.* I don't feel like working **evenings**.
***Wochentags** geht er früh schlafen.* **Weekdays** he goes to bed early.

The German equivalents of "tonight," "last night," and "this afternoon" are idiomatic.

***Heute Abend** muss ich arbeiten.* **Tonight** I have to work.
***Gestern Abend** ging ich ins Kino.* **Last night** I went to a movie.
***Heute Nachmittag** erwarte ich Besuch.* I am expecting company **this afternoon**.

Morgen means both "morning" and "tomorrow."

Guten Morgen! **Good morning**!
***Morgen** fahren wir nach Hause.* **Tomorrow** we are going home.

"Tomorrow morning" is expressed by *morgen früh*.

***Morgen früh** besucht er mich.* **Tomorrow morning** he is visiting me.

Chapter 14

BASIC VOCABULARY

PARTS OF THE BODY/ILLNESS

der Kopf (¨-e) – head   *die Brust (¨-e)* – chest
der Mund (¨-er) – mouth   *die Zehe (-n)* – toe
der Bauch (¨-e) – stomach   *die Schulter (-n)* – shoulder
der Finger (-) – finger   *die Hand (¨-e)* – hand
der Rücken (-) – back   *das Gesicht (-er)* – face
der Hals (¨-e) – throat   *das Knie (-)* – knee
der Arm (-e) – arm   *das Auge (-n)* – eye
der Fuß (¨-e) – foot   *das Ohr (-en)* – ear
der Zahn (¨-e) – tooth   *das Haar (-e)* – hair
die Nase (-n) – nose   *das Bein (-e)* – leg

Ich fühle mich nicht wohl. I don't feel well.
Was fehlt Ihnen? What's wrong with you?
Ich habe Kopfschmerzen. I have a headache.
    ...Halsschmerzen – sore throat
    ...Ohrenschmerzen – earache
    ...Magenschmerzen – stomachache
    ...Zahnschmerzen – toothache
    ...Fieber – a fever
    ...Husten – a cough
    ...Verstopfung – constipation
    ...Durchfall – diarrhea

Ich möchte bitte etwas gegen Kopfschmerzen usw. I would like something for a headache, etc.

ARTICLES OF CLOTHING/SHOPPING

For women   **For men**
der BH (-s) – bra   *der Anzug (¨-e)* – suit
die Bluse (-n) – blouse   *das Hemd (-en)* – shirt
die Hose (-n) – pants   *die Hose (-n)* – pants

der Hut (¨-e) – hat
das Kleid (-er) – dress
das Kostüm (-e) – suit
der Mantel (¨-) – coat
der Rock (¨-e) – skirt
der Slip (-s) – slip
die Strickjacke (-n) – cardigan
die Strümpf (¨-e) – stockings
die Strumpfhose (-n) – panty hose

der Hut (¨-e) – hat
die Krawatte (-n) – tie
der Mantel (¨) – coat
der Pullover (-) – sweater
die Socke (-n) – socks

Was wünschen Sie bitte? What would you like, please?
Ich möchte einen Pullover. I would like a sweater.
Welche Größe? What size?
Größe 36. Size 36.
Welche Farbe? What color?
Wieviel kostet das? How much does that cost?
Gut, ich nehme den/die/das. Good, I'll take that one.

COLORS

beige – beige
blau – blue
braun – brown
gelb – yellow
grau – grey
grün – green
lila – lilac

orange – orange
rosa – pink
rot – red
schwarz – black
violett – violet
weiß – white

bunt – colorful
dunkel – dark
gestreift – striped

hell – light
kariert – checked
silbern – silver

ASKING AND RECEIVING DIRECTIONS/ TRANSPORTATION

Entschuldigen Sie bitte! Excuse me, please.
Wie komme ich zur Bank? How do I get to the bank?
...zur Post? post office?
...zum Bahnhof? train station?
...zum Hotel? Hotel?
...zum Restaurant? Restaurant?
...zum Stadtzentrum? center of town?
...zum Flughafen? airport?

...zur Bushaltestelle? bus stop?
...zur Straßenbahnhaltestelle? street car stop?
...zum Markt? market?

Gehen Sie dort links/rechts. Go to the left/right there.
...um die Ecke. around the corner.
...geradeaus. straight ahead.
...in die nächste/erste/zweite Straße links/rechts. in the next/
first/second street to the left/right.

Fahren Sie mit dem Bus/Taxi/Auto/Zug. Go by bus/taxi/car/train.
...mit der Straßenbahn. by street car.
...mit der U-Bahn. by subway.

FAMILY

die Eltern – parents
das kind (-er) – child(ren)
die Geschwister – siblings
die Großeltern – grandparents
das Enkelkind (-er) – grandchild
die Schwiegereltern – parents-in-law

der Vater (¨-) – father	*die Mutter (¨-)* mother
der Sohn (¨-e) – son	*die Tochter (¨-)* – daughter
der Bruder (¨-) – brother	*die Schwester (-n)* – sister
der Großvater (¨-) – grandfather	
die Großmutter (¨-) – grandmother	

der Onkel (-) – uncle	*die Tante (-n)* – aunt
der Cousin (-s) – cousin	*die Kusine (-n)* – cousin
der Neffe (-n) – nephew	*die Nichte (-n)* – niece

der Schwager (¨-) – brother-in-law
die Schwägerin (-nen) – sister-in-law
der Schwiegersohn (¨-e) – son-in-law
die Schwiegertochter (¨-) – daughter-in-law
die Schwiegervater (¨-) – father-in-law
die Schwiegermutter (¨-) – mother-in-law

Stief... – step... (e.g., *die Steifmutter* – stepmother)
Ur... – great... (e.g., *der Urgroßvater* – great-grandfather)

FOOD AND DRINK/ORDERING

das Brot – bread
der Kuchen – cake

das Brötchen – roll
der/das Keks – cookie

der Fisch – fish
das Geflügel – poultry
das Hühnchen – chicken
das Kalbfleisch – veal
die Leber – liver
das Rindfleisch – beef
der Schinken – ham
das Schweinefleisch – pork
der Speck – bacon
die Wurst – sausage
die Butter – butter
der Joghurt – yogurt
der Käse – cheese
die Margarine – margarine
die Sahne – cream

der Blumenkohl – cauliflower
die Bohne (-n) – bean
die Erbse (-n) – pea
die Gurke (-n) – cucumber
die Kartoffel (-n) – potato
der Kohl – cabbage
die Möhre (-n) – carrot
der Reis – rice
der Rosenkohl – Brussel sprouts
der Salat – salad; lettuce
der Spargel – asparagus
der Spinat – spinach
die Tomate (-n) – tomato
die Zitrone (-n) – lemon
die Zwiebel (-n) – onion

die Cola – coke
das Bier – beer
der Wein – wine
das Wasser – water
das Mineralwasser – mineral water

der Milch – milk
der Kaffee – coffee
der Tee – tea
die Limonade– soft drink

der Apfel (¨-) – apple
die Apfelsine (-n) – orange
die Beere (-n) – berry
die Birne (-n) – pear
die Kirsche (-n) – cherry
die Melone (-n) – melon

die Pampelmuse (-n) – grapefruit
der Pfirsisch (-e) – peach
die Erdbeere (-n) – strawberry
die Himmbeere (-n) – raspberry
die Stachelbeere (-n) –
       gooseberry

Herr Ober! Die Speisekarte bitte! Waiter, the menu, please.
Was möchten Sie bitte? What would you like?
Ich hätte gern Hühnchen und Salat. I would like chicken and salad.
Und zum Trinken? And to drink?
Ein Glas Fruchsaft bitte. A glass of fruit juice, please.
Herr Ober! Die Rechnung bitte. Waiter, the check, please.
Getrennt oder zusammen? Separate or together?

GREETINGS

Guten Morgen! Good morning!
Guten Tag! Good afternoon!/Hello!
Guten Abend! Good evening!
Gute Nacht! Good night.
Wie geht es dir/Ihnen? How are you?
Gut, danke, und dir/Ihnen? Fine, thank you. And you?
Auf Wiedersehen! Good-bye.

GLOSSARY

aber – but
abfahren – to depart
alle – all
alles – everything
als – than, when
alt – old
an – on
Angestellte, der – employee
Angst, die – fear
anstatt – instead of
antworten – to answer
arbeiten – to work
ärgern, sich…über – to be annoyed at
Arzt, der – doctor
auf – on
aus – out of
außer – besides
bei – by, at the home of
begegnen – to meet
Bekannte, der – acquaintance
bestellen – to order
bevor – before
bewegen, sich – to move
Bild, das – picture
bis – until
bleiben – to remain
bringen – to bring
Buch, das – book
da – because
danken – to thank
dass – that
dein – your
denken – to think
denken an – think of/about
deutsch – German
Deutsch, das – German (language)
Deutsche, der, die – German (person)
dich – you (accusative)
dick – fat
Dienstag, der – Tuesday

dieser – this
dir – to you (dative)
Dom, der – cathedral
Donnerstag, der – Thursday
du – you
durch – through
dürfen – to be allowed
ehe – before
Einfluß, der – influence
Eltern, die – parents
empfehlen – to recommend
endlich – finally
er – he, it
erzählen – to tell
es – it
essen – to eat
etwas – something
euch – you (acc. and dat.)
euer – your
fahren – to drive
Farbe, die – color
Fenster, das – window
finden – to find
fliegen – to fly
fragen – to ask
Freitag, der – Friday
Freund, der – friend
freundlich – friendly
Freundschaft, die – friendship
frisch – fresh
für – for
Fuß, zu – on foot
geben – to give
Geburtstag, der – birthday
gefallen – to please
gegen – against
gehen – to go
gehören – to belong to
Geld, das – money
gestern – yesterday
glauben – to believe
glücklich – happy
gratulieren + dat. – to congratulate
groß – big
gut – good

haben – to have
hängen – to hang
Hause, zu – at home
heiß – hot
heißen – to be named
helfen – help
Herr, der – gentleman
herrlich – magnificent
heute – today
hinter – behind
hoch – high
Hund, der – dog
ich – I
ihm – to him, to it (dative)
ihn – him, it (accusative)
ihnen – to them (dative)
Ihnen – to you (dative, formal)
ihr – her, their
ihr – to her (dative)
Ihr – your (formal)
interessant – interesting
interessieren, sich für – to be interested in
Jahr, das – year
jeder – each
jung – young
Junge, der – boy
kalt – cold
Katze, die – cat
kaufen – to buy
kein, keine, kein – no
kennen – to be acquainted with
Klasse, die – class
kommen – to come
können – can
kosten – to cost
Krankenhaus, das – hospital
Kuchen, der – cake
Kuh, die – cow
lachen – to laugh
Land, das – country
laufen – to run
leben – to live
Leben, das – life
Lehrer, der – teacher
lesen – to read

machen – to do
Mädchen, das – girl
man – one
mancher – some
mein – my
meinen – to think
Meinung, die – opinion
Mensch, der – human being
mich – me (accusative)
mir – to me (dative)
mit – with
Mittwoch, der – Wednesday
möchten – would like to
Montag, der – Monday
morgen – tomorrow
Morgen, der – morning
müssen – must, have to
nach – to (a place), after
Nachbar, der – neighbor
nachher – afterwards
nah – near
neben – beside, next to
nehmen – to take
neu – new
nicht – not
nichts – nothing
Note, die – grade
ob – whether, if
Obst, das – fruit
obwohl – although
oft – often
ohne – without
Paar, ein – pair, couple
paar, ein – several
reich – rich
Reise, die – trip
reparieren – to repair
sagen – say to
Samstag, der – Saturday
schlafen – to sleep
schlank – thin
schließen – to close
schließlich – finally
schnell – fast
schreiben – to write

schreiben an – to write to
Schreibmaschine, die – typewriter
Schule, die – school
Schüler, der – pupil
sehen – to see
sein – to be
sein – his, its
seit – since
setzen, sich – seat (to…oneself)
sie – she/her, it, they/them
Sie – you (formal)
singen – to sing
solcher – such
sollen – should (to be supposed to)
sondern – but, on the contrary
Sonnabend, der – Saturday
Sonne, die – sun
Sonntag, der – Sunday
sprechen – to speak
sprechen von – to talk of/about
statt – instead of
Stock, der – floor
Straße, die – street
studieren – to study
teuer – expensive
Tisch, der – table
tragen – to carry, to wear
treffen – to meet
trinken – to drink
trotz – in spite of
tun – to do
über – above, over
um – around, at
Universität, die – university
uns – us
unser – our
unter – under
Verlobte, der/die – fiancé(e)
Versicherung, die – insurance
Verwandte, der/die – relative
viel – much
viele – many
von – from, of
Vorstellung, die – performance
Wagen, der – car

während – during
Wand, die – wall
wann – when
warten auf – to wait for
warum – why
was – what
waschen – to wash
wegen – because of
weil – because
Wein, der – wine
welcher – which
wem – who (dative)
wen – who (accusative)
wenig – little
wenn – if, when
wer – who (nominative)
werden – to become
wessen – whose
Wetter, das – weather
wie lange – how long
wieso – why
wie viele – how many
wieviel – how much
Wind, der – wind
wir – we
wissen – to know a fact
wo – where
Woche, die – week
wollen – want to
Würde, die – dignity
Wurst, die – sausage
zeigen – to show
zu – to
zuhören – to listen to
zuletet – finally
Zustand, der – condition
zwischen – between

SAT II: SUBJECT TEST IN GERMAN

PRACTICE TEST I

GERMAN PRACTICE TEST I

PART A

Time: 1 Hour
80 Questions

DIRECTIONS: Each of the sentences in this part has a blank space indicating that a word or phrase has been omitted. From the four choices select the ONE that when inserted in the sentence fits grammatically and logically with the sentence as a whole. Then blacken the corresponding space on the answer sheet.

1.   Hast du _____ den Arm gebrochen?

   (A) dich

   (B) sich

   (C) dir

   (D) dein

2.   Der Hund soll nur zweimal am Tage _____ .

   (A) essen

   (B) fressen

   (C) tafeln

   (D) schmausen

3.   Der Kurs beginnt jede(n)_____ um 19 Uhr, gleich nach dem Abendessen.

   (A) Abend

   (B) Nacht

   (C) Nachmittag

   (D) Morgen

4.	Max hat jeden Mittwoch um 19 Uhr einen Deutschkurs. Er fährt jede(n) _____ mit dem Bus hin.

(A)	Abend

(B)	Morgen

(C)	Nacht

(D)	Nachmittag

5.	Frau Kunz _____ jeden Morgen mit dem Bus zur Arbeit.

(A)	geht

(B)	reitet

(C)	fährt

(D)	reist

6.	Die Studentin nahm _____ Band von dem Bücherregal und las über _____ Schild und das Schwert des römischen Soldaten.

(A)	das … das

(B)	den … den

(C)	der … dem

(D)	den … das

7.	Das Buch hat _____ drei Dollar gekostet.

(A)	den Mann

(B)	der Mann

(C)	dem Mann

(D)	eines Mannes

8.   Dieser Bauer wohnt außerhalb _____ .

(A) das Dorf

(B) des Dorfes

(C) dem Dorf

(D) dessen Dorf

9.   Herr Hans Ingels war ein ausgezeichneter Pianist; er spielte einfach _____ .

(A) großartig

(B) farblos

(C) trotzig

(D) feige

10. Hier können wir ein Picknick abhalten, denn um uns sind nur Blumen und grünes Gras auf_____ .

(A) diesem Sand

(B) diesem Feld

(C) diesem Felsen

(D) dieser Wiese

11. Schnell zog sich Paul an. So hat er wieder _____ .

(A) Geld

(B) Eile

(C) eine Erkältung

(D) etwas zu essen

12. Das ist der Herr, _____ gestern hier war.

   (A) er

   (B) wer

   (C) der

   (D) dessen

13. Herr Braun ist älter _____ Herr Schmidt.

   (A) als

   (B) dann

   (C) denn

   (D) wie

Questions 14–15 are one sentence.

14. Fritz _____, wo das Hofbräuhaus steht,

   (A) kann

   (B) kennt

   (C) weiß

   (D) wird

15. denn er _____ München sehr gut.

   (A) kann

   (B) kennt

   (C) weiß

   (D) wird

16. Sie hat uns das allein machen _____ .

    (A) ließ

    (B) lassen

    (C) zu lassen

    (D) gelassen

17. Ich habe Paul vor einem Monat kennengelernt. Er ist ein netter _____ .

    (A) Freund

    (B) Liebling

    (C) Bekannter

    (D) Schatz

18. Wir klagen ihn _____ an.

    (A) der Diebstahl

    (B) des Diebstahls

    (C) dem Diebstahl

    (D) den Diebstahl

19. "Auf die Dauer wurde den Studenten das Gestammel des jungen, nervösen Professors unerträglich." Das bedeutet, _____ .

    (A) die Studenten hören seine Vorlesung nicht

    (B) den Studenten gefällt seine Vorlesung

    (C) die Studenten mögen die Vorlesung nicht

    (D) die Studenten finden die Vorlesung sehr interessant

20. Spricht er oft von seinem Vater? Ja, er spricht oft _____ .

(A) darauf

(B) davon

(C) darüber

(D) von ihm

21. _____ komme ich zu dir und bleibe_____ .

(A) Ein Tag … der ganze Tag

(B) Eines Tages … des ganzen Tages

(C) Einen Tag … den ganzen Tag

(D) Eines Tages … den ganzen Tag

22. Auf Ihrer Liste verstehe ich diese fünf deutschen _____ nicht.

(A) Wörter

(B) Worte

(C) Worten

(D) Wort

23. Der Tisch ist sehr schön. Aber _____ ist zu groß für meine Wohnung.

(A) es

(B) er

(C) sie

(D) Sie

24. Ich kaufe _____ ein schönes Buch.

    (A) mich

    (B) sich

    (C) mein

    (D) mir

25. "Der Student hat die Bibliotheksbücher nur nach der Leihfrist zur Bibliothek zurückgebracht." Mit anderen Worten, er hat die Bücher _____ .

    (A) gestohlen

    (B) rechtzeitig zurückgebracht

    (C) nie geborgt

    (D) über die Leihfrist hinaus behalten

26. Thomas hat alle_____ Schrauben weggeworfen.

    (A) schlechte

    (B) schlechter

    (C) schlechtem

    (D) schlechten

27. Wenn Sie wirklich nicht _____ , dann müssten wir Sie be- strafen.

    (A) bezahlst

    (B) bezahltest

    (C) bezahlte

    (D) bezahlten

28.   Sammelt Hans _____ Briefmarken?

(A) alle diese

(B) alle dieser

(C) alle diesen

(D) alle diesem

29.   Ist das der Wagen des _____ oder des _____?

(A) Students ... Tourists

(B) Studentes ... Touristes

(C) Studenten ... Touristen

(D) Student ... Tourist

30.   Je mehr Geld wir haben, _____ besser für uns.

(A) so

(B) dann

(C) desto

(D) denn

31.   Herr Braun isst nicht im Ratskeller, _____ im Hotel-restaurant.

(A) aber

(B) sondern

(C) und

(D) wie

9

32. Wir haben unsere Meinung _____ .

(A) gewechselt

(B) verwechselt

(C) verändert

(D) geändert

33. Fritz _____ lange vor der Tür gestanden.

(A) wurde

(B) ist

(C) hat

(D) kann

34. Die Polizei _____ gestern.

(A) kam

(B) kamt

(C) kammt

(D) kamen

35. Alles, _____ er uns vorgelesen hatte, war Unsinn.

(A) das

(B) was

(C) welches

(D) wessen

36. Gestern kaufte der Junge dem Vater ein schönes Buch, und_____ .

   (A) brachte er ihm es heute

   (B) brachte er es ihm heute

   (C) er brachte ihm es heute

   (D) er brachte es ihm heute

Questions 37–38 are one sentence.

37. Der Kaufmann schrieb, es _____ ein großes Problem,

   (A) sei

   (B) ist

   (C) wird

   (D) mag

38. das er aber lösen _____ .

   (A) kann

   (B) könne

   (C) wird

   (D) können

PART B

DIRECTIONS: Read the following passages carefully for comprehension. Each passage is followed by a number of incomplete statements or questions. Select the completion or answer that is best according to the passage and blacken the corresponding space on the answer sheet.

Mein Freund hatte ein Arbeitszimmer voller Bücher. Ich musste ihn sofort wegen seiner Ordnung loben. Er hatte viele Bücher und hatte sie in drei Abteilungen geordnet und diese drei durch ein Schildchen gekennzeichnet. Auf dem Schild der ersten Gruppe stand: "Bücher, die ich gelesen habe." Diese Gruppe war weitaus die kleinste Gruppe. Das Schild der zweiten, genauso kleinen Gruppe trug die Aufschrift: "Bücher, die ich lesen will." Die Bezeichnung der dritten, weitaus größten Gruppe lautete: "Bücher, die ich wohl nie lesen werde."

39. Man vermutet, der Freund liest Bücher _____ .

    (A) ungern

    (B) leidenschaftlich gerne

    (C) überhaupt nicht

    (D) immer wieder

40. Man vermutet weiter, sein Arbeitszimmer _____ .

    (A) ist ein schlampiges Zimmer

    (B) ist ein ordentliches Zimmer

    (C) hat wenige Bücher

    (D) hat viele Schilder

41. Der Erzähler hat zuerst die _____ im Arbeitszimmer gemerkt.

(A) Ordnung

(B) Abteilungen

(C) Gruppe

(D) Schilder

42. Die meisten Bücher hat der Freund _____ gelesen.

(A) schon   (C) nicht

(B) bald   (D) alle

"Ich muss Informationen über Sie, Ihre Anlageziele und Ihre Finanz-mittel einholen. Es ist meine Pflicht, Ihre Aufträge zum Kauf, Verkauf oder Tausch von Wertpapieren auszuführen. Nach Erhalt Ihres Auftrages habe ich die Transaktionen auf der Börse oder auf dem Markt auszuführen. Ich bin verantwortlich für die Verwahrung des Bargelds und der Wertpapiere auf Ihrem Konto bzw. in Ihrem Depot. Für die Zahlung von Geld und die Aushändigung von Wertpapieren bin ich ebenfalls verantwortlich."

43. Was bin ich von Beruf?

(A) Wissenschaftler

(B) Journalist

(C) Börsenmakler

(D) Bankier

44. Bevor dieser Herr für seine Kunden arbeiten kann, was muss er tun?

   (A) Er muss die Aktien seiner Kunden kaufen, verkaufen, oder tauschen.

   (B) Er muss unter anderem, Auskunft über die Kunden sammeln.

   (C) Er muss die Transaktion auf dem Markt ausführen.

   (D) Er muss die Wertpapiere aushändigen.

45. Dieser Mann, während er seine beruflichen Pflichten ausführt, darf für seine Kunden Wertpapiere nicht _____ .

   (A) stehlen   (C) verkaufen

   (B) kaufen   (D) tauschen

46. Wo findet man meistens ein Konto?

   (A) im Krankenhaus

   (B) im Rathaus

   (C) auf der Börse

   (D) auf der Bank

Per Autostop durch Deutschland

Da sie nicht sehr viel Geld zur Verfügung hatten, entschlossen sich Nicole und Chris per Autostop durch Deutschland zu reisen. Nachdem sie für einige Tage in Berlin gewesen waren, das im Norden Deutschlands liegt, wollten sie gerne zum Bodensee, der sich im südlichen Teil von Deutschland befindet. Sie wollten eine Freundin in Konstanz besuchen. Nicole und Chris machten sich auf den Weg zur Autobahn, wo sie vor der Auffahrt mit einem Schild "nach Konstanz" standen. Sie hatten Glück, ein Auto blieb nach nicht all zu langer Zeit stehen. Der Fahrer, der an der technische Universität Berlin studierte, erklärte ihnen, er fähre nicht zu der gewünschten Stadt, jedoch nach Tuttlingen, eine in der Nähe gelegene Stadt, die etwa eine Stunde von

Konstanz entfernt liegt. Sie nahmen das Angebot gerne an. Der Fahrer erklärte ihnen, sie könnten das letzte Stück mit dem Zug fahren und dass es nicht sehr viel kosten würde.

Als sie in Tuttlingen ankamen war es jedoch schon spät am Abend. Der Fahrer ließ sie vor dem Bahnhof aussteigen, wo sie kurz darauf feststellen mussten, dass der letzte Zug nach Konstanz vor etwa einer Stunde abgefahren war. Somit saßen sie in dieser kleinen Stadt fest und wussten nicht wo sie diese Nacht verbringen sollten. Der Bahnhof war sehr abgelegen. Die Möglichkeit per Autostop von hier weiterzukommen war sehr gering. Die Abfahrt der Autobahn lag einige Kilometer zurück. Nicole und Chris waren müde und hungrig. Der Weg zur Autobahn schien endlos weit entfernt. Völlig erschöpft kamen sie an einer Telefonzelle vorbei. Chris sagte zu Nicole, ihm wäre es sogar recht, wenn er in der Telefonzelle schlafen könnte. Als sie sich für eine kurze Pause niedersetzten, kam eine Auto vorbei. Es war die Polizei. Die Polizisten fragten Nicole und Chris was sie hier so spät abends machen. Sie erzählten in ihrem besten Deutsch von ihrem Unglück mit der Zugverbindung. Die Polizisten verlangten ihre Reisepässe und baten sie ins Auto einzusteigen. Nicole und Chris waren sich nicht im Klaren wo die Polizisten mit ihnen hinfahren würden. Mussten sie die Nacht im Gefängnis verbringen? Als Chris es dann doch wagte zu fragen, erfuhren sie, daß sie Richtung Autobahn fahren.

Die Polizisten brachten die Studenten zu einer Raststätte an der Autobahn, wo sie sich aufwärmen und etwas zu essen kaufen konnten. Nicole und Chris waren von der Freundlichkeit der Polizei überrascht. Einige Stunden später konnten sie mit einem LKW-Fahrer nach Konstanz fahren. Sie erreichten die Freundin um vier Uhr morgens, wo sie dann endlich in ein warmes Bett fallen konnten.

47. Warum sind die zwei Amerikaner nicht mit dem Zug gefahren?

   (A) Sie wollten lieber zu Fuß gehen.

   (B) Sie konnten sich die Fahrkarten nicht leisten.

   (C) Sie hatten Lust auf ein Abenteuer.

   (D) Sie konnten den Bahnhof nicht finden.

48. Chris und Nicole wollten im Süden _____ .

   (A) einige Tage verbringen

   (B) einen Kurs an der Universität besuchen

   (C) nach Berlin fahren

   (D) eine Freundin besuchen

49. Das erste Angebot kam von _____ .

   (A) einer Frau

   (B) der Polizei

   (C) einem Studenten

   (D) der Freundin von Chris und Nicole

50. Ein Kumpel ist _____ .

   (A) ein Hund

   (B) eine Art Brot

   (C) ein Freund

   (D) eine Krankheit

51. "Der Bahnhof war sehr abgelegen" bedeutet _____ .

   (A) er war wegen Feuer abgebrannt

   (B) er war außerhalb der Stadt

   (C) nur die Polizei darf mit dem Zug fahren

   (D) es gibt eine große Party im Bahnhof

52.	Die Polizisten haben _____ .

(A)	Chris und Nicole angeschrien

(B)	gedacht, Chris und Nicole sind Verbrecher

(C)	die zwei Amerikaner zu ihrer Freundin gefahren

(D)	die Reisepässe der Amerikaner angeschaut

53.	Nicole und Chris haben die Nacht _____ verbracht.

(A)	im Gefängnis

(B)	in der Raststätte der Autobahn

(C)	in einer Telefonzelle

(D)	bei ihrer Freundin am Bodensee

54.	Nach ein paar Stunden in der Raststätte sind Chris und Nicole _____ .

(A)	eingeschlafen

(B)	mit dem Bus nach Konstanz gefahren

(C)	weiter gefahren

(D)	hungrig geworden

PART C

DIRECTIONS: The sentences below contain blank spaces indicating omissions in the text. Below each blank are four choices. Select the choice that is grammatically correct in the context and blacken the corresponding space on the answer sheet. Be sure to read the sentences first.

Questions 55–59 are connected.

Brigitte läuft __(55)__ Bibliothekssaal, um ein Buch über Irland

55. (A) auf den

(B) zu dem

(C) nach dem

(D) in den

__(56)__ suchen, weil sie bald __(57)__ Irland fliegt.

56. (A) so   57. (A) auf

(B) aus   (B) in

(C) zu   (C) nach

(D) an   (D) zu

Der Dieb __(58)__ gestern von dem __(59)__ nebenan beobachtet.

58. (A) ist   59. (A) Herr

(B) war   (B) Herrn

(C) wird   (C) Herren

(D) wurde   (D) Herres

Der Dieb _(60)_ gerade jetzt wieder von ihm beobachtet.

60.　(A) ist

　　(B) war

　　(C) wird

　　(D) wurde

"_(61)_ schreiben Sie?" fragte ich den Journalisten.

61.　(A) Wer

　　(B) Wessen

　　(C) Wem

　　(D) Wen

Questions 62–64 are connected.

Er antwortete, er _(62)_ gerade über den Präsidenten, der auf der

62.　(A) schrieb

　　(B) schrieben

　　(C) schreibe

　　(D) schreiben

Universität gewesen _(63)_ und der zu lange geredet_(64)_.

63.　(A) ist　　　64.　(A) hat

　　(B) war　　　　　(B) hatte

　　(C) sei　　　　　(C) habest

　　(D) wird　　　　(D) habe

Questions 65–68 are connected.

" _(65)_ Kurt das letzte Mal hier war, sagte er, er wisse

65.   (A) Als

(B) Wann

(C) Wenn

(D) Ob

nicht, _(66)_ er dich wieder _(67)_ Geburtstag besuchen
kann," sagte

66.   (A) als   67.   (A) als

(B) wann   (B) für

(C) wenn   (C) zu

(D) weil   (D) zum

_(68)_ mein Vater.

68.   (A) mich

(B) zu mich

(C) mir

(D) zu mir

Die Mutter hat uns einen guten Kuchen _(69)_ , und ich
esse _(70)_ gern, denn er ist gut, aber ich esse lieber Torte,
denn sie ist _(71)_ .

69.   (A) backen   70. (A) er   71. (A) gerner

(B) gebukt   (B) es   (B) lieber

(C) gebackt   (C) ihn   (C) guter

(D) gebacken   (D) ihm   (D) besser

PART D

Die Watussi meinen, dieses Tier sei der König aller Tiere, denn dieses Geschöpf ist sehr groß, stark, und stolz. Es hat keine Feinde; kein anderes Tier kann ihm ernsthaft etwas antun und auch die schärfste Lanzenspitze macht ihm genaugenommen nicht sehr viel aus, denn seine Haut ist zu dick. Wenn es aber etwas töten, vernichten, oder zerstören will, braucht es nur daraufzutreten, ohne sich anzustrengen, weil es so viel Kraft hat. Trotz seiner Stärke aber, ist es ein gutmütiges Tier.

72. Das Tier, das hier beschrieben wird, ist _____ .

   (A) der Löwe

   (B) der Elefant

   (C) der Gorilla

   (D) die Giraffe

73. Wie wissen die Watussi, daß eine Lanze dem Tier wenige Schaden zufügen kann?

   (A)   Die Elefanten fressen Lanzen.

   (B)   Die Watussi haben sich es wahrscheinlich ausgedacht.

(C)   Die Watussi haben wahrscheinlich früher einmal versucht, das Tier mit Lanzen umzubringen.

(D)   Es wurde ihnen von Naturwissenschaftler aus Amerika erklärt.

74.   Die Watussi schätzen die _____ des Tieres am meisten.

(A)   List

(B)   Schüchternheit

(C)   Reizbarkeit

(D)   Überlegenheit

75.   Die Watussi _____ dieses Tier nicht.

(A)   hassen

(B)   verehren

(C)   mögen

(D)   kennen

76.   Wieso kann dieses Tier ein anderes, bloß beim Darauftreten töten?

(A)   Es kann es nicht tun.

(B)   Es ist so schwer und stark, dass es andere Tiere zerdrückt.

(C)   Es tritt auf ein anderes und dann verprügelt es das Tier, bis es tot ist.

(D)   Ein anderes Tier wird vom Anblick des großen Tieres auf der Stelle zu Tode erschrocken.

Wir kennen alle die Geschichte von dem Mann, der im Abteil eines Zuges saß und einer Dame so frech antwortete. Er rauchte eine Zigarre, also hustete die Dame. Da der Mann die Zigarre nicht weglegte, blickte die Dame streng über den Brillenrand und sagte ihm, man rauche nicht in Gegenwart einer Dame. Der Mann erwiderte ganz frech: "Wenn es Ihnen nicht gefällt, so setzen Sie sich woanders hin!" Die Frau ärgerte sich und rief: "So eine Unverschämtheit. Wären Sie mein Mann, würde ich Sie vergiften." Der Mann lächelte, rauchte weiter und sagte ihr: "Ja, und wäre ich Ihr Mann, so würde ich das Gift gerne nehmen."

77. Wer trägt hier eine Brille?

   (A) Der Mann

   (B) Die Dame

   (C) Beide Personen

   (D) Weder der Mann noch die Frau

78. Man kann annehmen, dass _____ .

   (A) der Qualm der Zigarre die Dame störte

   (B) der Mann der Dame gefallen hat

   (C) die Zigarre der Dame gefiel

   (D) die Dame auch Zigarren raucht

79. Die Antwort des Mannes, er würde das Gift nehmen, gibt zu verstehen, dass er _____ .

   (A) gerne Gift nimmt

   (B) sich lieber vergiften lässt, als bei dieser Frau als Ehemann zu leben

   (C) der Dame das Gift geben würde

   (D) gerne der Ehemann der Dame sein würde

80.   Der Mann ist _____ .

(A)   rücksichtsvoll

(B)   gutmütig

(C)   höflich

(D)   ohne Anstand

SAT II:
SUBJECT TEST IN GERMAN

PRACTICE TEST I

ANSWER KEY

1.	C	21.	D	41.	A	61.	C
2.	B	22.	A	42.	C	62.	C
3.	A	23.	B	43.	C	63.	C
4.	A	24.	D	44.	B	64.	D
5.	C	25.	D	45.	A	65.	A
6.	B	26.	D	46.	D	66.	B
7.	A	27.	B	47.	B	67.	D
8.	B	28.	A	48.	D	68.	C
9.	A	29.	C	49.	C	69.	D
10.	D	30.	C	50.	C	70.	C
11.	B	31.	B	51.	B	71.	D
12.	C	32.	D	52.	D	72.	B
13.	A	33.	C	53.	B	73.	C
14.	C	34.	A	54.	C	74.	D
15.	B	35.	B	55.	D	75.	A
16.	B	36.	D	56.	C	76.	B
17.	C	37.	A	57.	C	77.	B
18.	B	38.	B	58.	D	78.	A
19.	C	39.	A	59.	B	79.	B
20.	D	40.	B	60.	C	80.	D

GERMAN PRACTICE TEST I

DETAILED EXPLANATIONS OF ANSWERS

1.   (C)
The dative reflexive pronouns (*mir, dir, sich, uns, euch, sich*) are used when referring to parts of the body in combination with the definite article (where English uses the possessive). This dative reflexive pronoun is used only if there is a direct object in the sentence (*Arm* in this sentence).

2.   (B)
Menschen essen, Tiere fressen. Tafeln, reserved for people, is too fancy: "to dine, sup." *Schmausen* is rather colloquial, meaning more "to feast"; a person feasts, an animal does not.

3.   (A)
Abend is generally the time between 6 and 10 p.m. (18:00 and 22:00 on the 24-hour clock). Only after 10 p.m. (22:00) can we designate the time *Nacht*.

4.   (A)
Abend is generally the time between 6 and 10 p.m. After 10 p.m. we can designate an event with the word *Nacht*. Since Max's class starts at 7 p.m., it's an "evening class" in German, not a "night class" (because it begins between 6-10 p.m.). To be a night class, it would have to begin after 10 p.m. Likewise, "I go every night at 8 p.m. to his house" would be rendered *jeden Abend* in German, and not *jede Nacht*.

5.   (C)
The generic term is *gehen*. When it expresses locomotion, it indicates walking: *Er geht jeden Tag in den Park* means he walks to the park

every day. But if a vehicle is involved, *fahren* must be used unless the distance is so great that it precludes walking. If the vehicle has wheels and it is mentioned (as it is here), then *fahren* must be used.

Reiten is used for riding animals (horses, donkeys, etc.); *reisen* is for long journeys (it means "to journey").

6.   (B)
Watch nouns that have different genders and, therefore, different meanings: *der Band* (book volume), *das Band* (ribbon, tape, band, tie); *der Schild* (shield), *das Schild* (sign, door plate). The student took the book volume and read about the Roman soldier's shield (and sword). So the masculine forms are appropriate. Since both nouns are accusative singular, both *der* become *den*. Likewise: *der See* (lake), *die See* (sea, ocean); *der Gehalt* (contents), *das Gehalt* (salary); *der Tor* (a fool), *das Tor* (a gate); and so on.

7.   (A)
Only a select number of verbs will (must) take a double accusative. The most common of these are *lehren, nennen, fragen, schimpfen (schelten),* and *kosten.* Thus, in this sentence, *Mann* and *Dollar* are both in the accusative case.

8.   (B)
Außerhalb – like *innerhalb* and *oberhalb* and the more common prepositions *trotz, (an)statt, während, wegen* – requires that the genitive case follow the preposition: *innerhalb des Dorfes* (within the village), *trotz des Wetters* (in spite of the weather), and so on.

9.   (A)
A good synonym for *ausgezeichnet* is *großartig*, especially in the expression *einfach großartig*. The other adjectives/adverbs given here as possible choices all express criticism rather than praise.

10.   (D)
Feld should be used only for plowed, cultivated, tilled land. If it is a field of permanently green grass or a huge field of wildflowers, weeds,

etc., then *Wiese* is preferred or compounds of it (*Feld-* and *Wiesenblumen*).

11. (B)

If Paul dresses quickly then one may infer that he is in a hurry. There is no indication that by getting dressed, he has or will have money, a cold, or something to eat.

12. (C)

When a relative pronoun is used, use the form of *der, die, das/die* (etc.) or *welcher, welche* (etc.), which corresponds with gender, case, and number. *Wer* is not a relative prounoun, but rather an interrogative pronoun and so cannot be used. *Wer* is used for direct and indirect questions: *Wer ist das?* (direct question); *Ich weiß nicht, wer das ist* (indirect question).

13. (A)

Just as the word "than" is used in the comparative in English (older than, slower than, more beautiful than, etc.), *als* is used in the comparative in German: *älter als, langsamer als, schöner als,* etc.

14. (C)

See explanation no. 15.

15. (B)

Wissen means to have information about something and refers to facts, situations, data, etc. Thus, it's a fact that Fritz knows where the *Hofbräuhaus* is. Also: *Ich weiß, zwei und zwei ist vier.* I know (as a fact) two plus two is four.

    Kennen means to be acquainted with or know a person, place, or thing. Fritz knows Munich very well (a place); he knows where major attractions are, what the city has, etc. Likewise: *Ich kenne Frau Turner.* "I know Mrs. Turner. I have made her acquaintance." *Ich kenne das Lied.* "I know that song; I've heard it before; I know the words to it."

16.   (B)

As a general rule, *lassen* functions like the modals and so forms double infinitives in the perfect tenses. The auxiliary verb *haben* is always used. *Er hat das Buch liegen gelassen* sometimes occurs, but the double infinitive *liegen lassen* is preferred. This is also true of *hören* and *sehen*: *Ich habe das Auto nicht kommen hören/sehen.*

17.   (C)

Freund/in is used only for referring to very close and intimate friends on a *du* basis. Such a close friendship usually takes years to form. If it is not such a relationship, one uses *Bekannte,* which means "acquaintance" as well as "friend." It always means "acquaintance" if it is on a *Sie* basis.

18.   (B)

There are a few verbs that take as their object the accusative of person but the genitive of thing: "We accuse him (accusative of person) of theft (genitive of thing)": *Wir klagen ihn* (acc.) *des Diebstahls* (gen.) *an.* Another example: *Wir versichern ihn* (acc.) *unserer Treue* (gen.): "We assure him of our loyalty." A few other verbs in this category besides *anklagen* and *versichern* are *bedürfen, gedenken* and *sich schämen.*

19.   (C)

This question tests your knowledge of vocabulary. If the students find the lecture to be "*Gestammel*" and "*unerträglich,*" they find it "unbearable"; they surely do not care for his lecture.

20.   (D)

A *da-* compound refers only to things or ideas and not to a person. When referring back to a person, use the preposition plus pronoun, as here: *von* (plus) *ihm.*

21.   (D)

To express an indefinite point in past or future time, use the genitive case. In English, it usually means "one" or "some" as here: "One day" or "Some day" (*Eines Tages*). "One/some winter" (*eines Winters*), etc.

Note, too: Though *Nacht* is feminine, use the masc./neuter genitive form: "One/some night" is thus *eines Nachts.* To express a definitive point in time (when?) or a duration (length) of time (how long?), use the accusative case. Here: *den ganzen Tag* (acc.) is correct because it answers the question, "How long?" for the duration of a day (duration of time). Thus, we have here: One/Some day" (*Eines Tages*) I'll come (to your place) and stay "for the whole day" (duration of a whole day) (*den ganzen Tag*).

22.   (A)

Wörter are words used as single entities, that is, as disconnected words, such as in a list. *Worte* are words in connected discourse, that is, with a context: *Der Gast sagte ein paar freundliche Worte und setzte sich.*

23.   (B)

Replace nouns with pronouns that designate the same gender (and number) of the noun being replaced. Here, since *Tisch* is masculine, use the pronoun designating masculine gender nouns (*er*). When referring to a thing (e.g., a table), translate the *er* (and *sie*) with "it" and not with "he" (or "she"). *Er/sie* means "he/she" only when referring to males/females.

24.   (D)

The dative reflexive pronouns (*mir, dir, sich, uns, euch, sich*) are frequently used where more than just minimal interest is expressed (and, therefore, called the "dative of interest"). The dative of interest is optional and occurs with verbs such as *kaufen, holen, bestellen,* etc. This dative reflexive pronoun is used only if there is a direct object in the sentence ("*Buch*" in this sentence).

25.   (D)

If the student brought the book back only after the due date, he obviously had checked the books out and had returned them, although tardily; he did not steal them or return them on time.

26.   (D)

As with the definite article (*der, die, das*), a modifying adjective following *alle* takes an *en* in the plural: *alle braven Kinder; alle kleinen Autos;* etc. But when demonstrative or possessive adjectives follow *alle*, they take the same ending that *alle* has: *alle diese; aller solcher; allen meinen,* etc. In other words, a parallelism rather than a weak ending is applied.

27.   (B)

The general subjunctive (Subjunctive II) is used for unreal conditions; i.e., situations contrary-to-fact. It can deal with the future, present, or past. To form the future and present unreal condition, use the indicative past tense form (e.g., *bezahlte, bezahltest, bezahlte/bezahlten, bezahltet, bezahlten*) for weak verbs.

28.   (A)

When demonstrative adjectives (*dies-, jen-, solch-,* etc.) or possessive adjectives (*mein, dein,* etc.) follow *alle* these adjectives will take the same ending that *alle* has: *alle diese, aller solcher, allen meinen,* etc. In other words, there is a parallelism (parallel, same endings). But when adjectives that are neither demonstrative nor possessive follow *alle,* weak endings [i.e., the same endings as those adjectives following the definite article ("*der, die,*" etc.)] are required.

29.   (C)

Weak masculine nouns, also called "n-nouns," usually designate a male's station in life (profession, livelihood, activity, nationality), and have an *(e)n* ending in the genitive singular case, instead of the usual *(e)s* ending. Such nouns often end in *t* (*Student, Tourist, Polizist*), in *ph* (*Philosoph, Geograph*), and in *nom* (*Astronom*). Thus, "*Der Wagen des Studenten/Touristen/Philosophen/Astronomen.*" *Herr* and *Junge* (masculine) are included here.

30.   (C)

"The more, the better; the older, the weaker" and so on; this is expressed in English with "the...the." In German this pairing is *"je...desto"* or *je...je* or *je...um so: Je größer das Volumen, je kleiner der Druck* (the larger the volume, the smaller the pressure); *je billiger, desto (um so) besser für uns* (the cheaper, [so much] the better for us).

31. (B)
Both *aber* and *sondern* convey the English "but." However, only *sondern* is correct when it meets two conditions: The first clause has some kind of negation in it, and the meaning "but on the contrary, but instead, but rather" is implied; often a contrast is inferred. Otherwise, use *aber* which means "but, however." Here, Mr. Braun is not (negative, a negation) eating in the Rathskeller but on the contrary/but rather/but instead (*sondern*) he is eating in the hotel restaurant.

32. (D)
Ändern is best because it means "to make different" and here, to make one's mind "different" – to change one's mind. *Wechseln* is an exchange (not a change) between two different things (e.g., money); *verändern*, usually reflexive, means "to become different": *Er hat sich sehr verändert* – he has "become different" – he has changed a lot. *Verwechseln* means "to get mixed up, confused"; e.g., mix up, confuse an address and so arrive at the wrong destination: *die Adresse verwechseln.*

33. (C)
Though one sees the use of the auxiliary *sein* in the perfect tenses with this verb in southern Germany and in some Austrian areas, *stehen* should take a form of *haben* to form its perfect tenses.

34. (A)
"Polizei" (like *"Volk"*) is a collective noun that takes the singular form (singular verb) in German, whereas in English "police" has a plural form (verb): "The police are coming."

35. (B)
Was must be used as the relative pronoun for all indefinite pronoun

antecedents, or when referring to an entire clause (idea) (*alles, nichts, vieles, etwas*): *Sie gab mir ein schönes Buch, was mich sehr freute. Was* refers back to the entire clause here, to the entire idea, that "I was pleased that she gave me something."

36. (D)
The dative object usually precedes the accusative object, unless the accusative object is a pronoun. Here *es* (a book – *ein Buch*) is the neuter accusative object and so precedes *"ihm"* (referring to *Vater* (him)), the masculine dative (indirect) object.

   In addition, it must be *er brachte* and not *brachte er* because *und* is a coordinating conjunction and does not affect word order (i.e., it takes regular, not inverted, word order).

37. (A)
See explanation no. 38.

38. (B)
The subjunctive is often used in indirect discourse, especially in cautious reporting (where there is some question as to the truth or accuracy of the statement by a second party) or in more formal noncommittal reporting. For indirect discourse/questions, the special subjunctive (Subjunctive I) can be used if its form is not identical with the indicative verb forms. If it is the same, the general subjunctive (Subjunctive II) should be used. Subjunctive I is formed by adding *e, est, e/en, et, en* to the verb infinitive stem; e.g., *spreche, sprechest, spreche,* etc. For Subjunctive II, add the same endings to the past tense stem (and add umlauts to "*a, o, u*" for strong verbs): *spräche, sprächest, spräche,* etc. The special subjunctive of *sein* is *sei, seiest, sei/seien, seiet, seien.*

   In present time situations (present subjunctive), use only the main verb in the form(s) described above.

39. (A)
If the books that the friend probably will never read (*"die ich wohl nie lesen werde"*) represent, by far, the largest group of books in the study, then we can assume he is not exactly an avid reader, though he did read

some, but that was, by far, the smallest group (*"weitaus die kleinste Gruppe"*).

40.   (B)
The room is no doubt orderly because the visitor compliments his friend for that fact in the second sentence of the passage.

41.   (A)
Of the listed items, the visitor first mentions his friend's sense of order (*"sofort wegen seiner Ordnung loben"*).

42.   (C)
Obviously, if the largest groups of books are those the friend has not yet read (the second group) and those he probably will never read (the third group), then of course most books in this study are those he has "not read" (*"nicht gelesen"*).

43.   (C)
A person who buys, sells, or exchanges securities on the stock market is a stock broker and cannot be described as a scientist, journalist, or banker.

44.   (B)
One must first get information about a potential client before one can buy, sell, or trade stocks and before one can complete buy/sell orders or deliver securities.

45.   (A)
The broker can buy, sell, or trade stocks/securities for his clients, but he may not steal them for himself or for his clients.

46. (D)

One finds a money account most often in a bank.

47. (B)

It is doubtful that the two Americans could not find the train station in Berlin (D) or that they chose to walk several hundred miles from Berlin to Konstanz (A). Although they may very well have wanted to have an adventure, answer (C) is not the best choice of those given. To answer correctly, you must know that *"nicht sehr viel Geld zur Verfügung haben"* means the same thing as *"sich etwas nicht leisten können."* Basically, Nicole and Chris did not have a lot of money and could not afford to buy train tickets to Konstanz.

48. (D)

This question tests your reading comprehension. Since Chris and Nicole departed from Berlin, where they had spent *"einige Tage"* and there is no mention of how long they plan to visit their friend, answers (A) and (C) can be ruled out. The text does explain that Konstanz and the Bodensee are *"im südlichen Teil von Deutschland."* From the information provided in the text, there is no reason to assume that the two Americans want to take a course at the university (B).

49. (D)

The text very clearly states that Chris and Nicole received their first offer of a ride from a student.

50. (C)

This is a test of your vocabulary. To answer correctly, you must know that in colloquial speech *Kumpel* is a synonym for friend. It is not "a dog," "a kind of bread," or "a disease."

51. (B)

According to the text, the last train to Konstanz had departed an hour before Chris and Nicole arrived in Tuttlingen. Therefore, answer (A), which says the train station had burned down, is not possible. There is no mention of any special trains reserved for police (C), or of any party at the station.

52.   (D)

This question tests your vocabulary. *"Angeschrien"* is the past participle of the verb *anschreien*, which means to yell or scream at someone.
The police did not scream at the two Americans (A). A *Verbrecher* is
a criminal and since there is no evidence that the police suspected Chris
and Nicole of criminal activity, answer (B) does not apply. Answer (C)
suggests that the police drove Chris and Nicole to Konstanz, which is
not true; they drove them to the *Autobahn* rest-stop. The verb
anschauen means to look at. The police did ask to see Chris and
Nicole's passports, therefore (D) is the correct answer.

53.   (B)

The text states that Chris and Nicole spent several hours that night at
the rest-stop on the *Autobahn*. They did not spend the night in jail or in
a telephone booth. Since they did not arrive in Konstanz until 4 a.m.,
they did not spend the night at their friend's house.

54.   (C)

The text states that after a few hours at the rest-stop, the two Americans
got a ride and, so, were able to continue on their journey to Konstanz
(*"weiter fahren"*). The two Americans did not go to Konstanz by bus
but by hitching a ride (*"per Autostop"*) with an *LKW-Fahrer*, or truck
driver. Since the text tells you that they have something to eat while
they are at the rest-stop, they do not become hungry while there. They
also do not fall asleep after several hours.

55.   (D)

Prepositions are tricky to use in any language. The English "to" in
German is no exception. Generally, *"an"* means "to" when going
toward furniture or bodies of water: *Er geht an den Tisch/See.* "Zu"
could also be used here. The German *in* means "into;" i.e., use *"in"*
when going to (into) an interior, such as into a room. Thus, *in den
Bibliothekssaal, in den Wald, ins Theater,* etc. *Auf* can mean "to/
toward" in some expressions (*Er geht auf die Bank/Bude/Universität*),

but it generally means "on," not "to."

56.   (C)

The preposition *"um"* requires the preposition *"zu"* to introduce an infinitive clause/phrase that expresses a purpose or intention. Thus, *"um"* and *"zu"* go in pairs (*um...zu*) (here: "in order to look for a book about Ireland"). Likewise, *"(an)statt"* and *"ohne"* also combine with *"zu"* and mean "instead of" and "without": *(an)statt/ohne ein einziges Wort zu sagen* – "instead of/without saying a single word."

57.   (C)

For almost all geographical names, for all of the "3 C's" (City, Country, Continent), *"nach"* is used for "to." Thus, *"sie fliegt nach Irland"*: she is flying to Ireland.

In summary (nos. 55–57), somewhat oversimplified, but still a good guideline: *an* = to (furniture, water); *in* = into; *auf* = on; *nach* = to the 3 C's.

58.   (D)
See explanation no. 59.

59.   (B)

Weak masculine nouns, also called "n-nouns," usually designate a male's station in life (profession, livelihood, activity), and they will have an *"(e)n"* in all oblique cases (i.e., in all but the nominative, singular case). Thus, here the *Herr* becomes *Herrn* because *"Herr Wachtmeister"* is in the dative case (the name follows *"von,"* a preposition requiring the dative). Other weak masculine nouns requiring *"(e)n"* in all oblique cases are *Junge, Student, Tourist, Mensch, Polizist,* etc.

60.   (C)

The true passive is formed by using a combination of *werden* plus the past participle (p.p.) of the main verb. The perfect tenses, an additional form of *sein* with a final *worden* is used. This combination of verbs determines the English meaning and tense as follows:

Present tense:
present tense of *werden* + p.p. = is/are being + p.p.

Der Brief wird geschrieben = The letter is being written

Past tense:
past tense of *werden* + p.p. = was/were + p.p.

Der Brief wurde geschrieben = The letter was written

Likewise:

Present perfect tense:
present tense of *sein* + p.p. + *worden* = has been + p.p.

Past perfect tense:
past tense of *sein* + p.p. + *worden* = had been + p.p.

Future tense:
present tense of *werden* + p.p. + *werden* = will be + p.p.

Future perfect tense (seldom used):
present tense of *werden* + p.p. + *worden* + *sein* = will have been + p.p.

61.　　(C)
The indirect object (here: "To whom" are you writing?) is expressed with the dative case. This is also true of the interrogative pronoun "who," which in the dative changes from *wer* to *wem*.

62.　　(C)
The subjunctive is often used in indirect discourse, especially in cautious reporting (where there is some question as to the truth or accuracy of the statement by a second party) or in formal noncommittal reporting. For indirect discourse/questions, the special subjunctive (Subjunctive I) can be used if its form is not identical with the indicative verb forms. If it is the same, the general subjunctive (Subjunctive II) should be used. Subjunctive I is formed by adding *"e, est, e, en, et, en"* to the verb infinitive stem; e.g., *spreche, sprechest, spreche,* etc. And here: *schreibe, schreibest, schreibe,* etc. For subjunctive II, add the

same endings to the past tense stem (and add umlauts to *"a, o, u"* for strong verbs): *spräche, sprächest, spräche,* etc. The special subjunctive of *"sein"* is *sei, seiest, sei, seien, seiet, seien.*

63.   (C)
See explanation no. 64.

64.   (D)
For a discussion of the subjunctive in indirect discourse, see explanation number 62, above. In that item, the indirect discourse for present/future time situations was given. Here we have a past time situation. In past time situations (past subjunctive), use a *sei* form for *sein* or a subjunctive I or II form for *haben* (*er habe/hätte,* etc.) plus the past participle of the main verb: *der Präsident sei gewesen* (no. 63) and *der Präsident habe geredet* (no. 64).

65.   (A)
Als is used when the reference is to a single event, act, or state in the past ("at the time when"). Here: "When Kurt was here the last time,..." Likewise: *Sie winkten, als ich abfuhr.* (They waved as/when I left.) Thus *als* will be seen with past tense forms.

66.   (B)
Wann is used only as an interrogative to introduce direct or indirect questions ("at what time"): *Wann kommen Sie morgen?* Or with indirect questions (interrogative clauses): *Shirley weiß nicht, wann sie fertig ist.* (Shirley doesn't know when she'll be finished; when will Shirley be finished?) And here: He doesn't know when *(wann)* he can visit you again: *"..., wann er dich wieder besuchen kann."*

67.   (D)
Prepositions are always tricky because they can usually not be translated word for word (literally). For instance, "for" cannot always be translated with *für* or "to" with *zu.* Thus, doing or receiving something for Easter, Christmas, New Year's Eve, one's birthday, etc., or being on or going for a holiday or vacation is not expressed with *"für"* but with

just about every German preposition except *"für"*: use *"zu"* for the holidays (*zu Ostern/Weihnachten/Silvester*); *"zum"* for one's birthday (*zum Geburtstag*); *"auf" Urlaub gehen, "auf, in, im" Urlaub sein, "in" Urlaub fahren; "in" die Ferien gehen/fahren, "in" den Ferien sein,* and so on. These various uses and meanings of the prepositions must be memorized.

68.   (C)
In German, indirect objects are expressed in the dative case (*"mir"* is dative). Therefore, if "Father says something to me," "to me" in the indirect object, *mir*. The "to" in "to me" is already built into the German meaning by using the dative form. Thus, *"zu mir"* would be redundant ("to to me") and is not correct in this sentence.

69.   (D)
The forms are *backen – backte – gebacken* (it's a strong verb). One occasionally sees *gebackt*, which is probably accepted in certain dialects, but is not an acceptable form in Hochdeutsch. *"Gebukt"* doesn't exist.

70.   (C)
Ich esse den Kuchen gern becomes *"Ich esse ihn gern"* when using a pronoun to replace the noun (*Kuchen*). Stay with the gender. Since *Kuchen* is masculine, use the corresponding masculine pronoun (*"er"*). The *"er"* becomes *"ihm"* in the dative case and *"ihn"* in the accusative case. Here it is accusative because it's a direct object: "I eat it (*ihn*), the cake (*den Kuchen*)."

71.   (D)
When comparing two things (here, *"Kuchen"* with *"Torte"*), use the comparative forms. (Use the superlative form when comparing more than two things.) The comparative form for *gern* (gladly) is *lieber* (more gladly) and for *"gut"* is *"besser."* These are irregular comparative forms and must be memorized.

72.   (B)

Watch for certain clues: "*sehr groß; Haut ... dick; braucht es nur daraufzutreten.*" Of the four animals, only the elephant has a skin thick enough to withstand some spears; only it is big enough to crush something simply by standing on it. From these clues, one can infer which creature is being discussed here.

73.   (C)

This question tests your logic. Obviously, the answer is not expressly stated in the passage, but by using one's good judgment, a little common sense and logic, one realizes that the tribe knows this fact from personal experience when hunting animals, including the elephant, and certainly not by reading about it in a library or from American scientists.

74.   (D)

The main impression one should derive from this passage is that the Watusi tribe feels somewhat in awe of the elephant's air of superiority. The passage made no mention of whether or not elephants are cunning, shy, or irritable.

75.   (A)

Read between the lines to find that if this African tribe finds the elephant to be the king of all animals and finds it good-natured, then certainly the tribe does not hate the animal. But they certainly honor, like, and know about the elephant (choices B, C, and D). Read the sentence carefully and don't overlook the final "*nicht.*" The tone of this paragraph clearly reveals that the Watusi do not despise this largest of all land animals.

76.   (B)

The elephant will crush most other animals simply by "stepping on them" because it is that big and strong: "*Wenn es aber etwas töten ... will, braucht es nur daraufzutreten, ... weil es so viel Kraft hat.*"

77.   (B)

The lady is wearing a pair of glasses. The clue is that she looks over the rim of her glasses to tell the man he shouldn't smoke: "...*blickte die Dame streng über den Brillenrand....*"

78.   (A)

Don't let the transposed word order of the dative case (for *gefallen*) confuse you. Read it carefully. We can surely assume the smoke disturbed the lady though she never came out and said so. We can assume this since she looked at him severely and didn't hesitate to remind him of his manners about smoking in her presence.

79.   (B)

He would rather poison himself than live with this woman. Though he doesn't say this, his final remark implies this and carries that message to her probably more effectively than if he had actually come out and said it.

80.   (D)

We can see that the man is without much decorum, good behavior, or manners (*ohne Anstand*). He is not caring and he doesn't sound terribly good-natured.

SAT II:
SUBJECT TEST IN
GERMAN

PRACTICE
TEST II

GERMAN PRACTICE TEST II

PART A

Time: 1 Hour
        80 Questions

DIRECTIONS: Each of the sentences in this part has a blank space indicating that a word or phrase has been omitted. From the four choices select the ONE that when inserted in the sentence fits grammatically and logically with the sentence as a whole. Then blacken the corresponding space on the answer sheet.

1.   Er hat es immer _____ .

      (A) schnell

      (B) rasch

      (C) eilig

      (D) geschwind

2.   Ich bin _____ nach Deutschland gefahren.

      (A) in 1987

      (B) im Jahre 1987

      (C) am Jahre 1987

      (D) im Jahr 1987

3.   Brahms _____ am 7. Mai 1833 geboren.

      (A) wird

      (B) werde

      (C) wurde

      (D) ist

44

4. _____ kommt er zu mir.

   (A) Hin und her

   (B) Auf und ab

   (C) Ab und zu

   (D) Hier und dort

5. _____bringt Briefe.

   (A) Der Postmann

   (B) Der Briefbringer

   (C) Der Postträger

   (D) Der Briefträger

6. Wo _____ du die Schule?

   (A) gehst

   (B) besuchst

   (C) lernst

   (D) unterrichtest

7. Ich denke nicht _____.

   (A) daran

   (B) an dem

   (C) woran

   (D) voran

8.   Er hat _____, hier zu bleiben.

(A) die Absicht

(B) die Aussicht

(C) die Sicht

(D) die Aufsicht

9.   Das ist _____alles völlig egal.

(A) mich

(B) mir

(C) meinetwegen

(D) ihn

10.   _____ kommst du _____ kommt er.

(A) Entweder...noch

(B) Entweder...oder

(C) Weder...oder

(D) Wieder...noch

11.   Er _____ die Frage.

(A) verantwortet

(B) antwortet

(C) beantwortet auf

(D) beantwortet

12. Er ist _____ alt _____ ich.

   (A) als…als

   (B) so…als

   (C) so…wie

   (D) als…wie

13. Ich habe _____ dem Zahnarzt.

   (A) Angst vor

   (B) Angst für

   (C) Angst an

   (D) Ängste vor

14. _____ Briefe hast du denn von ihm bekommen?

   (A) Was vor

   (B) Was für

   (C) Was für einen

   (D) Welche für

15. Hast du das Gedicht _____ ?

   (A) inwendig gelernt

   (B) auswendig gelesen

   (C) auswendig gelernt

   (D) auswendig gelehrt

16. Ist das wirklich _____?

    (A) der Mühe wert

    (B) die Mühe wert

    (C) des Mühes wert

    (D) wert der Mühe

17. Ich interessiere mich _____ die Musik von Mozart.

    (A) in

    (B) für

    (C) auf

    (D) an

18. Helfen Sie _____ doch!

    (A) ihn

    (B) sie

    (C) ihm

    (D) es

19. Er hat sich hoffnungslos in _____.

    (A) mich beliebt

    (B) mich verliebt

    (C) mir verliebt

    (D) mich geliebt

20. Das ist der Mann, _____ ich gestern sah.

    (A) der

    (B) die

    (C) dem

    (D) den

21. Er stellte die Flasche auf _____ Tisch.

    (A) dem

    (B) der

    (C) die

    (D) den

22. Ich habe _____ gearbeitet.

    (A) der ganze Tag

    (B) den ganzen Tag

    (C) dem ganzen Tag

    (D) des ganzen Tages

23. Er weiß nicht, _____ ich bin.

    (A) wer

    (B) der

    (C) wen

    (D) wem

24. Wann kommt er gewöhnlich _____?

   (A) zu Hause

   (B) nach Hause

   (C) in dem Haus

   (D) nach dem Haus

25. Leider habe ich _____ Geld.

   (A) nicht

   (B) keins

   (C) kein

   (D) nein

26. Gefällt _____ sein Haus?

   (A) dich

   (B) dir

   (C) sie

   (D) ihn

27. "_____ zuletzt lacht, lacht am besten."

   (A) Wer

   (B) Wen

   (C) Wem

   (D) Wo

28.   Wann kommt er _____?

(A) vor

(B) an

(C) in

(D) zu

29.   _____ das _____ verstehen, mußt du das Buch lesen.

(A) In...Ordnung

(B) Um...zu

(C) Um...nach

(D) In...zu

30.   Wir haben etwas _____ zu berichten.

(A) Wichtiges

(B) Wichtigen

(C) Wichtig

(D) Wichtiger

31.   Ein _____war bei uns zu Besuch.

(A) Deutsch

(B) Deutsche

(C) Deutscher

(D) Deutschen

32. _____ kam er unerwartet.

   (A) Ein Tag

   (B) Eines Tages

   (C) Einen Tag

   (D) Einem Tag

33. Ich weiß nicht _____ er meint.

   (A) was

   (B) welchem

   (C) wer

   (D) wem

34. Ich erinnere _____ noch an die Zeit in Wien.

   (A) sich

   (B) selbst

   (C) mich

   (D) mir

35. Bist du verrückt? _____ doch langsam!

   (A) Fähr

   (B) Fährst

   (C) Fahrt

   (D) Fahre

36. Es _____ viele Leute, die gern Fußball spielen.

(A) gibt

(B) geben

(C) sind

(D) ist

37. _____ ich dort wohnte, war ich jung.

(A) Wenn

(B) Als

(C) Wann

(D) Obwohl

38. Wohnt er _____ in Köln?

(A) immer nicht

(B) immer noch

(C) immer wieder

(D) immer mehr

PART B

DIRECTIONS: Read the following passages carefully for comprehension. Each passage is followed by a number of incomplete statements or questions. Select the completion or answer that is best according to the passage and blacken the corresponding space on the answer sheet.

Im Jahre 1284 erschien ein merkwürdiger Mann in Hameln. Er trug einen vielfarbigen, bunten Rock und behauptete Rattenfänger zu sein. Er sagte, er könne gegen ein gewisses Geld die Stadt von allen Mäusen und Ratten befreien. Die Bürger erklärten sich bereit, diesen Lohn zu bezahlen. Der Rattenfänger zog sein Pfeifchen heraus und spielte. Ratten und Mäuse krochen aus allen Häusern hervor and sammelten sich um ihn herum. Als er meinte, dass alle da waren, ging er aus der Stadt hinaus. Der ganze Haufen folgte ihm, stürzte ins Wasser und ertrank. Als die Bürger sich von ihrer Plage befreit sahen, wollten sie nicht mehr den Lohn bezahlen. Der Mann ging verbittert weg. Kurz danach kehrte er zurück. Diesmal war er als Jäger gekleidet und trug einen roten, wunderlichen Hut. Während alle Bürger in der Kirche versammelt waren, ließ er seine Pfeife wieder in den Gassen ertönen. Jetzt kamen nicht Ratten und Mäuse, sondern Kinder, vom vierten Jahr an, gelaufen. Diese führte er hinaus und verschwand. Nur zwei Kinder wurden gerettet. Das eine war blind und konnte den Ort nicht zeigen und das andere war stumm und konnte nicht erzählen. 130 Kinder wurden verloren. (Nach Brüder Grimm "Deutsche Sagen.")

Die Sage ist eine der bekanntesten Sagen in aller Welt. Sie wurde in ca. 30 Sprachen übersetzt und gehört in vielen Ländern zum Standardprogramm im Schulunterricht. Ihre genaue Klärung ist bis heute nicht möglich gewesen. Sie besteht jedoch aus einer Verbindung von verschiedenen Geschichten, die zur Zeit der Rattenplagen in Europa entstanden sind. Es ist wahrscheinlich, dass es zu der Zeit Rattenfänger gab, aber sie haben bestimmt realistischere Methoden verwendet als der sagenhafte Rattenfänger von Hameln.

39.   Der Mann behauptete, _____ .

(A) er könnte die Stadt umsonst von Ratten befreien

(B) er könnte Ratten und Mäuse von der Stadt entfernen

(C) er könnte gegen Austausch von Kindern die Stadt von Ratten befreien

(D) er könnte gegen ein gewisses Geld die Kinder aus der Stadt führen

40. Was war das Resultat seines Spielens?

(A) Die Bürger wollten das Geld nicht bezahlen.

(B) Die Ratten folgten ihm in die nächste Stadt.

(C) Die Ratten sind im Fluss umgekommen.

(D) Ein Haufen Bürger stürzte ins Wasser und ertrank.

41. Was war das Resultat seines Erfolgs?

(A) Er ging enttäuscht und unglücklich weg.

(B) Die Leute wollten den Lohn nicht bezahlen, aber er bekam ihn trotzdem.

(C) Er verkleidete sich als Jäger und erschoss die Bürger der Stadt.

(D) Er bekam endlich sein Geld.

42. Diese Sage _____ .

(A) ist in aller Welt weniger bekannt, als andere Sagen

(B) wird oft in Schulen gelesen

(C) ist heute völlig geklärt worden

(D) hat nichts mit dem Leben im 13. Jahrhundert zu tun

Wegen des engen Zusammenlebens in einer Großstadt kann es oft zu Streit zwischen Nachbarn kommen. Die Chancen für solche Streitereien steigen, wenn Tiere auf der Bildfläche erscheinen. Das war der Fall in einem ländlichen Stadtteil von München, wo ein Jurist einen Nachbarn mit einem Hahn namens "Fredi" hatte. Der entnervte Jurist behauptete Fredis Krähen sei genauso störend wie der Lärm von Baumaschinen. Da Baumaschinen zwischen 22 und 7 Uhr nicht benutzt werden dürfen, sollte Fredi auch nicht während dieser Zeit krähen dürfen. Vor dem Landgericht in München wurde Fredi aber dazu verurteilt, täglich von 20 bis 8 Uhr in seinem schalldichten (sound proof) Stall eingesperrt zu werden. Das war also länger als die Ruhezeit für Baumaschinen. An Sonn-und Feiertagen durfte er auch nicht zur Mittagszeit frei herumlaufen. Fredis Besitzer war nicht damit zufrieden und es gab einen zweiten Prozess. Diesmal kam Fredi besser davon weg. Als Resultat dieses Prozesses musste Fredi nur noch zur üblichen Ruhezeit zwischen 22 und 7 Uhr den Schnabel halten.

43. In einer Großstadt gibt es oft Schwierigkeiten zwischen Nachbarn, weil _____ .

   (A) man wenig Platz hat

   (B) man gern streitet

   (C) man die Nachbarn nicht mag

   (D) Tiere mit einander streiten

44. Warum beklagte sich Fredis Nachbar?

   (A) Weil Fredi seine Baumaschine kaputtmachte.

   (B) Weil Fredi viel Lärm machte.

   (C) Weil Fredi entnervt war.

   (D) Weil Fredi zwischen 22 und 7 Uhr die Baumaschine benutzte.

45.	Warum war Fredis Strafe ungerecht?

(A) Weil Fredis Krähen doch nicht so störend war, wie die Baumaschine.

(B) Weil Fredi in einem Stall eingesperrt werden musste.

(C) Weil Fredi länger ruhig sein musste, als die Baumaschine.

(D) Weil Fredi keine Baumaschine war, sondern ein Hahn.

46.	Warum war der zweite Prozess günstiger für Fredi?

(A) Jetzt mussten die Baumaschine zwischen 20 und 8 Uhr ruhig sein.

(B) Jetzt durfte sein Besitzer frei herumlaufen.

(C) Jetzt durfte Fredi weggehen.

(D) Jetzt durfte Fredi längere Zeit krähen.

Wie wurde man Rockstar in der Deutschen Demokratischen Republik? Die Antwort auf diese Frage fand man in der Lebensgeschichte von Tamara Danz, der bekanntesten Sängerin der DDR. Tamara Danz galt als "deutsche Tina Turner." Nach ersten musikalischen Versuchen auf Partys und kleinen Veranstaltungen, schien sie zuerst den normalen Weg einschlagen zu wollen. Sie immatrikulierte sich an der Humbolt-Universität für das Fach Germanistik. Nebenbei trat sie als Sängerin einer Rockgruppe auf. In ihrer Studienzeit lernte sie andere Sänger in Ostberlin kennen und beschloss, ihr bisheriges studentisches Leben aufzugeben. Stattdessen wollte sie an der Berliner Hochschule für Musik weiterstudieren, aber diese Hoffnung erfüllte sich nicht. Später behauptete sie, das wäre das Beste, was ihr hätte passieren können, weil die meisten Hochschulabsolventen in der Rockmusik keinen Erfolg haben. Aber in der DDR mußte man einen Berufsausweis für Musiker haben. Um in den Besitz dieses Ausweises zu gelangen, besuchte Tamara Danz eine kleine Musikschule in Berlin, wo Klavier und Gesang im Vordergrund standen. Über ihre Ausbildung behauptet Tamara Danz, sie hatte sich selbst alles beibringen müssen, was sie kann, aber die Ausbildung schade nichts, man werde schließlich nicht blöder davon. Im Jahre

1978 entstand ihre Band "Silly." Diese Gruppe Wurde Nr. 1 in der DDR und ihre LP wurde von der Kritik zum "Meilenstein" in der DDR-Rockgeschichte erklärt. Sie macht Tourneen durch die Schweiz und Westdeutschland und träumt vom Auftritt in London, fürchtet aber, dass die Engländer sich wenig für deutschsprachige Texte interessieren, wurden.

47. Dieser Aufsafz stellt die Frage wie _____ .

   (A) man Rockstar in Westdeutschland wird

   (B) man überhaupt Rockstar wird

   (C) man eine deutsche Tina Turner wird

   (D) man Rockstar in Ostdeutschlands wird

48. Tamara Danz _____ .

   (A) wollte an der Berliner Hochschule für Musik studieren

   (B) wollte vom Anfang an Germanistik studieren

   (C) wollte nur nebenbei als Sängerin auftreten

   (D) wollte ihr bisheriges studentisches Leben weiterführen

49. Was hält sie davon, dass ihr Auftrag für die Berliner Hoch-schule für Musik abgelehnt wurde?

   (A) Sie ist immer noch sehr enttäuscht.

   (B) Sie freut sich.

   (C) Sie hofft immer noch, dort angenommen zu werden.

   (D) Sie glaubt, die Hoffnung wird sich erfüllen.

50. Warum besuchte sie eine kleine Musikschule in Berlin?

   (A) Weil man doch Klavier lernen muss.

   (B) Weil sie einen Berufsausweis brauchte.

   (C) Weil Klavier und Gesang bei ihr im Vordergrund stehen.

   (D) Weil die kleine Schule besser ist als die größere.

51. Über die Ausbildung meinte Tamara Danz:

   (A) Die Ausbildung ist blöd.

   (B) Man wird schließlich dümmer davon.

   (C) Man kann doch etwas davon lernen.

   (D) Sie musste alles selbst lernen.

52. Eine LP der Band "Silly" _____ .

   (A) wurde für wichtig gehalten

   (B) wurde für die Rockgeschichte für unbedeutend gehalten

   (C) wurde gar nicht von den Kritikern beachtet

   (D) machte die Gruppe Nr. 1 in der DDR

53. Was hielt Tamara Danz von einem Auftritt in London?

   (A) Sie fürchtete, den Engländern würde ihre Musik nicht
       gefallen.

   (B) Sie fürchtete, die Engländer würden die deutschen Texte
       nicht interessant finden.

   (C) Sie dachte nicht daran.

   (D) Sie wollte nur Westdeutschland und die Schweiz besuchen.

PART C

DIRECTIONS: The sentences below contain blank spaces indicating omissions in the text. Below each blank are four choices. Select the choice that is grammatically correct in the context and blacken the corresponding space on the answer sheet. Be sure to read the sentences first.

Questions 54–57 are one sentence.

In Berlin (54) der (55) Mann (56)

54. (A) hat   55. (A) junger   56. (A) jeden Abend

    (B) hatte   (B) jung   (B) jeder Abend

    (C) wurde   (C) jungen   (C) jedes Abend

    (D) ist   (D) junge   (D) jede Abend

 (57) Theater gegangen.

57.   (A) ins

       (B) in

       (C) in der

       (D) in den

Questions 58–60 are one sentence.

 (58) er Zeit und Geld gehabt, (59) er länger

58.   (A) Hat   59.   (A) wäre

       (B) Hatte   (B) war

       (C) Habe   (C) hätte

       (D) Hätte   (D) hatte

in Deutschland geblieben, __(60)__ .

60.   (A) und einen Roman schreiben

       (B) um einen Roman zu schreiben

       (C) um einen Roman schreiben

       (D) um zu schreiben einen Roman

Questions 61–65 are connected.

Helga ist eine __(61)__ Dame, __(62)__ in der

61.		62.	
(A) altere		(A) die	
(B) ältere		(B) wer	
(C) alteren		(C) welcher	
(D) alter		(D) wo	

Nachbarschaft __(63)__ .

63.   (A) arbeite

       (B) gearbeitet ist

       (C) arbeitete

       (D) gearbeitet war

__(64)__ Mutter wohnte bei __(65)__ .

64.		65.	
(A) Ihre		(A) sie	
(B) Seiner		(B) dich	
(C) Ihrer		(C) ihr	
(D) Sein		(D) mich	

Questions 66–67 are one sentence.

_(66)_ Frühling gibt es immer noch viele _(67)_ Tage.

66. (A) Im   67. (A) kalten

     (B) In der   (B) kalte

     (C) Zu   (C) kalt

     (D) In   (D) kalter

Questions 68–70 are one sentence.

Er _(68)_ neben _(69)_ , weil wir unsere Reise

68. (A) standete   69. (A) mich

     (B) stande   (B) mir

     (C) stand   (C) mein

     (D) stehte   (D) meiner

_(70)_ .

70. (A) zu besprechen wollten

     (B) besprechen wollten

     (C) besprechen gewollt

     (D) besprechen wollt

PART D

DIRECTIONS: Read the following passages carefully for comprehension. Each passage is followed by a number of incomplete statements or questions. Select the completion or answer that is best according to the passage and blacken the corresponding space on the answer sheet.

Der bekannte Dichter Bertolt Brecht war eine Art Lebenskünstler, der es verstand, sich in schwierigen Lagen durchzuschlagen, ob in Nazi-Deutschland, in Amerika oder in der späteren DDR. Dass diese Überlebens-Fähigkeit sich ziemlich früh merken ließ, sieht man in einer Geschichte, die von einem Schulkameraden aus ihrer gemeinsamen Schulzeit erzählt wurde. Eines Tages bekamen die Schüler schriftliche Arbeiten zurück, die vom Klassenlehrer korrigiert worden waren. Bei Brecht gab es viele Fehler, die nicht zu übersehen waren, wegen des roten Stiftes, den der Lehrer reichlich benutzt hatte. Da er für diese Arbeit eine schlechte Note bekam, war Brecht unzufrieden. Nach kurzer Überlegung nahm er selber einen roten Stift und umkreiste einige Antworte, die richtig waren. Dann nahm er die Arbeit wieder zum Lehrer, zeigte auf die neuen "Fehler" und fragte, wieso die Antworten falsch seien. Der Lehrer sah sie sorgfältig an und gab dann zu, er habe sich offenbar geirrt und einige richtige Antworte aus Versehen für falsch gehalten. Es blieb ihm keine Wahl. Er musste die von Brecht umkreisten Punkte zu der ersten, schlechten Note rechnen, mit dem Resultat, dass Brecht am Ende eine befriedigende Note bekam.

71. Bertolt Brecht gilt als Lebenskünstler, weil _____ .

   (A) er viele Gedichte schrieb

   (B) er bekannt war

   (C) er andere geschlagen hat

   (D) er sich in schwierigen Zeiten retten konnte

72. Da Brecht mit seiner Note unzufrieden war, _____ .

(A) hat er seine Arbeit weggeworfen

(B) umkreiste er einige richtige Antworten, als ob sie falsch wären

(C) zeigte er den Lehrer an

(D) umkreiste er einige falsche Antworten, als ob sie richtig wären

73. Was machte der Lehrer, als Brecht ihm die Arbeit wieder zeigte?

(A) Er behauptete, Brecht habe sich geirrt.

(B) Er sagte, Brecht habe keine Wahl. Er müsste die Note akzeptieren.

(C) Er sagte, Brechts Note wäre schon befriedigend.

(D) Er dachte, er hatte sich geirrt und gab Brecht eine bessere Note.

74. Diese Geschichte zeigt, daß _____ .

(A) Brecht schlau, aber nicht immer ehrlich, war

(B) Brecht ein braver, gehorsamer Schuler war

(C) Brecht Angst vor seinem Lehrer hatte

(D) Brecht immer ohne Weiteres befriedigende Noten bekam

Ein Deutscher, der nie in Amerika war und wenig Englisch konnte, hatte große Lust, San Francisco kennenzulernen. Obwohl er Angst vorm Fliegen hatte, nahm er sich zusammen und kaufte ein Flugticket nach Kalifornien. Der Flug war lang, aber angenehm und alles lief planmäßig. Als das Flugzeug in Amerika landete, verstand er nicht, was angesagt wurde, aber er freute sich, endlich aus dem Fluzeug auszusteigen und die Beine ausstrecken zu können. Drei Tage lang besichtigte er die Stadt, aber er wunderte sich, dass sie so klein war. Endlich kam er zum Schluß, daß er in einem Vorort und nicht im Stadtzentrum von San Francisco war. Also stieg er in ein Taxi ein und sagte dem Taxifahrer, er möchte ins Stadtzentrum fahren. Der Taxifahrer war verblüfft, weil sie schon da waren. Er wollte jedoch den deutschen Touristen nicht beleidigen und fragte ihn so höflich wie möglich, in welches Stadtzentrum er denn fahren möchte. Der Deutsche sagte etwas empört, dass er selbstverständlich ins Stadtzentrum von San Francisco fahren wollte. Der Taxifahrer sah ihn fassungslos an und erklärte ihm, das sei mindestens 3000 Meilen von dieser Stadt entfernt. Jetzt war der Deutsche fassungslos aber es gelang ihm doch den Taxifahrer zu fragen, in welcher Stadt er nun sei. Es stellt sich heraus, dass sein Flugzeug eine Zwischenlandung in Bangor, Maine hatte und er war ungefähr vier Stunden und 3000 Meilen zu früh ausgestiegen. Nachdem es dem Taxifahrer klar wurde, was passiert war, fand er die Geschichte ganz lustig und sie kam in die Bangorer Zeitung. Daraufhin wurde der Deutsche vom Bürgermeister und verschiedenen Bürgern der Stadt-Bangor eingeladen. Er blieb noch zwei Wochen dort und ist wegen der Gastfreundlichkeit in Bangor nie weiter nach San Francisco gefahren. Am Ende seiner Aufenhalt in Bangor ist er ganz vergnügt wieder ins Flugzeug eingestiegen, um nach Deutschland zurückzufliegen. Beim Abschied teilte er den Bürgern von Bangor mit, er hätte vor, nächstes Jahr wieder seinen Urlaub bei ihnen zu verbringen.

75. Warum ist der Deutsche falsch ausgestiegen?

(A) Er verstand wenig Englisch.

(B) Er wollte die Stadt Bangor besichtigen.

(C) Der Flug war ihm zu lang.

(D) Er wollte die Beine ausstrecken.

76. Warum stieg er in ein Taxi ein?

   (A) Er war müde.

   (B) Er wollte ins Stadtzentrum fahren.

   (C) Er wollte einen Vorort von San Francisco sehen.

   (D) Er wollte 3000 Meilen mit dem Taxi fahren.

77. Der Taxifahrer war verblüfft, weil _____ .

   (A) sie schon in San Francisco waren

   (B) der Deutsche ihn beleidigte

   (C) er den Deutschen nicht beleidigen wollte

   (D) sie bereits im Stadtzentrum waren

78. Der Deutsche war fassungslos, weil _____ .

   (A) der Taxifahrer nicht fahren wollte

   (B) er nicht gewusst hatte, dass das Flugzeug eine Zwischen-
       landung hatte

   (C) er San Francisco doch nicht besuchen wollte

   (D) der Taxifahrer 3000 Meilen in 4 Stunden fahren wollte

79. Der Deutsche _____ .

   (A) war überall zu Gast

   (B) fand die Gastfreundlichkeit in Bangor unausstehlich

   (C) ist sofort weiter nach San Francisco gefahren

   (D) wollte nächstes Jahr unbedingt nach San Francisco fahren

80. Die Geschichte zeigt, was passieren kann, wenn _____ .

   (A) man nach San Francisco fährt

   (B) man die Sprache nicht beherrscht

   (C) man aus einem Flugzeug aussteigt

   (D) man einen Taxifahrer etwas fragt

SAT II:
SUBJECT TEST IN GERMAN

PRACTICE TEST II

ANSWER KEY

1.	C	21.	D	41.	A	61.	B
2.	B	22.	B	42.	B	62.	A
3.	C	23.	A	43.	A	63.	C
4.	C	24.	B	44.	B	64.	A
5.	D	25.	C	45.	C	65.	C
6.	B	26.	B	46.	D	66.	A
7.	A	27.	A	47.	D	67.	B
8.	A	28.	B	48.	A	68.	C
9.	B	29.	B	49.	B	69.	B
10.	B	30.	A	50.	B	70.	B
11.	D	31.	C	51.	D	71.	D
12.	C	32.	B	52.	A	72.	B
13.	A	33.	A	53.	B	73.	D
14.	B	34.	C	54.	D	74.	A
15.	C	35.	D	55.	D	75.	A
16.	A	36.	A	56.	A	76.	B
17.	B	37.	B	57.	A	77.	D
18.	C	38.	B	58.	D	78.	B
19.	B	39.	B	59.	A	79.	A
20.	D	40.	C	60.	B	80.	B

GERMAN PRACTICE TEST II
DETAILED EXPLANATIONS
OF ANSWERS

1.   (C)

All of the choices have to do with being fast. However, only the word *"eilig"* fits here. The words *es* and *hat* reveal it to be part of the idiom *es eilig haben*. The English equivalent is "to be in a hurry." *Schnell, rasch*, and *geschwind* all mean "fast." Examples:

> *Er läuft schnell.* (He runs fast.)
> *Er entschließt sich oft zu rasch.* (He often decides hastily.)
> *Das geht nicht so geschwind.* (That doesn't go so fast.)

2.   (B)

There are two possibilities in German for expressing the English equivalent of "in the year____." One can either say *im Jahre_____* or simply state the year without a preposition. For example, the above sentence could also read: *Ich bin 1987 nach Deutschland gefahren.* Choice (A) is one of the most common mistakes made by English speaking students of German because it is closest to English. Remember, use either the whole phrase or nothing. The preposition *"am"* in (C) is used before days of the week (*am Montag, am Dienstag,* etc.), or for dates in which the day is also given: *Am 1. Juli 1987.* The preposition *zu*, like all prepositions, has many uses, but in time expressions it appears in conjunction with holidays: *zu Weihnachten, zu Ostern,* ("at Christmas," "at Easter") or like the English "for" in *zum Geburtstag* ("for [one's] birthday") where *zum* is a contraction of *zu dem*.

3.   (C)

To state the birth date of a deceased person, the imperfect of the verb *werden* is used. For a living person, the present of *sein* is used: *Ich bin*

1959 geboren. Since Brahms is no longer living, choice D is incorrect. (A) is incorrect because it is the present tense of the verb *werden.* (B) is the first person singular present tense of the verb *werden.* It is incorrect because it is the wrong tense and also because it would have to be third-person singular to agree with the subject *Brahms.*

4.   (C)

Ab und zu means "now and then" and fits the context of the sentence. All other choices listed have to do with location. Choice (A), *"hin und her,"* does not fit because it means "back and forth." Choice (B), *"auf und ab,"* means "up and down." Choice (D), *"hier und dort,"* is the equivalent of "here and there" in English.

5.   (D)

Choice (A) is a literal translation of "mailman" and does not exist in German. Choice (B) is also an invention and literally means "letter bringer." Choice (C) is a combination of fact and fantasy. The words *Post* and *Träger* exist, but not in this combination. The correct answer, *Briefträger* means literally "letter carrier." *Träger* is a noun derived from the verb *tragen,* "to carry."

6.   (B)

Eine Schule besuchen is an idiom meaning "to attend school." The other choices all have to do with school, but would have to be used with a preposition:

    (A) *Gehst du heute in die Schule?* (Are you going to school today?)

    (C) *Was lernst du in der Schule?* (What are you learning at school?)

    (D) *Unterrichten Sie in dieser Schule?* (Do you teach in this school?)

7.   (A)

"Daran" is a *"da(r)*-construction." It replaces a preposition and a pronoun referring to a thing. *"Ich denke nicht daran"* means "I am not thinking about it." If the sentence were "I am not thinking about him,"

it would not be possible to express the prepositon + pronoun with the *da(r)* - construction: *"Ich denke nicht an ihn."* Choice (B) is not possible because the expression *denke an* is always followed by the accusative and *dem* is dative. Choice (C) is a *wo(r)* - construction and is used to replace a preposition + *was*. For example: *"Woran denkst du?"* (What are you thinking about?) Choice (D) simply means "ahead" and does not fit. An example of its use would be *Er geht voran* (He's going ahead).

8. (A)
Die Absicht haben means "to have the intention." Choices (B) and (C) mean "view" and do not fit the context. Examples of their use are:
> *Von dem Fenster im Hotel hatte er eine schöne Aussicht.*
> (From the hotel window he had a beautiful view.)
> *Bei diesem Wetter ist die Sicht gut.*
> (The view/visibility is good in this weather.)

Choice (D) has to do with watching over and supervising:
> *Sie hatten die Aufsicht über die Kinder.*
> (They were in charge of the children.)

9. (B)
The idiom *"Das ist mir egal"* means "That's all the same to me" or "I don't care." The person who doesn't care is always in the dative case. For example, "He doesn't care" would be: *Das ist ihm egal.* Since none of the other forms given are dative, they are incorrect. Choice (A) is the accusative form of the first-person singular pronoun. Choice (C) *meinetwegen* means "as far as I am concerned" or "for my sake and on my account." Examples:
> *Meinetwegen brauchst du das nicht zu tun.*
> (You don't have to do that on my account.)
> *Darf ich mitkommen? Meinetwegen.*
> (May I come along? As far as I'm concerned.)

10. (B)
The English equivalent of *entweder...oder* is "either...or." The sentence reads: "Either you come, or he [comes]." The combinations in

(A), (C) and (D) do not exist. The other legitimate form is *"weder...noch."* It means "neither...nor." Example:

> *Weder mir noch ihm gehört das Buch.*
> (The book belongs to neither me nor him.)

11.   (D)

There are two ways to express "to answer a question" in German. One is *beantworten* + the accusative case and the other is *antworten* + *auf* + the accusative case. Choice (B) is incorrect because *antworten* would have to be followed by *auf*. Choice (A) is from the verb *verantworten*. It means "to answer for" or "to account for." Choice (C) is wrong, because the preposition *auf* should not be used with *beantworten*.

12.   (C)

In comparing two things that are equal, the combination *"so...wie"* is used. The English equivalent is "as...as." Choice (A) is a direct translation of the English equivalent and is incorrect. The combinations in (B) and (C) do not exist.

13.   (A)

In order to answer this correctly, you must know the German idiom *"Angst haben vor,"* which means "to be afraid of." The preposition is always *vor*. Therefore, choices (B) and (C) are incorrect. The word for "fear" in Choice (D) is plural. It always remains singular in this expression.

14.   (B)

"Was für" means "what kind of." The sentence reads, "What kind of letters did you receive from him?" The combination in choices (A) and (D) do not exist. Choice (C) is possible. It means "what kind of a." Since *einen* is masculine accusative, it would have to be used in a sentence in which it is followed by a masculine direct object. For example:

> *Was für einen Koffer hattest du?*
> (What kind of a suitcase did you have?)

15. (C)

In order to answer correctly, you need to know the expression *etwas auswendig lernen*. The English equivalent is "to learn something by heart." The other combinations are not possible. The word *inwendig* in choice (A) means "internal." In choice (B), *gelesen* is the past participle of the verb *lesen,* "to read." In choice (D), *gelehrt* is the past participle of the verb *lehren,* which means "to teach." None of these can be used with *auswendig*.

16. (A)

The idiom *"der Mühe wert"* is equivalent to the English expression "worth the trouble." If one thinks of it as meaning "worthy of the trouble," it is easier to remember, because *"Mühe"* is in the genitive case. For this reason, choice (B) is incorrect, since *"die Mühe"* is not genitive. Choice (C) appears to be genitive, but it is not, since *"Mühe"* is feminine. *"Des"* is the genitive definite article for the masculine and neuter. Choice (D) is incorrect because of the word order. In this expression, the noun comes first, unlike in the equivalent English expression.

17. (B)

"To be interested in" is rendered into German by *interessieren an* + dative, or *sich interessieren für* + accusative. Since *"die Musik von Mozart"* is in the accusative, the only possibility is *sich interessieren für*. Choices (A) and (C) are not possible.

18. (C)

"Helfen" is a verb that takes a dative object. All of the pronouns listed here are accusative except for *"ihm."*

19. (B)

In order to answer correctly, you must be familiar with the idiom *sich in jemanden* (accusative) *verlieben*. The English equivalent is "to fall in love with someone." Choice (A) does not exist. The word *beliebt* alone means "beloved" or "popular." Choice (C) is incorrect, because the object must be in the accusative case. *Mir* is the dative. In choice

(D), everything is correct except the verb. *Geliebt* is the past participle of the verb *lieben*, "to love," and does not fit here. One can say *Er hat mich geliebt*. (He loved me.)

20.   (D)

Missing here is a relative pronoun. In order to use relative pronouns, you must know two things: the gender of the word it refers to (antecedent) and how it is used in the relative clause. Here the antecedent is *Mann* and it is the direct object (accusative case) of the verb *sah*. Except for the genitive forms (*dessen, deren, dessen, deren*) and the dative plural (*denen*), relative pronouns look like the definite article. Just as the masculine, definite article in the accusative case is *den*, so is the relative pronoun. Choice (A) could be a relative pronoun, but it is the wrong case to fit here. Choice (B) could also be a relative pronoun, but it is the wrong gender for this relative clause. Choice (C) could also be a relative pronoun, but it is in the dative case.

21.   (D)

In order to answer correctly, you need to know that *auf* is a "two way" preposition. This means that it can either be followed by the dative or the accusative case. If motion toward a goal is described, as is the case here, the accusative is used. The bottle was placed on the table. You also need to know that *Tisch* is masculine. Another way of looking at it is that *stellen* is a verb of motion. If the verb were *stehen*, there would be no motion involved and the dative case would be used. For example, *Die Flasche steht auf dem Tisch*. (The bottle is on the table.)
This explains why choice (A) is incorrect. Choice (B) is wrong, because it is either the wrong case (nominative), or the wrong gender (feminine, dative or genitive). Choice (C) can either be feminine nominative or accusative. Therefore, it is incorrect on all counts.

22.   (B)

Definite time expressions such as this one, which means "the whole day" are in the accusative case. Choice (A) is incorrect, because it is in the nominative case. Choice (C) is in the dative case. Choice (D) is in the genitive case. There are time expressions in the genitive case, but they are indefinite time expressions, such as *eines Tages* (one day).

23.   (A)
The interrogative "who" has three forms in German, depending upon its case. The case here is nominative. Therefore, *wer* is the correct form. Choice (B) does not fit because it is not an interrogative form. Choice (C) is accusative. An example of its use would be:

> *Wen hast du gesehen?*
> (Whom did you see?)

Choice (D) is dative. An example of its use is:

> *Wem hast du das Buch gegeben?*
> (To whom did you give the book?)

24.   (B)
The idiom *"nach Hause"* is used after verbs of motion to mean "home." Choice (A) is used after other verbs and means "at home." For example:

> *Er ist nicht zu Hause.*
> (He isn't at home.)

The prepositional phrase in choice (C) means "in the house" and doesn't fit here, because of the motion verb *kommen*. Choice (D) is not possible. The preposition *nach* generally means "to" when followed by a proper name:

> *Er fährt nach Berlin.*
> (He is driving to Berlin.)

25.   (C)
Kein has the same endings as the indefinite article *ein*. It is used to negate nouns without an article, as in this example. It also replaces *nicht + ein*. For example:

> *Ich habe kein Buch von ihm gelesen.*
> (I haven't read a book by him.)

Choice (A) negates a verb. For example:

> *Ich habe das Buch nicht gelesen.*
> (I haven't read that book.)

Choice (B) is incorrect because neuter, accusative *"ein"*-words have no ending. Choice (D) is used to answer a question in the negative.

26.   (B)
Gafallen is a verb that takes a dative object. The best way to think of it is that it means "to be pleasing to." The person or thing that is pleasing is in the nominative case and the person to whom it is pleasing is in the dative case. In the example, *"sein Haus"* is nominative and *"dir"* is dative. The literal meaning is: "Is his house pleasing to you?" Since *dich* in choice (A), *sie* in choice (C) and *ihn* in choice (D) are all accusative, they do not fit.

27.   (A)
This is a well-known proverbial saying in both English and German: "He who laughs last, laughs best." In the German version, *wer* is the subject of the verb *lacht*. Choice (B) is incorrect because it is accusative. Choice (C) is incorrect because it is dative. Choice (D) means "where" and doesn't fit.

28.   (B)
In order to answer this, you must know the verb *ankommen*, which means "to arrive." There is also the verb *vorkommen*, as in choice (A), but it means "to happen" and doesn't fit here. An example of its use:

  Das Kommt oft vor.

  (That happens often.)

Choices (C) and (D) are prepositions which need an object. Therefore, they do not fit. *An* in the test example is not a preposition, but a separable prefix. It is part of the verb.

29.   (B)
"Um...zu" is the German equivalent of "in order to." The expression *in Ordnung* given in (A) exists, but doesn't fit here. It means "in order." For example:

  Seine Sachen sind in Ordnung.

  (His things are in order.)

The combinations in (C) and (D) do not exist.

30.   (A)
After *"etwas,"* an adjective can be turned into a neuter noun. It always ends in *-es*. Other examples are *etwas Gutes* (something good), *etwas Schönes* (something beautiful), etc. Choices (B), (C), and (D) all have the wrong ending.

31.   (C)
An adjective used as a noun after *ein* has the same ending it would have if it were simply used as an adjective. *"Ein Deutscher"* is masculine, nominative in this sentence. Therefore, the adjective ending is *-er*. Choice (A) is incorrect because it has no ending. As it stands, it refers to the language, German. For example:
> *Er lernt Deutsch.*
> (He is learning German.)

Choice (B) would be correct if the article were *eine* (feminine, nominative or accusative). For example:
> *Eine Deutsche war bei uns zu Besuch.*
> (A German [woman] was visiting us.)

Choice (D) would be correct if the article were *einen* (masculine, accusative). For example:
> *Ich sah einen Deutschen.*
> (I saw a German [man]).

32.   (B)
Indefinite time expressions are in the genitive case. That is the case in this sentence, which means: "One day he came unexpectedly." Choice (A) is nominative and doesn't fit grammatically. Choice (C) is accusative and choice (D) is dative. Neither fits here.

33.   (A)
When a relative pronoun is necessary and there is no specific word to which it refers, *"was"* is used. That is the case here. Choice (B) could also be used if *welcher* were in the accusative case. *Ich weiß nicht, welchen er meint* translates as "I don't know which one he means." The antecedent for *welchen* would have to be masculine. Choice (C) is also

incorrect because of its case. In order to be used here, it would have to be accusative.

Ich weiß nicht, wen er meint means "I don't know whom he means." Choice (D) is in the dative case and could fit into this sentence only if the verb were changed, since *meinen* takes an accusative object.

34.   (C)

To answer this question, you need to know that this is a reflexive verb (*sich erinnern*). With the first person singular pronoun, there are always two possibilities when the verb is reflexive. The reflexive can be either *mich* (accusative) or *mir* (dative). The accusative form is used when there is not another accusative object of the verb in the sentence. *Die Zeit* is the object of the preposition *an*. Answer (D) would be possible in a sentence with an accusative object of the verb.

Example:	*Ich wasche mir*	*die Hände.*
	dat. reflexive	acc. object

Answer (A) would be the correct reflexive form for third-person singular and plural (*er, sie, es, sie*) or for the formal you (*Sie*). *Selbst* is an intensifier and can be used in addition to the reflexive pronoun but not in place of it.

35.   (D)

The exclamation point at the end of the sentence shows that an imperative form is needed. The preceding sentence shows that the imperative is being addressed to one person with whom the speaker is on a familiar basis. Therefore, you must decide which is the correct *du* imperative form of the verb *fahren*. In order to eliminate (A), you must know that verbs which add an umlaut to the stem of the *du* form in the present tense drop the umlaut in the imperative. *Du fährst → Fahre.* Answer (B) is also incorrect because the *du* imperative also drops the -*st* ending of the present tense. (C) would be correct if the speaker were addressing more than one person with whom he is on a familiar basis. It is the *ihr* form of the imperative and would be correct had the sentence read: *Seid ihr verrückt?*

36.   (A)

Es gibt corresponds to the English "there is/there are." It is always singular even when followed by a plural noun and translated "there are" into English. Since it is always singular, answer (B) is incorrect. Answer (C) translates literally as "there are," but *es sind* is a more specific statement than *es gibt* and would be inappropriate here. *Es gibt* refers to the existence of something or someone, as in the statement above. Perhaps the difference is best illustrated by these examples:

> *Es gibt weiße Mäuse.*
> (There are white mice.)
> *Es sind zwei weiße Mäuse in diesem Zimmer.*
> (There are two white mice in this room.)

The last possibility is least likely, since it neither fits the meaning of the sentence, which expresses merely the existence of people who like to play football, nor would it fit grammatically.

If the verb "to be" were possible at all here, it would have to be plural.

37.   (B)

There are three words in German which correspond to the English word "when." They are *wann, als,* and *wenn.* Of these three, the easiest to remember how to use is *wann.* It is always used in questions, direct or indirect and in any tense. For example:

> *Wann kommst du?*
> *Weisst du, wann du gekommen bist?*

The next easiest is *als.* It is always used in the past tense to express a one time past action. This is the case in this question. *Wenn* is the most difficult because it can be used in any tense. When used in the past, it expresses a repeated past action. It often corresponds to the English "whenever." For example:

> *Wenn ich nach Deutschland fuhr, nahm ich immer meinen*
> *Hund mit.*
> (Whenever I went to Germany, I always took my dog along.)

Choice (D) means "although" and would not fit logically into the sentence.

38.   (B)

"Immer noch" corresponds to "still" in English. Except for *immer nicht,* which doesn't exist as a phrase, the other examples are legitimate but do not fit into the context of the sentence. Choice (C) means "again and again." Choice (D) means "more and more." *Immer* + a comparative, as in the last example, corresponds to the English comparative construction "(more) and (more)."

Other examples: *immer schwerer* (more and more difficult)
immer schöner (more and more beautiful)
immer billiger (cheaper and cheaper)

39.   (B)

This is a well-known legend and should cause no problems. However, in order to find the correct answer, it helps to know that the verb *entfernen* means "to remove." The verb used in the text, *"befreien,"* means "to free" or "to liberate." The Pied-Piper did not want to free the city of the plague of rats for nothing (*umsonst*) (A), or free it from rats in exchange for children (C), nor was it his original intention to lead the children out of the city (D).

40.   (C)

The result of his playing was that the rats and mice followed him out of the city and drowned in the river. In the text, the verb meaning "to drown" (*ertrinken*) was used. In answer (C), the verb *umkommen* (to die) was used. It is true, as stated in question (A), that the citizens did not want to pay him, but that was not the result of his playing. The rats and mice did not follow him into the next city, as stated in answer (B), but into the river. Answer (D) states that a lot of citizens threw themselves in the water and drowned.

41.   (A)

The result of his success was not what he had expected. Rather than finally receiving his money (D), he went away disappointed (*enttäuscht*) and unhappy (*unglücklich*). It is true that the people did not want to pay him; it is not true that he received the money anyway (B).

He returned dressed as a hunter but he did not shoot the citizens of the city (C).

42.   (B)
As stated in the reading, this myth is often read in schools. However, this assertion is worded slightly differently than in answer (B). The text stated that it is a standard part of school instruction *("...gehört...zum Standardprogramm des Schulunterrichts")*. Answer (A) claims it is less well-known than other myths. Answer (C) asserts that the story has now been completely explained. This is not the case. Answer (D) says it has nothing to do with life in the thirteenth century. This is also not true. The story originated during the time in which Europe was plagued by rats and is probably based upon tales told about means of ridding cities of rats.

43.   (A)
There are often problems between neighbors in large cities because of lack of space *("man hat wenig Platz")*. In the text this idea is expressed as *"das enge Zusammenleben."* Literally translated, this means "narrow co-existence." We can hope that it is not true, as stated in answer (B), that people like to fight with each other. Needless to say, it can happen that one doesn't like one's neighbors (C), but this is not the reason given in this reading for the problems. We also cannot blame problems of co-existence upon animals fighting with each other, as suggested in answer (D).

44.   (B)
Fredi's neighbor complained because Fredi made too much noise with his crowing, not because he ruined the construction machinery (A) or because he used it (D). It was the lawyer who had wracked nerves *("entnervt")*, not Fredi (B).

45.   (C)
Fredi's punishment was unfair because he had to be quiet longer than the construction machinery with which the lawyer had compared him.

Answer (A) is probably also true. Fredi's crowing was probably not as disturbing as the construction machinery, but this is not the reason given in the text for considering his treatment unfair. The same is true for answer (B). It might have been unfair to lock him in a stall, but this is not the reason given in the text. Answer (D) states his treatment was unfair because he was a rooster and not a piece of construction machinery. This might also be true, but is not based on the text.

46.   (D)
The second trial was more favorable for Fredi because he had to be quiet only between the hours of 10:00 p.m. and 7:00 a.m., not between 8:00 p.m. and 8:00 a.m. He could crow longer. The time for use of construction machines was not changed, as stated in (A). There was also no change in the life of Fredi's owner. He was always allowed to run free (B). It was never a question of Fredi's going away (C).

47.   (D)
This reading is concerned with how one became a rock star in the German Democratic Republic (*"in Ostdeutschlands"* = in East Germany) and not in West Germany (A). It is not concerned with the general question of how to become a rock star (B). Although the reading states that Tamara Danz had become the German Tina Turner, it does not explain how one becomes a Tina Turner (C).

48.   (A)
Tamara Danz wanted to study at the Berlin *"Hochschule für Musik."* It is not true that she only wanted to study German from the beginning (B). She was always interested in a career in music. She was not satisfied to appear as a singer "on the side" (*nebenbei*) (C). She did not want to continue the student life she had led (D). After meeting other singers in Berlin, she decided to give up (*aufgeben*) the student life.

49.   (B)
She was later happy that her application to study at the Berlin *"Hochschule für Musik"* had been turned down; she was not disap-

pointed (*enttäuscht*) anymore (A). She was no longer hoping to be accepted there (C) and did not believe her dream would have been fulfilled (D) by studying there.

50. (B)
She attended a small music school in Berlin because one needed a professional certification (*"Berufsausweis"*) to practice any profession in the GDR. She did not attend that school because one must learn to play the piano, as stated in answer (A). The text does not state that piano and singing are in the foreground for her (C), but for the music school. She also did not attend it because it is better than the larger school (D).

51. (D)
Tamara Danz maintains that she had to teach herself everything she knows. Nevertheless, she does not consider education stupid (*"blöd"*) (A), but says at least one doesn't become more stupid (*"blöder"*) from having received an education. Answer (B) maintains that one does indeed become more stupid from an education. Answer (C) says that one will learn from an education. This idea is not expressed by Tamara Danz.

52. (A)
 The band's LP was considered very important, a milestone (*"Meilenstein"*) in GDR Rock history. Therefore, it is not considered insignificant (*Unbedeutend*) (B), nor is it left unnoticed by critics (C). The group "Silly" was already no. 1 when this LP came out. It did not make them no. 1 (D).

53. (B)
It was her dream to perform in London, but she feared the English would not be interested in German texts. She wasn't worried about the music itself (A). Since it was her dream to perform in London, answer (C) (She didn't think about it) and (D) (She only wanted to visit West Germany and Switzerland) are false.

54. (D)

In order to answer correctly, you must first find the past participle at the end of the sentence. *Gegangen* is the past participle of the verb *gehen,* which forms its perfect tenses with *sein.* Most verbs in German form the perfect tenses with *haben.* However, verbs which (1) have no object and (2) indicate a change of location or condition form the perfect tenses with *sein.* Since *gehen* has no object and indicates a change of location, it forms its perfect tenses with *sein.* That eliminates choices (A) and (B). Choice (C) is the imperfect of the verb *werden* and does not fit grammatically.

55. (D)

The masculine nominative adjective ending is *-e* when preceded by a *der*-word. An easy way to remember this is that the masculine marker *(-r)* only appears once. When preceded by *der,* it's already there. However, when preceded by *ein,* it isn't and must be included: *Ein junger Mann....* For this reason, choice (A) is wrong. Choice (B) is incorrect because there is no adjective ending and all attributive adjectives (adjectives which come before a noun) must have an ending. Choice (C) would be correct for the masculine accusative. Actually more adjectives end in *-en* than anything else. So, if forced to guess, *-en* is always the best guess, but it doesn't work here.

56. (A)

Definite time expressions like this one (every evening) are in the accusative case. Therefore choice (B) (nominative) is incorrect. Choice (C) is the wrong gender (neuter). Choice (D) is also the wrong gender (feminine).

57. (A)

In is a preposition which can be followed by either the accusative or the dative case. If it answers the question *wo?,* i.e., if it shows no motion, it is followed by the dative. If it answers the question *wohin?,* i.e., if it shows motion, it is followed by the accusative. That is the case here. *Ins* is a contraction of *in das.* Choice (B) has no article and is therefore wrong. The article in choice (C) is dative or genitive feminine. Choice (D) would be correct if "Theater" were masculine. Like most words of foreign origin in German, it is neuter.

58.   (D)

Hätte is the Subjunctive II form of the verb *haben.* In this sentence it is used as an auxiliary to form the past tense in the subjunctive. *"Hätte er Zeit und Geld gehabt..."* means "If he had had time and money...." The Subjunctive II is used here because it is an "if" (*wenn*) clause with the "if" (*wenn*) omitted. Such clauses are easy to recognize because the verb is in first place and the punctuation shows that it is not a question. The formation of the Subjunctive II is based on the *wir* form of the imperfect tense. Irregular verbs with the vowels *a, o,* or *u* add an umlaut.

The Subjunctive II is used primarily to express contrary-to-fact conditions. Choice (A) is incorrect because it is clear from the context of of the sentence that this is a contrary-to-fact condition (he had no time and money) and *hat* is not a subjunctive form. The same applies to choice (B). Since it has no umlaut, it is clear that it is not a subjunctive form. Choice (C) is either the *ich* form of the present tense of *haben* or the *ich* and *er, sie, es* Subjunctive I form of *haben.* Subjunctive I does not fit here since Subjunctive I does not describe contrary-to-fact conditions. It is used in indirect discourse.

59.   (A)

Choice (A) is the Subjunctive II form of the verb *sein.* Here it is an auxiliary to form the Past Subjunctive II. Following the rules of formation stated above. Choice (B) is not a subjunctive form. Choice (C) is a subjunctive form, but the verb *bleiben* forms its perfect tenses with *sein.* Choice (D) is not a subjunctive form.

60.   (B)

This is an infinitive phrase formed with *um...zu,* which means "in order to." Choice (A) means "and to write a novel" and does not fit into the context of the sentence. Choice (C) is not complete because the *zu* is missing. Choice (D) has incorrect word order. In this, and in other infinitive phrases, the *zu* comes before the infinitive and the infinitive comes at the end of the phrase. Therefore, choice (D) has two mistakes in word order. It is a direct translation of English word order: in order to write a novel.

61.   (B)
This is a comparative form. Most one syllable adjectives with the vowels *a, o,* or *u* add an umlaut in the comparative and superlative forms. That is the case with *alt*. The next step in forming the comparative is to add the *-er*. Because this is an attributive adjective, it must also have an adjective ending. The ending is *-e,* because it is preceded by the indefinite article and is feminine nominative. Choice (A) is wrong because there is no umlaut. Choice (C) is missing an umlaut and is also the wrong case (accusative) and gender (masculine). Choice (D) is missing the umlaut and the adjective ending.

62.   (A)
Die is a relative pronoun. It is feminine because it refers to *Dame* and nominative because it is the subject of the relative clause. Choice (B) can only be used in questions. Choice (C) means "which" or "which one." The masculine -er ending eliminates it for use here. Choice (D) means "where" and does not fit the context.

63.   (C)
Choice (C) is the imperfect of the verb *arbeiten*. Choice (A) does not agree with the subject. It is the present tense *ich* form. Choices (B) and (D) are incorrect because *arbeiten* forms its perfect tenses with *haben*. If the choice were *gearbeitet hat* or *gearbeitet hatte* they would be correct and would mean "worked" and "had worked."

64.   (A)
Ihre means "her" in this sentence. Choice (B) would be possible as far as its meaning goes (his), but the -er ending is incorrect for the nominative case. The same is true for choice (C). Choice (D) would also be possible in meaning (his), but it needs an -e ending, since *Mutter* is feminine.

65.   (C)

The preposition *"bei"* is followed by the dative case. For this reason, choices (A), (B) and (D) are incorrect. They are all accusative forms.

66.   (A)

Before seasons the preposition *in* + the definite article is used. It is contracted to *im*. Other examples: *im Herbst, im Sommer, im Winter*. Since all the seasons are masculine, *im* is always used. Choice (B) has the wrong gender (feminine). Choice (C) is the wrong preposition. Choice (D) is missing the definite article.

67.   (B)

Since the word *"viele"* has no effect on adjective endings, this is an unpreceded adjective. The unpreceded adjective endings follow the pattern of the definite article, except in the genitive. Genitive endings are *-en*. In other cases, simply substitute the definite article to find out what the ending is. Here we would substitute *die* because *Tage* is plural. Therefore, the ending is *-e*. Choice (A) would be the correct plural adjective ending if *Tage* were preceded by the definite article. Choice (C) is wrong because it has no ending. All adjectives before nouns have an ending in German. Choice (D) would be the correct ending for a singular, unpreceded, masculine noun. For example:
> *Kalter Wein schmeckt mir.*
> (Cold wine tastes good to me.)

68.   (C)

The simple past tense (imperfect) of the verb *stehen* is irregular: *ich stand, du standest, er stand, wir standen, ihr standet, sie standen.* Choice (A) has confused the irregular form, which has no ending in the third person with a regular form like *arbeitete*. Choice (B) doesn't exist. Choice (D) has failed to take into account the vowel change in the irregular verb and has simply treated it as a regular verb by adding the regular past tense ending *-te* to the stem.

69.   (B)

Neben can be followed by an accusative or by a dative object, depending upon whether it indicates motion toward a goal (accusative) or no motion (dative). Here there is no motion, so the object is dative. Therefore, choice (A) is incorrect because it is in the accusative. Choice (C) means "my" and does not fit. Choice (D) also means "my."

70.   (B)

Here the conjugated verb *wollten* goes to the end of the clause because of the subordinating conjunction *weil*. Therefore choice (C) is wrong. Choice (A) is incorrect because there is no *zu* before the infinitive when the conjugated verb is a modal. Choice (D) is incorrect because the conjugated verb does not agree with the subject. It is the *ihr* form.

71.   (D)

Bertolt Brecht was considered a sort of "artist-of-life" (he knew how to live) because he was able to survive in difficult times (*"er verstand es, sich in schwierigen Lagen durchzuschlagen"*). This is stated slightly differently in (D): He knew how to save (*retten*) himself in difficult times. One is considered an artist (*Künstler*), but not a *Lebenskünstler* when one writes poetry (A). One is not considered a *Lebenskünstler* just because one is well-known (*bekannt*) (B). He was not considered a *Lebenskünstler* because he beat (*schlagen*) others, but because he could survive (*sich durchschlagen*) (C).

72.   (B)

Since Brecht was not satisfied with his grade, he circled a few correct answers as if they had been marked incorrect. He did not throw his paper away (*wegwerfen*) (A), or report his teacher to the police (*anzeigen*) (C). He did not circle some incorrect answers, as if they were correct (D).

73.   (D)

When Brecht showed the teacher his work again, the teacher thought he had made a mistake (*sich irren*) and gave Brecht a better grade. He did not say Brecht had made a mistake (A), nor did he say Brecht had no choice and must accept his grade (B). He also did not say Brecht's grade was satisfactory (*befriedigend*) (C).

74. (A)

This story shows that Brecht was sly (*schlau*), but not always honest (*ehrlich*). It does not show that he was a good (*brav* means "good" in the sense of "well-behaved"), obedient (*gehorsam*) student (B). It certainly does not show that he was afraid of (*Angst haben vor*) his teacher (C). Furthermore, the story does not indicate that Brecht always got good grades without any effort (*ohne Weiteres*) (D).

75. (A)

The German got off the plane at the wrong place (*"ist falsch ausgestiegen"*) because he did not understand enough English (*"er konnte wenig Englisch"*). He did not want to visit Bangor (B). *Besichtigen* means "to visit, tour, look around." The flight might have been too long (C) and he might have wanted to stretch his legs (D), but that was no reason to get off in Bangor, Maine, when he wanted to go to San Francisco.

76. (B)

He got into a taxi because he wanted to go into the center of town, not because he was tired (A). He did not get into the taxi because he wanted to see a suburb of San Francisco but because he thought he was already in a suburb (C). He also did not intend or want to travel 3,000 miles by taxi (D).

77. (D)

The taxi driver was perplexed because they were already in the center of town, not because they were already in San Francisco (A). He was not perplexed because the German had insulted him (B), or because he did not want to insult the German (C).

78. (B)

The German was astonished because he had not known that the plane had a stopover (*Zwischenlandung*) before landing in San Francisco. He was not surprised because the taxi driver did not want to go or because he did not want to visit San Francisco after all (C). The taxi driver did not want to drive 3,000 miles in 4 hours (D).

79. (A)

The German was invited everywhere. He did not find the hospitality in Bangor unbearable (*unausstehlich*) (B), nor did he fly on to San Francisco immediately (C). He planned to return to Bangor next year, not to San Francisco (D).

80. (B)

The story shows what can happen when one has not mastered a language (*eine Sprache beherrschen* = to master a language), not what can happen when one goes to San Francisco (A). It also does not show what happens when one gets off a plane (C) or when one asks a taxi driver something (D).

SAT II:
SUBJECT TEST IN
GERMAN

PRACTICE
TEST III

GERMAN PRACTICE TEST III

PART A

Time: 1 Hour
        80 Questions

DIRECTIONS: Each of the sentences in this part has a blank space indicating that a word or phrase has been omitted. From the four choices select the ONE that, when inserted in the sentence, fits grammatically and logically with the sentence as a whole. Then blacken the corresponding space on the answer sheet.

1.   Dieser Rennfahrer fuhr wieder _____ .

   (A) dem schnellsten

   (B) am schnellen

   (C) schnellsten

   (D) am schnellsten

2.   Ich stehe schon stundenlang draußen im Schnee und _____!

   (A) ich bin kalt

   (B) mir ist kalt

   (C) ich bin heiß

   (D) ich habe heiß

3.   Wir fuhren mit dem neuen Wagen _____ See.

   (A) an den

   (B) auf den

   (C) nach dem

   (D) in den

4. Weil das Buch und der Film sehr langweilig waren, nehmen wir an, dass ____ das Buch ____ der Film sehr interessant gewesen waren.

(A) weder ... noch

(B) entweder ... oder

(C) entweder ... noch

(D) weder ... oder

5. Euer heute morgen ____ Buch war eine schöne Überraschung.

(A) angekommene

(B) angekommener

(C) angekommenes

(D) angekommenen

6. Wir hörten überhaupt nichts, ____ er sagte.

(A) das

(B) was

(C) welches

(D) dessen

7. Wenn Maria _____, würde sie ja auch staunen.

(A) dorthingehe

(B) dorthingeht

(C) dorthinging

(D) dorthinginge

8. _____ Mittagessen gibt es Fisch und Kartoffeln.

   (A) Für

   (B) Zu

   (C) Zum

   (D) Am

9. Robert bekommt ein neues Radio entweder _____ Geburtstag oder _____ Weihnachten.

   (A) für … für

   (B) vor … bei

   (C) zum … zu

   (D) am … an

10. Paul hat die Mutter den Weg entlang kommen _____.

    (A) sehen

    (B) gesehen

    (C) sieht

    (D) sah

11. Wir fragten ihn, aber er _____ uns nicht.

    (A) klingelte

    (B) bratete

    (C) erwiderte

    (D) lenkte

12.   Ich wasche _____ die Hände.

(A) sich

(B) mein

(C) mir

(D) mich

13.   Der alte Mann war _____.

(A) totmüde

(B) todmüde

(C) totenmüde

(D) todesmüde

14.   Meine drei _____ merken nicht, wie sehr ich sie liebe.

(A) Hund

(B) Hunde

(C) Hunden

(D) Hünde

15.   Die zwölf _____ im Park wurden frisch gestrichen.

(A) Bänke

(B) Bänken

(C) Banke

(D) Banken

16.   Wir haben hier eine Nummer, eine Ziffer, und diese Nummer ist _____ Fünf.

(A) eines

(B) einer

(C) ein

(D) eine

17.   Paula hat das Auto _____ Tür kaputt ist, gefahren.

(A) wessen

(B) das

(C) des

(D) dessen

18.   Der Kranke wurde auch _____ über 100 Pillen nicht geheilt.

(A) durch

(B) von

(C) bei

(D) mit

19.   Dieses neue Auto ist _____ als das alte Auto.

(A) schön

(B) schöner

(C) mehr schön

(D) mehr schöner

20. Sie wünscht, dass sie ein neues Auto kaufen _____.

    (A) kann

    (B) kannte

    (C) konnte

    (D) könnte

21. Während _____, aß er viel Schokalade.

    (A) die Film

    (B) dem Film

    (C) des Film(e)s

    (D) der Film

22. Wenn Herr Huber meint, dass er morgen um 11 Uhr vorbei-
    komme, dann besucht er mich also morgen _____.

    (A) früh

    (B) vormittag

    (C) nachmittag

    (D) mittag

23. Um 19 Uhr essen wir _____.

    (A) Abend

    (B) Abendessen

    (C) zu Abend

    (D) zum Abendessen.

24. _____ heißt Ihr Vater?

(A) Wie

(B) Was

(C) Wo

(D) Wessen

25. Ilse und Ingrid _____ gestern arbeiten.

(A) mussen

(B) müssen

(C) müssten

(D) mussten

26. Der Arzt kommt zum Kranken _____ er kann.

(A) sobald

(B) so bald

(C) so bald als

(D) so bald wie

27. Er hat ein "A" bekommen, weil er an dem Tag vor der Prüfung
sehr fleißig _____ hat.

(A) studiert

(B) gelernt

(C) geschlafen

(D) gespielt

28. Der Chef hat uns geschrieben, dass Frau Hansel momentan nicht sehr fleißig _____.

(A) arbeiten

(B) arbeitet

(C) arbeite

(D) arbeitest

29. Der Politiker bestand darauf, dass er gestern tatsächlich dahingefahren _____!

(A) sei

(B) sein

(C) ist

(D) hat

30. Obwohl Herr Schmidt der jungen Inge oft finanziell half, _____ Inge den Herrn Schmidt nie.

(A) konnte

(B) kennte

(C) kannte

(D) könnte

31. Miriam fährt nächste Woche _____ Frankreich.

(A) nach

(B) in

(C) zu

(D) an

32. Die _____ Kinder klingen schön.

    (A) singen

    (B) singenen

    (C) singend

    (D) singenden

33. Ich sagte dem _____, dass es die Flugkarte des _____ sei.

    (A) Pilot ... Student

    (B) Pilot ... Students

    (C) Pilots ... Students

    (D) Piloten ... Studenten

34. Als Hans in New York war, hatte er Angst, die Unterführung
    _____.

    (A) zu fressen.

    (B) nach fressen.

    (C) zu benutzen.

    (D) nach gebrauchen.

35. Du holst _____ schnell ein Programm.

    (A) dir

    (B) dich

    (C) sich

    (D) euch

36. _____ er uns das gestern gesagt, dann wären wir nicht sofort abgefahren.

   (A) Hat

   (B) Hatte

   (C) Hätte

   (D) Wäre

37. Wenn er gestern abend gesungen hätte, dann _____ wir langer geblieben.

   (A) waren

   (B) wären

   (C) hatten

   (D) hätten

38. Paula kann nicht mitkommen, denn _____.

   (A) sie ist krank

   (B) ist sie krank

   (C) sie krank ist

   (D) ist krank

PART B

DIRECTIONS: Read the following passages carefully for comprehension. Each passage is followed by a number of incomplete statements or questions. Select the completion or answer that is best according to the passage and blacken the corresponding space on the answer sheet.

Ich bin für alle Tag und Nacht da. Ich koche, bediene und spüle mindestens dreimal am Tage ab, jeden Tag der Woche. Ich bin Putzfrau, Betreuer, Krankenschwester, Lehrerin, Beraterin, Sekretärin, alles in einem. Wenn ich nicht in der Küche bin, so bin ich im Waschraum mit der Wäsche oder im Lebensmittelgeschäft oder ich sitze im Auto als Chauffeur und bringe die Kinder zum Spielplatz, zur Geburtstagsparty, zum Arzt oder Zahnarzt und wer weiß, sonst noch wohin. Meine Dienststunden sind nicht von 9 bis 5, sondern sie haben kein Ende weil meine Arbeit kein Ende hat. Sie fängt immer wieder neu an. Dabei verdiene ich keinen Pfennig und nur selten ein "Danke schön." Die Personen, für die ich das alles mache, sind nicht besonders dankbar. Sie nehmen alles im Kauf.

39. Was bin ich?

    (A) Ärztin

    (B) Dienstmädchen

    (C) Hausfrau

    (D) Verkäuferin

40. Diese Dame ist offenbar sehr _____.

    (A) verschwenderisch

    (B) faul

    (C) zerstreut

    (D) fleißig

102

41. Für diese Arbeit wird sie _____.

(A) nicht bezahlt

(B) schlecht bezahlt

(C) gut bezahlt

(D) schwer bestraft

42. Wo arbeitet die Dame am meisten?

(A) Im Geschäft

(B) Im Auto

(C) Zu Hause

(D) In der Schule

43. Wer sind die Personen, die "nicht besonders dankbar" sind?

(A) Angestellte

(B) Patienten

(C) Arbeitskollegen

(D) Familienmitglieder

44. Diese Personen halten die Arbeit der Dame für selbstverständlich. Das heißt, dass sie _____.

(A) für den Dienst dieser Dame bezahlen

(B) die Leistung der Dame ohne weiteres erwarten

(C) mit der Hausarbeit helfen

(D) sehr dankbar für die fieberhafte Tätigkeit der Dame sind und sich täglich sehr dankbar zeigen

Er steht hinter dem Haus und ist von einem Zaun eingeschlossen.
Hier wachsen drei Bäume, viel Gras und sogar im Sommer Gemüse
und Obst. Er braucht viel Arbeit im Frühling und im Sommer, z.B., man
muss dann mähen und Beete gießen. Aber deshalb ist alles auch
friedlich, schön und bunt. Dann macht er uns viel Freude. Die Kinder
spielen dort, Peter, z.B., setzt sich oft auf die Schaukel und lässt sich
die Sonne auf die Nase scheinen. Und wir essen dort ab und zu an einem
Tisch oder der Vater sitzt in einem Stuhl und tut nichts und erholt sich.
Die Vögel besuchen uns, besonders die frechen Spatzen.

Im Winter wird er vom Schnee bedeckt.

45.   Er ist unser _____.

(A) Haus

(B) Park

(C) Gras

(D) Garten

46.   Was könnte hier "bunt" sein?

(A) Der Vater

(B) Der Schnee

(C) Die Blumen

(D) Der Rasen

47.   Ein Spatz ist ein _____.

(A) Schnee

(B) Gartengerät

(C) Vogel

(D) Insekt

48.   Der Vater erholt sich sehr wahrscheinlich von _____.

(A) den Ferien

(B) der Arbeit

(C) seinem Mittagsschläfchen

(D) der Sonne

49.   "Er macht uns viel Freude" heißt, dass _____.

(A) es uns Spaß macht

(B) er uns viel Kummer bringt

(C) es viel Arbeit bedarf

(D) es uns nur Sorgen macht

Unser Sonnenschein und treuer Kamerad, unser unvergesslicher Fritz, ist heute im Alter von knapp 8 Jahren für immer friedlich eingeschlafen. Bis zum letzten Atemzug hat er uns nur Freude und Anhänglichkeit geschenkt. Jeder, der ihn kannte, hat ihn lieb gewonnen. Er hinterließ zwei traurige Herzen und viele Freunde.

In aller Stille haben wir ihn zur letzten Ruhe gebettet. Möge der liebe Gott Deine kleine, reine Seele bei sich aufnehmen und behüten, lieber Fritz. Wir behalten Dich in glücklicher Erinnerung.

50.   Der "Kamerad" ist sehr wahrscheinlich ein(e) _____.

(A) Mann

(B) Teddybär

(C) Puppe

(D) Haustier

51. Was ist dem Kamerad passiert?

(A) Er hat diese Leute verlassen und wohnt jetzt irgendwoanders.

(B) Nichts ist ihm passiert.

(C) Er ist gestorben.

(D) Er ist für die Nacht schlafengegangen.

52. Der Kamerad wohnte bei _____.

(A) zwei Personen, möglicherweise einem Ehepaar

(B) einem alten, traurigen Mann

(C) einer alten, traurigen Dame

(D) einer Familie mit Kindern

53. Die Leute sind _____, dass der Kamerad nun weg ist.

(A) froh

(B) traurig

(C) unbekümmert

(D) wütend

54. Der Kamerad ist _____.

(A) eine Katze

(B) ein Pferd

(C) ein Hund

(D) ein Drache

55. Der Kamerad wurde _____.

(A) vergessen

(B) ausgestopft

(C) weggeworfen

(D) begraben

PART C

DIRECTIONS: The sentences below contain blank spaces indicating omissions in the text. Below each blank are four choices. Select the choice that is grammatically correct in the context and blacken the corresponding space on the answer sheet. Be sure to read the sentences first.

Questions 56–59 are one sentence.

Wissen Sie, einige (56) Freunde von (57) ,

56.		57.	
(A) gute		(A) Sie	
(B) gutes		(B) Ihnen	
(C) gutem		(C) du	
(D) guten		(D) dir	

 (58) ich in Deutschland besucht habe, fuhren voriges Jahr (59) .

58.		59.	
(A) die		(A) nach Schweiz	
(B) deren		(B) in Schweiz	
(C) denen		(C) in die Schweiz	
(D) den		(D) in der Schweiz	

Questions 60–63 are one sentence.

Sie erwiesen Paula (60) dreimal, (61) aber nur einmal;

60. (A) diese Ehre   61. (A) ich

    (B) dieser Ehre   (B) mir

    (C) diesen Ehre   (C) mich

    (D) dieses Ehre   (D) mein

sie hat also diese Auszeichnung (62) erhalten als (63) .

62. (A) oft   63. (A) ich

    (B) öfter   (B) mir

    (C) öfters   (C) mich

    (D) öfterer   (D) mein

Questions 64–67 are connected.

Warum schreiben sie immer über (64) Onkel? Alles, (65) sie

64. (A) ihre   65. (A) dessen

    (B) ihrer   (B) welches

    (C) ihrem   (C) was

    (D) ihren   (D) das

in (66) Brief geschrieben haben, hat immer etwas (67) , von dem alten Kerl, zu tun.

66. (A) der   67. (A) von ihm

    (B) des   (B) davon

    (C) dem   (C) von ihn

    (D) den   (D) darüber

Questions 68–71 are one sentence.

Jürgen ist ein __(68)__ Student __(69)__ wird er __(70)__ ,

68. (A) nette   69. (A) Ein Tag   70. (A) Arzt

    (B) netter   (B) Einen Tag   (B) ein Arzt

    (C) nettem   (C) Einem Tag   (C) einer Arzt

    (D) netten   (D) Eines Tages   (D) einen Arzt

denn er möchte __(71)__ Menschen helfen.

71.   (A) andere

     (B) anderer

     (C) anderen

     (D) anderem

PART D

DIRECTIONS: Read the following passages carefully for comprehension. Each passage is followed by a number of incomplete statements or questions. Select the completion or answer that is best according to the passage and blacken the corresponding space on the answer sheet.

Der Löwe, der Tiger und der Wolf haben starke Zähne und scharfe Krallen. Der Elefant hat Stoßzähne und einen Rüssel. Der Stier, das Nashorn und der Büffel haben Hörner. Die Schildkröte hat einen Panzer, der Igel Stacheln, manche Schlangen Gift und manche Insekten Tarnung. Anderen Tieren, wie dem Hasen und der Gazelle, hat die Natur ihre Schnelligkeit gegeben.

72. Es ist hier über _____ der Tiere geschrieben.

(A) das Temperament

(B) die Waffen und den Schutz

(C) die Größe und Geschwindigkeit

(D) das Aussehen

73. Der Hase schützt sich gegen Feinde, indem er _____.

(A) stark beißen kann

(B) einen ekelhaften Geruch abgeben kann

(C) giftig ist

(D) geschwind weglaufen kann

74. Welches Tier hat keine Hörner?

(A) Der Stier

(B) Das Nashorn

(C) Der Elefant

(D) Der Büffel

Die Bürger im Dorfe Schilda sind sehr intelligente Leute. Wir sehen das, als wir schauen, wie sie ihr Rathaus bauen. Sie holten das Bauholz fürs Haus aus einem nahen Wald, schleppten die Stämme über den Berg und auf der anderen Seite des Berges trugen sie sie wieder hinunter. Da sagte plötzlich ein Schildbürger, "Warum tragen wir die schweren Stämme hinunter? Wir können sie ja hinunterrollen lassen. Das wäre einfacher und schneller." So holten sie alle Stämme aus dem Dorf hinaus (die sie vorhin hinuntergetragen hatten) und trugen sie wieder auf den Berg hinauf. Dann rollten sie die Stämme ins Dorf hinunter.

Danach bauten sie ihr Rathaus. Als sie damit fertig waren, merkten sie, dass es im Rathaus sehr dunkel war. (Es hatte keine Fenster.) "Wie bekommen wir Licht in das Haus hinein?" fragten sie sich. "Ganz einfach," sagte einer. "Wir müssen das Dach entfernen, dann haben wir genügend Licht." So entfernten sie das Dach und sie hatten viel Licht im Innern des Baues. Die Schildbürger waren glücklich und stolz auf ihre Klugheit.

75. Der Autor nennt die Schildbürger "klug." Damit will er _____ sein.

   (A) ehrlich

   (B) todernst

   (C) albern

   (D) sarkastisch

76. Schilda ist ein(e) _____.

   (A) Dorf

   (B) Stadt

   (C) Großstadt

   (D) Land

77. Das zweite "sie" im dritten Satz. "... trugen sie sie wieder hinunter," bezieht sich auf die _____.

   (A) Schildbürger

   (B) Stämme

   (C) Berge

   (D) die Seite des Berges

78. Diese Erzählung gibt uns _____ Beispiel(e) der Dummheit der Schildbürger.

(A) kein

(B) ein

(C) zwei

(D) drei

79. Die Stämme fürs Rathaus kommen von _____.

(A) einem Möbelgeschäft

(B) einer Betonfabrik

(C) dem Dorf Schilda

(D) Bäumen

80. Wir wissen, daß die Schildbürger _____ für das Rathaus vergessen hatten.

(A) das Dach

(B) die Wände

(C) die Fenster

(D) den Boden

SAT II: SUBJECT TEST IN GERMAN

PRACTICE TEST III

ANSWER KEY

1.	D	21.	C	41.	A	61.	B
2.	B	22.	B	42.	C	62.	B
3.	A	23.	C	43.	D	63.	A
4.	A	24.	A	44.	B	64.	D
5.	C	25.	D	45.	D	65.	C
6.	B	26.	A	46.	C	66.	C
7.	D	27.	B	47.	C	67.	A
8.	C	28.	C	48.	B	68.	B
9.	C	29.	A	49.	A	69.	D
10.	A	30.	C	50.	D	70.	A
11.	C	31.	A	51.	C	71.	C
12.	C	32.	D	52.	A	72.	B
13.	B	33.	D	53.	B	73.	D
14.	B	34.	C	54.	C	74.	C
15.	A	35.	A	55.	D	75.	D
16.	D	36.	C	56.	A	76.	A
17.	D	37.	B	57.	B	77.	B
18.	A	38.	A	58.	A	78.	C
19.	B	39.	C	59.	C	79.	D
20.	D	40.	D	60.	A	80.	C

GERMAN PRACTICE TEST III
DETAILED EXPLANATIONS
OF ANSWERS

1.   (D)

The superlative form of an adjective, used when comparing predicate adjectives or when comparing adverbs, uses *am* before the adjective/ adverb and has the suffix *-sten:*

> *schnell: am schellsten billig: am billigsten*

Most superlatives have umlauts also (e.g.,: *arm, am ärmsten*). But watch for the usual irregular forms (e.g.,: *viel, am meisten*; not *am vielsten*).

2.   (B)

In general, *sein* used with the predicate nominative indicates a more or less permanent state (*Ich bin dumm/klein*), not a temporary one. Thus, here and in similar situations, choice (A) (*Ich bin kalt*) is incorrect. Instead, use the dative without a grammatical subject: *Mir ist kalt/ warm/heiß* and never *Ich bin kalt/warm/heiß* for describing such temporary conditions.

3.   (A)

Prepositions are tricky to use in any language. The English "to" is no exception in German. Generally, English "to" is expressed in German with *"an"* when going toward furniture or bodies of water: *Er geht an den Tisch/den See. Zu* could also be used here. The German *in* is used for the English "into"; i.e., when going to (into) an interior, such as a room. Thus, *Wir fahren in den See* would mean to drive into the lake, which is unlikely. *Auf* can mean "to" in some expressions (*Er geht auf die Bude/Bank/Uni*), but it generally means "on," not "to."

4.   (A)
Neither (*weder*) the film nor (*noch*) the book was interesting according to the critic. *Entweder...oder* means "either...or" and does not make sense here. The other choices do not exist in German.

5.   (C)
After the possessive pronouns (*mein, dein,* etc.) the following descriptive adjectives take the primary ("strong") endings: *Mein altes Buch, euer altes Buch,* etc. The use of the extended adjective construction makes no difference: *Mein/Euer angekommenes Buch,* etc.

6.   (B)
Was must be used as the relative pronoun for all indefinite pronoun antecedents or when referring to an entire clause (idea). Thus, *was* follows *alles, nichts, vieles, etwas,* etc. *Alles/Nichts/Vieles, was er sagt, ist mir sehr klar.* In addition, it can follow an entire clause: *Sie gab mir ein schönes Buch, was mich sehr freute. Was* refers back to the entire clause here, to the entire idea, that I was pleased that she gave me something.

7.   (D)
The general subjunctive (Subjunctive Il) is used for unreal conditions, i.e., situations contrary-to-fact. It can deal with the future, present, or past. For weak verbs: To form the future and present contrary-to-fact (unreal) condition, use the indicative past tense form (e.g.: *bezahlte, bezahltest, bezahlte, bezahlten, bezahltet, bezahlten*). The general subjunctive form of a strong verb is achieved by adding the suffixes *-e, -est, -e, -en, -et,* and *-en* to the imperfect form of the third person singular; e.g.: *ging* (imperfect third person singular) + suffixes = *ginge, gingest, ginge, gingen, ginget, gingen.Wenn Maria dorthin ginge, würde sie ja auch staunen.* If Maria would go there, she would also be surprised.

If a strong verb has an a, o, or u in its imperfect stem, an umlaut is needed; e.g., *äße, äßest, äße, äßen, äßet, äßen: Wenn die Kinder nicht so viel äßen, so wären sie nicht so dick.* If the children would not eat so much, then they would not be so fat.

8.   (C)

The word "for," when used in such phrases as "for breakfast" or "for lunch," is translated as *zu* in German. The definite article of the meal is also used and is combined with *zu* to form the contraction *zum* (*zu dem*). *Zu* is used alone when it is followed by a holiday, as in *zu Ostern* (for Easter); no article is needed.

9.   (C)

This is similar to the previous exam item (no. 8, above) in that one again needs to determine which preposition to use for which situation. "For" cannot always be translated as *für* and "to" cannot always be translated as *zu.* Thus, doing or receiving something for Easter, Christmas, New Year's, one's birthday, etc., or being on or going for a holiday or vacation is not expressed with *für,* but with just about every German preposition except *für:* use *zu* for the holidays (*zu Ostern/ Weihnachten/Silvester*), *zum* for one's birthday (*zum Geburstag*). The other choices are incorrect because certain phrases call for certain prepositions and in the case given *zum* and *zu* are needed.

10.   (A)

Hören, sehen, lassen, helfen, heißen, and the modal auxiliaries do not take the past participle (*gehört, gesehen,* etc.) but their infinitive form whenever they are used in connection with another verb in the present perfect and past perfect tenses. Since we then have two infinitives, it is called appropriately the "double infinitive": *Paul hat ihn kommen sehen; Er hat es gestern liegen lassen; Ich habe nie kommen wollen* (a modal) and so on.

11.   (C)
Of the choices that are given, only *erwiderte* (he replied) makes sense in the context of the sentence. Choices (A), (B), and (D) translate respectively into "ring (a bell)," "roast," and "steer." Only (C) makes sense in this example.

12.   (C)
The dative reflexive pronouns (*mir, dir, sich, uns, euch,* and *sich*) are used when referring to parts of the body or clothing with the definite article (where English uses the possessive). This dative reflexive pronoun is used only if there is a direct object in the sentence (*Hände* in this sentence) and shows that the accusative object belongs to the subject of the sentence.

13.   (B)
Compound adjectives use the stem *"tod-"* (*todmüde, todernst, todsicher*, etc.) or *"toten-"* (*totenblass, totenstill*, etc.), but verbs use *"tot-"* (*totlachen, totschlagen*, etc.).

14.   (B)
Mastering German plurals is not easy because the rules are few and they are confusing. The tendency among English-speaking people is to want to add *"en"* to words ending in consonants, but that is only one way to pluralize nouns (e.g., *Held, Helden; Übung, Übungen*). Another way is simply to add *"e"* to the final consonant. Thus the plural of *Hund* is *Hunde*. Other words that pluralize by adding only *"e"* are *Tag* (*Tage*), *Monat* (*Monate*), and *Jahr* (*Jahre*). Adding *"en"* to them is incorrect (except in the plural dative case).

15.   (A)
Be careful of homonyms whose singular forms sometimes differ in gender (*der Band* [volume], *das Band* [band, ribbon, tape] and those whose singular forms are of the same gender (*die Bank* for "bench" and "bank"). These homonyms will often have different plural forms: *der*

Band, die Bande; das Band, die Bänder/Bande (depending on meaning). The plural here is *Bänke* (benches), not *Banken* (banks (for money)). Another example: *der Schild, die Schilde* (shield(s)); *das Schild, die Schilder* (sign(s), doorplate(s)).

16.   (D)
"We have a number, a numeral, here, and it is a five." Cardinal numbers have a feminine gender when used as nouns. Likewise: *Das Haus hat eine Sieben;* "The house has a (figure) seven"; *Er ist eine Null*: "he is a nobody (a zero, a nothing)."

17.   (D)
"Paula drove the car whose (*dessen*) door is broken." The relative pronoun in the genitive is *deren* (feminine and plural reference) or *dessen* (masculine and neuter reference). *Dessen* is used in this sentence because it refers to *das Auto,* a singular, neuter form.

18.   (A)
Von is used in passive sentence structures when the agent of the action that is performed on the subject is a person. The agent is then in its dative form. *Durch* is used when the agent is not a person. The agent is then in its accusative form. *Bei* and *mit* do not indicate agents of action.

19.   (B)
When comparing two things, add *"-er"* to the adverb/adjective stem; monosyllabic adjectives that have an *"a," "o,"* or *"u"* in their stems are usually umlauted *(alt, älter)*. Adjectives that have *"au"* are not umlauted *(laut, lauter)*. Unlike in English, adverbs/adjectives never form the comparative using *mehr*. Although one says "more beautiful," rather than "beautifuller," "more suitable" and not "suitabler," etc., in English, German uses *schöner* to express the idea "more beautiful."

20.   (D)
"She wishes that she could buy a new car."

Since the subordinate clause represents something that is contrary to fact, the subjunctive form of *können* must be used. *Kann* is the present indicative form, *kannte* is not a form of *können*, and *konnte* is the imperfect indicative form.

21.   (C)

The object of a phrase that is begun by *während* (during) is in the genitive case. *"Die Film"* does not exist in German (*"Film"* is masculine), *dem Film* is in the dative case and *der Film* is nominative.

22.   (B)

The time between about 9 a.m. and noon is *Vormittag, Morgen früh* is early morning (before about 9 a.m.). After 12 noon it is *Nachmittag,* the afternoon. *Mittag* is noontime.

23.   (C)

When speaking of eating lunch or supper, do not use the word *essen* twice in the same sentence (once as a verb and once in the noun denoting the meal). Thus, *Ich esse das Mittagessen/Abendessen,* in which *essen* appears twice, is incorrect. Instead, substitute the noun with *zu Mittag/Abend: Ich esse zu Mittag.* If *essen* is not used, then the complete noun is used: *Was gibt es zum Abendessen? Wir gehen in die Mensa zum Mittagessen.*

24.   (A)

When requesting identification, such as a name, the only form that can be used is *Wie heißt…? Was heißt* means *was bedeutet* (i.e., what does (something) mean). In other words, *was heißt* is a request for a definition, translation, or explanation.

25.   (D)

"Ilse and Ingrid had to work yesterday." The imperfect forms of all modal auxiliaries contain the *te, test, te,* etc., endings and have no umlauts. *Mussen* does not exist. *Müssen* is present tense and makes no sense with *gestern* (past tense). *Müssten* is a subjunctive form.

26.   (A)

So ... wie is used in comparisons before nouns (*so groß wie ein Elefant*) and before pronouns and adjectives (*so reich wie er; so bald wie möglich*). However, it is not used before clauses. In these cases *sobald* is used (spelled as one word).

27.   (B)

Studieren does not mean "to study" in the sense of "to do one's homework," "to prepare a lesson," "to study for a test or quiz," etc., a fact that is unfortunately not clearly stated (or simply incorrectly stated) in many textbooks. *Lernen* is appropriate for use in kindergarten to 12th grade as well as in university coursework. *Hausaufgaben machen/schreiben* would probably be more commonly used by German *Gymnasiasten* (middle- and high school students). *Studieren* is used in the sense of attending a university, being a university student (e.g., *Sie studiert vier Semester in Freiburg.*), learning an academic discipline (e.g., *Er studiert Jura.*), or, by extension, investigating or analyzing something (e.g., *Wir wollen dieses Problem eingehend studieren.*).

28.   (C)

The subjunctive is often used in indirect discourse, especially in cautious reporting (where there is some question as to the truth or accuracy of the statement by a second party) or in formal noncommittal reporting. In indirect discourse and in questions, the special subjunctive (Subjunctive I) can be used if its form is not identical with the indicative verb forms. If it is the same, the general subjunctive (Subjunctive II) should be used. Subjunctive I is formed by adding the suffixes *"-e," "-est," "-e," "-en," "-et,"* and *"-en"* to the verb's infinitive stem; e.g., *spreche, sprechest, spreche,* etc. And *arbeite, arbeitest, arbeite,* etc.

29.   (A)

For a discussion of the use of the subjunctive in indirect discourse, see explanation no. 28. In that item, the forms of indirect discourse for present and future time situations were explained. Here we have a past time situation. In past time situations (past subjunctive), use a Subjunctive I or II form (*sei/wäre*) for verbs requiring *sein* to form the perfect tense, or a Subjunctive I or II form of *haben* (*er habe/hätte*, etc.) and the past participle of the main verb. Thus, *Er sei dahingefahren,* since *fahren* requires *sein* here, is the correct answer.

30.   (C)
Kennen is like *denken, brennen,* and other "mixed" verbs or "irregular weak verbs" whose stem vowels, when the verb is in its imperfect form, change from *"e"* to *"a"* before the normal imperfect suffixes are attached: *ich kannte, du dachtest, es brannte, renne, senden,* etc. Thus, Inge never knew her benefactor, Mr. Smith: *"...kannte Inge den Herrn Schmidt nie." Konnte* (the imperfect form of *können*) and *könnte* (the present subjunctive form of *kann*) are incorrect choices because, as modal verbs, they require an infinitive. *Kennte* does not exist in German.

31.   (A)
Remember, for the "three c's" (c̲ity, c̲ountry, c̲ontinent) one most often uses *"nach"* to mean "to." Sometimes, if the country requires the definite article with it, and there are very few of these, one might use *"in"* to mean "to": *Er fährt morgen in die Schweiz.*

32.   (D)
The present participle is most widely used as a modifying adjective, and it is formed as follows: verb infinitive + *d* (+ adjective ending). It is translated most often in English as verb + "ing": *singen + d + en = singenden* = singing: "The singing children sound nice." Likewise: *fliegen + d + e* (adj. end.) = *der fliegende Adler* (the flying eagle): *Die suchende Mutter fand das weinende Kind,* (the searching mother found the crying child).

33.   (D)
Weak masculine nouns, also called "n-nouns," usually designate a male's station in life (profession, livelihood, nationality, activity,

pastime) and they will have *"(e)n"* endings in the oblique cases (accusative, dative, and genitive cases). Such nouns often end in *"-t"* (*Student, Tourist, Polizist*), in *"-ph"* (*Philosoph, Geograph*) and in *"-nom"* (*Astronom*). *Herr, Junge, Mensch* are also weak masculine nouns.

Thus, *Dem Piloten* (dative; indirect object), *des Studenten* (genitive; possession) are the correct answers.

34.   (C)
"When Hans was in New York, he was afraid to use the subway."

Infinitive constructions in German consist of *zu* and the infinitive. The use of *nach* is incorrect according to this definition. *Fressen* means "to eat" and is used when referring to an animal that is eating. Technically, choice (A) is grammatically correct, but it would make sense only under very specific conditions.

35.   (A)
The dative reflexive pronouns (*mir, dir, sich, uns, euch, sich*) are frequently used when more than just minimal interest is involved (and so is called the "dative of interest"). The dative of interest is optional and occurs with verbs such as *kaufen, holen, bestellen,* etc. This dative reflexive pronoun is used only if there is a direct object in the sentence (*"Programm"* in this sentence).

36.   (C)
An unreal (contrary-to-fact) condition in past time is expressed by a conditional clause (the *wenn* clause) whose verb is in its past subjunctive form; the past subjunctive form of a verb consists of the subjunctive form of *haben* or *sein* and the past participle of the verb itself. In the sentence, both *hätte gesagt* (had he said) and *wären abgefahren* (we would have gone) are in the past subjunctive.

37.   (B)
An unreal (contrary-to-fact) condition in past time also includes the conclusion (*dann/so* clause) expressed in the past subjunctive:

...dann/so wären wir länger geblieben.
...then we would have stayed longer.
...dann/so hätten wir mit Peter gesprochen.
...then we would have spoken with Peter.

38.   (A)
Denn, like all the other coordinating conjunctions, is followed by a phrase that has regular word order (subject – verb) choice (A), not inverted word order (verb – subject) choice (B) and not transposed word order (verb is last, as with subordinating conjunctions) choice (C). Choice (D) is not correct because the subject of the second clause is missing.

39.   (C)
If this person is doing laundry, chauferring children around, cleaning, carrying out other obligations and does this at all hours, yet does not see monetary reimbursement for all this work, she must be a homemaker.

40.   (D)
Such a hard-working person is not wasteful, lazy, flighty, absent-minded or anything else. She can only be hard-working and industrious to accomplish all these chores.

41.   (A)
She is not well-paid, poorly paid or otherwise; she is simply not paid at all. There is no remuneration for her work.

42.   (C)
Most of her work is accomplished at home. That is why she is known as a homemaker (*Hausfrau*).

43.   (D)
It is the family members who are not especially grateful or who usually do not show their thanks often enough for her untiring work.

44.   (B)

These family members too frequently take the homemaker's work for granted — work that they expect to be done without necessarily deserving it or having earned it.

45.   (D)

It is not the house and most people do not own and work in their own park. Grass is only part of what is being described. But it also includes a playing area with a *Schaukel,* an eating area with a *Tisch,* a resting area with a *Stuhl,* and a garden (*Beete gießen*). So it must be a family's *Garten,* which we understand as a "yard," and not strictly as a "garden," which would be more specifically labelled as *Blumengarten, Gemüsegarten, Obstgarten,* etc., to differentiate it from *Garten* in general: the backyard.

46.   (C)

The only thing that could be very colorful, or many-colored (*bunt*), is the flowers. The *Schnee* and *Rasen* are each one color (white and green, respectively), and this designation for father is ridiculous.

47.   (C)

A *Spatz* (also *Sperling*) is a sparrow. Do not confuse the word with *Spaten* (spade), a garden utensil (*Gartengerät*).

48.   (B)

Father would relax from work done at his job or done in his backyard. We doubt he would rest up from his vacation because one goes on vacation in order to relax. Likewise, one takes a nap to rest and not to relax from afterwards.

49.   (A)

If it is giving us pleasure (*Freude*), then it is giving us enjoyment (*Spaß*) and not worries (*Kummer, Sorgen*) or a lot of work (*Arbeit*).

50.　　(D)

One doubts a person would take such pains to bury a doll or teddy bear; they would not be designated with an age (*von knapp 8 Jahren*). It is not a *Mann,* since this being passed away *im Alter von knapp 8 Jahren.* It must be a pet.

51.　　(C)

The pet died. Clues: *für immer friedlich eingeschlafen, er hinter lässt, zur letzten Ruhe gebettet, Gott … Deine … Seele … aufnehmen.*

52.　　(A)

The pet lived with two people: *Er hinter läßt zwei traurige Herzen ….* The *Freunde* are people who knew the pet but surely did not live as part of the family with the pet.

53.　　(B)

Obviously, they are unhappy that the pet died (*traurige Herzen*). They are not untroubled or furious.

54.　　(C)

The pet is referred to as *er, ihn,* and *lieber.* Thus, it is not a *Katze* (*sie, liebe*). It is not a horse because it is a *kleine Seele,* making this a small animal and not one as large as a horse. Dragons are mythical, not actual beasts.

55.　　(D)

Wir haben ihn zur letzten Ruhe gebettet. Hence, he was buried. He was not forgotten, stuffed, or thrown away.

56.　　(A)

Limiting numerical adjectives, such as *einige, wenige, mehrere,* and *viele* are treated as unpreceded adjectives, i.e., the attributive (modifying) adjectives following them take the same (strong) endings, except in the genitive case; nominative and accusative: *einige gute Freunde;* dative: *einigen guten Freunden;* genitive: *einiger guten Freunde.*

57. (B)
Von requires objects in the dative case, so the dative personal pronoun *Ihnen* is required here; *dir* cannot be used because the person is being addressed as *Sie (Wissen Sie)*, a formal form, so that formal form must be used again (*Ihnen,* formal, not *dir,* the informal, familiar form).

58. (A)
The relative pronoun *die* refers to the *Freunde: Ich habe die [Freunde] besucht.* Thus, the relative pronoun is the object of the verb *besuchen.* Since direct objects are in the accusative case, the accusative plural relative pronoun, which is *die,* must be used here.

59. (C)
The names of a few countries are always preceded by some form of the definite article and they all happen to be feminine: *die Schweiz, die Türkei, die Slovakei* and a few others. So only the last two options are possible here. Since the friends "drove to Switzerland" (motion toward an object [*wohin?*]) we use the "accusative of motion toward," which, for the feminine singular, is *die.*

60. (A)
"They rendered Paula this honor three times." In this phrase, *sie* is the subject and is therefore in the nominative case. "Paula" is the indirect object and is therefore in the dative case (although it can only be understood as dative in context; "Paula" has no articles) and *Ehre* must therefore be in the accusative case; *Ehre* is feminine, so the correct adjective is *diese.*

61. (B)
The honor was paid to me; therefore, "me" is the indirect object. Since the indirect object is in the dative case, the dative pronoun *mir* is needed here.

62.   (B)

The comparative form of *oft* (often) is *öfter* (more often) and the superlative form is *am öftesten* (most often), not *öfters,* which means "frequently" and is not used very much except in more informal usage: *Sie sprachen öfters von ihm.* ("They talked frequently about him." "They mentioned him frequently.")

63.   (A)

"She received the honor more often than I." In both languages, the nominative form of "I" is correct; e.g., *Er ist größer als ich/du* (He is taller than I/you.). In German, as in English, the case of the first noun in a comparison (*sie,* which is nominative) determines the cases of any other nouns in that comparison (*ich,* which is also nominative).

64.   (D)

Usually when you have a verb that is used with *über,* then the noun following *über* is in the accusative case: *Du schreibst/klagst* (etc.) *über das Wetter/den Mann,* (etc.). *Über,* in this sentence, means "about," and, in such instances, always takes objects that are in their accusative forms.

65.   (C)

Was must be used as the relative pronoun for all indefinite pronoun antecedents or when referring to an entire clause (idea). Thus, *was* follows *alles, nichts, vieles, etwas,* etc., because these are indefinite pronouns.

66.   (C)

If the relative pronoun must answer the question "where?" (*wo?*), use the dative case (unless a preposition that takes a noun in the accusative or genitive case is used); therefore, *dem* (for the singular, dative masculine *Brief*) is the proper article.

67.   (A)

A *da(r)*-compound refers only to things or ideas, and not to a person.

When referring back to a person, use the preposition and a pronoun, as here: *von ihm.*

68.   (B)
Adjectives following *ein*-words have mixed (neither weak nor strong) declensions; i.e., they have the endings *"-e," "-es," "-er,"* or *"-en,"* depending on case, gender and number. Here *"Student"* is masculine, nominative and singular, so the adjective *nett* has an *"-er"* suffix: *netter.*

69.   (D)
Indefinite times, expressed as "one" or "some" in English (one day/ year, some day/year, etc.) are expressed in German by the "genitive of indefinite time." Therefore, "one day" becomes *eines Tages* (genitive form) and not *ein Tag* (nominative form).

70.   (A)
Nationalities, religions and professions usually do not include the indefinite article (*Er ist Amerikaner/Katholik/Arzt*) unless an adjective is included: *Er ist ein junger Amerikaner.*

71.   (C)
Menschen is in the dative plural case since *helfen* is a verb requiring the dative case. The adjective *"ander-"* is declined as strong since it has no *"der"*-word (weak declension) or *"ein"*-word (mixed declension) preceding it. Therefore, the proper suffix for the *"ander-"* root is *"-en."*

72.   (B)
Not the animals' temperament, size or general appearance but their weapons and types of protection are given here (teeth, horns, speed, etc.).

73.   (D)
The rabbit's best defense is its speed.

74.   (C)

Three animals are mentioned that have horns (*Stier, Nashorn, Büffel*);
the *Elefant* has tusks (*Stoßzähne*).

75.   (D)

Obviously, these people are pretty stupid. When the writer calls them
"intelligent," he is purposely being rather sarcastic.

76.   (A)

Schilda is the name of an imaginary village (*im Dorfe Schilda*, "in the
village of Schilda"). It is not a country or any kind of city.

77.   (B)

In the third sentence, "...*und auf der anderen Seite des Berges trugen
sie sie wieder hinunter,*" the second *sie* refers to the logs: "...and on the
other side of the mountain/hill, they carried them [the logs] down
again." The first *sie* refers to the *Schildbürger*, to the citizens of
Schilda.

78.   (C)

Two examples of the villagers' stupidity are given here: First, we see
how stupidly they carry the logs back up the mountain again just so they
can roll them down; second, we see that their solution to getting light
into the building is to permanently remove the roof, rather than to have
built windows in the first place!

79.   (D)

The logs for the *Rathaus* (city hall) come from trees in the nearby forest,
not from a concrete factory or from anywhere else. We can assume the
citizens chop down the trees in the nearby forest to obtain the logs for
their building.

80.   (C)
Since the citizens had no light in their completed building and they got no light until they removed the roof, we know they forgot to add windows in their original building plans.

SAT II:
SUBJECT TEST IN
GERMAN

PRACTICE
TEST IV

GERMAN PRACTICE TEST IV

PART A

Time: 1 Hour
    80 Questions

DIRECTIONS: Each of the sentences in this part has a blank space indicating that a word or phrase has been omitted. From the four choices select the ONE that, when inserted in the sentence, fits grammatically and logically with the sentence as a whole. Then blacken the corresponding space on the answer sheet.

1.   Wann _____ du geboren?

   (A) warst

   (B) wurdest

   (C) bist

   (D) wirst

2.   _____ Mann war mein Freund.

   (A) Diese

   (B) Dieser

   (C) Diesen

   (D) Dieses

3.   Welche Vorlesungen _____ du?

   (A) besuchst

   (B) versuchst

   (C) behandelst

   (D) nimmst

132

4.   Er setzte sich neben _____ .

        (A) die Dame

        (B) der Dame

        (C) einer Dame

        (D) einem Dame

5.   Was nimmst du? _____ du eine Cola?

        (A) Möchtest

        (B) Mag

        (C) Mögt

        (D) Mögen

6.   Es ist schwer, _____ 6 Uhr aufzustehen.

        (A) zu

        (B) am

        (C) um

        (D) an

7.   Er macht _____ Sorgen, dass sie nicht kommt.

        (A) ihn

        (B) sich

        (C) ihm

        (D) sein

8.   Was fehlt _____?

(A) dir

(B) dein

(C) dich

(D) sich

9.   Er ist _____ als ich.

(A) größere

(B) größer

(C) großer

(D) größt

10.   Das _____ weh!

(A) macht

(B) tun

(C) tut

(D) ist

11.   Das ist die Dame, _____ Handtasche ich fand.

(A) dessen

(B) der

(C) deren

(D) wessen

12.   Das war Liebe auf den ersten _____!

(A) Schlag

(B) Blick

(C) Aussicht

(D) Blickwinkel

13.   _____ Mann hast du gesehen?

(A) Welch für einen

(B) Welch für ein

(C) Was für einen

(D) Welche für ein

14.   Was du sagst, ist _____ egal.

(A) mir

(B) sie

(C) dich

(D) mich

15.   Er glaubt, dass er immer _____.

(A) recht ist

(B) recht hat

(C) richtig hat

(D) Rechnung hat

16. Nimmst du _____ Teil?

   (A) davor

   (B) da an

   (C) daran

   (D) darüber

17. Er ist stolz _____ seine Kinder.

   (A) an

   (B) vor

   (C) über

   (D) auf

18. Trinken Sie _____ Milch oder Tee?

   (A) liebst

   (B) gerner

   (C) lieber

   (D) lieb

19. Wie hast du das Buch _____?

   (A) gekommen

   (B) bekommt

   (C) gekommt

   (D) bekommen

20. Sie _____ immer gut _____.

(A) sieht . . . an

(B) sieht . . . aus

(C) sieht . . . um

(D) sieht . . . über

21. Karl _____ gestern von einem Hund angefallen.

(A) werde

(B) wär

(C) wurde

(D) wären

22. Das höre ich _____ in meinem Leben!

(A) zum erstenmal

(B) für das Ersten Mal

(C) vorerst

(D) zuerst

23. Er hat _____ Mai Geburtstag.

(A) in

(B) zu

(C) am

(D) im

24. Mit Welchem Zug _____ er _____?

   (A) kommt…um

   (B) kommt…vor

   (C) kommt…mit

   (D) kommt…an

25. Hans ist _____.

   (A) Student

   (B) ein Student

   (C) einen Studenten

   (D) ein Studenten

26. Ich komme direkt von _____.

   (A) zu Hause

   (B) Hause

   (C) nach Hause

   (D) Haus

27. _____ soll man das nicht machen.

   (A) In meiner Meinung

   (B) Nach meiner Meinung

   (C) Meine Meinung

   (D) Meiner Meinung nach

28. Wenn ich will, kann ich Pilot _____.

   (A) werden

   (B) bekommen

   (C) werde

   (D) bekomme

29. _____ kalt.

   (A) Ich bin

   (B) Mich ist

   (C) Zu mir ist es

   (D) Mir ist

30. _____ Buch ist das?

   (A) Wessen

   (B) Wer

   (C) Wem

   (D) Wen

31. Er kommt _____ vorbei.

   (A) heute Abend

   (B) heute Nacht

   (C) gestern Abend

   (D) gestern Nacht

32.   Er _____, wie ich heiße.

   (A) kennt

   (B) weiß

   (C) weißt

   (D) kannte

33.   _____ Kind kann brav sein.

   (A) Jeder

   (B) Jeden

   (C) Jede

   (D) Jedes

34.   Er _____ die Haare schneiden.

   (A) verlässt sich

   (B) lässt sich

   (C) verlässt

   (D) lässt

35.   Das Buch gehört _____ nicht.

   (A) ihr

   (B) sie

   (C) ihn

   (D) dich

36. _____ Koffer hast du?

(A) Welcher

(B) Welchen

(C) Welches

(D) Welche

37. Sie möchte nach Deutschland _____.

(A) führen

(B) gefahren

(C) zu fahren

(D) fahren

38. _____ Brötchen sind schwer zu finden.

(A) Gutes

(B) Guten

(C) Gute

(D) Gut

PART B

Eines Tages wollten eine Mutter und ihre Tochter, wie sie es gewohnt waren, zusammen in die Stadt fahren, um Einkaufe zu machen. Diesmal war die Mutter an der Reihe, die Tochter abzuholen. Als sie aus der Einfahrt fuhren, sah die Mutter den alten, treuen Familienhund, der vor dem Haus schlief. Nach einigen Stunden in der Stadt machten die Frauen sich auf dem Rückweg. Unterwegs trafen sie plötzlich auf einen toten Hund in der Straße, der von einem Auto überfahren worden war. Die Mutter erkannte ihn sofort und fragte die Tochter erschrocken, ob das nicht ihr Hund sei. Die Tochter traute sich nicht, aus dem Auto auszusteigen, um den Hund genauer anzusehen. Endlich machte die Mutter es und kam mit der traurigen Nachricht zurück, das sei tatsächlich ihr lieber "Waldi." Als die zwei Damen ratlos da standen und fast hysterisch weinten, kam ein Mann vorbei und fragte, ob er ihnen irgendwie behilflich sein könnte. Die Mutter, die sich einigermaßen gefasst hatte, bat ihn, den Hund in den Kofferraum zu legen, damit sie ihn nach Hause bringen und begraben könnten. Das machte er und die beiden fuhren dann tränenerstickt nach Hause. Unterwegs überlegten sie, wie sie es den Kindern sagen würden usw. Als sie in die Einfahrt fuhren, fing die Mutter an, laut zu lachen: Dort vor dem Haus schlief immer noch der alte, treue Familienhund! Wem gehörte der fremde Hund im Kofferraum??!

39.   Die Mutter und die Tochter_____ .

(A) haben in der Stadt gewohnt

(B) fuhren selten zusammen in die Stadt

(C) wollten zusammen in der Stadt wohnen

(D) wollten zusammen einkaufen gehen

40. Die Mutter _____ .

   (A) wurde von der Tochter abgeholt

   (B) holte die Tochter ab, weil das ihre Gewohnheit war

   (C) holte manchmal die Tochter ab

   (D) holte immer die Tochter ab

41. Auf dem Rückweg _____ .

   (A) haben sie einen Hund in der Straße überfahren

   (B) haben sie einen überfahrenen Hund in der Straße
       gesehen

   (C) haben sie einen toten Hund überfahren

   (D) haben sie einen überfahrenen, aber noch nicht toten
       Hund in der Straße gesehen

42. Der Mann _____ .

   (A) legte den überfahrenen Hund in den Kofferraum

   (B) fragte, ob er ihr Hund sei

   (C) hat aus Versehen den Hund überfahren

   (D) wollte den Hund begraben

43. Als sie den toten Hund fanden _____ .

   (A) weinten sie vor Freude

   (B) wurden sie fast hysterisch

   (C) glaubten sie "Waldi" sei noch zu Hause

   (D) wollten sie ihn dort lassen

44.   "Waldi" _____ .

   (A) musste begraben werden

   (B) wurde vom Mann im Garten begraben

   (C) freute sich als die Frauen ankamen

   (D) schlief noch vor dem Haus

Eine Amerikanerin, deren Deutsch nicht einwandfrei war, studierte an der Universität Heidelberg. Wie viele von ihren Kommilitonen, ist sie im Laufe des Jahres in finanzielle Schwierigkeiten geraten. Sie war verzweifelt. Die Eltern waren weit weg; eine Stelle zu finden kam wegen der Schwierigkeiten eines Ausländers, eine Arbeitsgenehmigung zu bekommen nicht in Frage und Geld von den genauso armen Freunden zu borgen war unmöglich. Nach langen Zögern und länger Überlegung entschloss sie sich, Blut zu spenden—eine Lösung, die nicht selten auch von deutschen Studenten gefunden wird. Also eines Tages nahm sie sich zusammen und suchte die Stelle auf, wo man Blut spenden könnte. Der junge, gutaussehende Krankenpfleger, der hinter einem großen Schreibtisch saß, schien sehr freundlich zu sein. Die Freunde der Studentin hatten ihr genau beigebracht, wie sie sich ausdrücken sollte. Zu ihrer großen Erleichterung verstand er alles, was sie sagte, aber als er sie ansprach, hörte sie nur deutlich das eine Wort "ziehen." Schon in dem ersten Deutschkurs in Amerika hat sie das Wort "ausziehen" gelernt und wusste, was sie zu machen hatte. Obwohl es ihr etwas extrem schien, sich auszuziehen, um Blut zu lassen, zögerte sie nicht lange, weil sie Geld brauchte. Der Krankenpfleger war beschäftigt und arbeitete weiter am Schreibtisch, ohne sich um sie zu kümmern. Die Amerikanerin zog sich aus und hörte nicht auf, bis sie splitternackt vor ihm stand. Als der Krankenpfleger hochschaute, sah sie wie er sich zu beherrschen versuchte und gegen Gelächter kämpfte. Mit großer Anstrengung ist es ihm gelungen, genügend Herr über sich zu werden, um ganz langsam and deutlich sagen zu können: "Sie hätten nur den Ärmel hochziehen müssen!"

45.   Die Amerikanerin wollte Blut spenden, weil _____ .

   (A) sie Geld brauchte

(B) sie weit weg von ihren Eltern war

(C) sie eine Stelle suchte

(D) ihre Freunde ihr nicht helfen wollten

46. Sie konnte keine Stelle suchen, weil _____ .

(A) ihre Eltern dagegen waren

(B) ihre Freunde nicht arbeiteten

(C) Ausländer ohne Erlaubnis nicht arbeiten dürfen

(D) sie Geld von ihren Freunden borgen könnte

47. Die Studentin _____ .

(A) verstand alles, was der Krankenpfleger sagte

(B) verstand nur ein Teil davon, was der Krankenpfleger sagte

(C) verstand nichts davon, was der Krankenpfleger sagte

(D) verstand genau, was der Krankenpfleger sagte

48. Der Krankenpfleger kümmerte sich nicht um sie, weil _____ .

(A) er wusste, dass sie Geld brauchte

(B) er mit seiner Arbeit beschäftigt war

(C) er sich zu beherrschen versuchte

(D) er lachte

49. Die Studentin zog sich aus, weil _____ .

(A) der Arzt es ihr befahl

(B) sie nicht zögern wollte

(C) sie falsch verstanden hatte

(D) der Arzt es langsam und deutlich sagte

Die Schauspieler des Deutschen Schauspielhauses in Hamburg suchen einen ihrer Hauptdarsteller: den Hundestar "Aaron." Aaron ist ein Mischlingshund, der in Shakespeares "Wie Es Euch Gefällt" die Rolle eines Hirtenhundes spielt. Als er zum letzten Mal gesehen wurde, war er auf Urlaub in Bayern, wo er einen Spaziergang durch den Wald machte. Seitdem wartet nicht nur sein Besitzer, der den Schäfer in der klassischen Komödie spielt, sondern das gesamte Ensemble auf ein Lebenszeichen von ihm. Sie seien alle ganz verzweifelt und traurig, sagte eine Sprecherin des Schauspielhauses. Warum ist Aaron weggelaufen? Er ist wieder ein Opfer seiner Leidenschaften geworden.

Er hat sich nämlich in eine Hündin namens "Sissy" verliebt. Seit dieser Liebe auf dem ersten Blick ist das Paar verschwunden. Der mittelgroße, blonde Aaron hatte immer eine Vorliebe für große langbeinige Hundedamen. Das Ensemble will nicht die kleinste Chance auslassen, den Star wiederzubekommen. Sie wissen jedoch nicht, wie es weitergehen soll.

50. Wen suchen die Schauspieler des Deutschen Schauspielhauses?

(A) Einen weggelaufenen Hund

(B) Einen Mann, der einer ihrer Haupdarsteller ist

(C) Einen Hirtenhund, der die Rolle von Aaron spielt

(D) Einen Hund, der eine Rolle in einem Stück von Shakespeare spielen könnte

51. Wie ist der Hund verlorengegangen?

(A) Auf einer Reise nach Bayern hat er sich verfahren.

(B) Während eines Spazierganges ist er verschwunden.

(C) Er wollte allein durch den Wald laufen.

(D) Er wollte Urlaub in Bayern machen.

52.   Er ist weggelaufen weil _____ .

(A) er nicht mehr arbeiten wollte

(B) er sich verliebt hat

(C) er verschwinden wollte

(D) er weitergehen wollte

53.   Wer wartet auf sein Rückkehr?

(A) Nur sein Besitzer interessiert sich dafür

(B) Nur eine Sprecherin des Schauspielhauses ist daran
        interessiert

(C) Nur ein Schäfer macht sich Sorgen

(D) Nicht nur sein Besitzer, sondern auch die Schauspieler
        hoffen, daß er wiederkommt

54.   Aaron und Sissy sind vielleicht ein komisches Paar, weil
        _____ .

(A) Aaron Schauspieler ist

(B) Sissy keine Schauspielerin ist

(C) Aaron zu leidenschaftlich ist

(D) sie anders aussehen

PART C

DIRECTIONS: The sentences below contain blank spaces indicating omissions in the text. Below each blank are four choices. Select the choice that is grammatically correct in the context and blacken the corresponding space on the answer sheet. Be sure to read the sentences first.

Questions 55–58 are one sentence.

Ich __(55)__ nicht __(56)__ er kommt, aber wir

55. (A) weißte
    (B) wusste
    (C) wüsste
    (D) gewusst

56. (A) woher
    (B) wo
    (C) wohin
    (D) wozu

__(57)__ , dass wir aus dem __(58)__ Stadtteil von Berlin stammen.

57. (A) stellten fest
    (B) feststellten
    (C) haben gefeststellt
    (D) wurden festgestellt

58. (A) gleichen
    (B) gleiche
    (C) gleiches
    (D) gleich

Questions 59–62 are connected.

Gestern __(59)__ in __(60)__ Bibliothek

59. (A) ein Fremder hat mich   60. (A) der

    (B) hat ein Fremder mich   (B) die

    (C) mich ein Fremder hat   (C) dem

    (D) mich hat ein Fremder   (D) den

angesprochen. Er wollte wissen, __(61)__ ich je etwas von Hesse __(62)__ .

61. (A) wenn   62. (A) lesen wollen habe

    (B) obwohl   (B) lesen wollen hat

    (C) wen   (C) hat lesen wollen

    (D) ob   (D) habe lesen wollen

Questions 63–66 are one sentence.

An deiner Stelle __(63)__ ich __(64)__ gesagt,

63. (A) wäre   64. (A) er

    (B) hatte   (B) ihn

    (C) hätte   (C) ihm

    (D) hat   (D) es

er __(65)__ morgen __(66)__ .

65. (A) müsse
    (B) müsst
    (C) müssen
    (D) musst

66. (A) kommen wieder
    (B) wiederzukommen
    (C) zu wiederkommen
    (D) wiederkommen

Questions 67–69 are one sentence.

__(67)__ , __(68)__ ich Lust,

67. (A) Nachdem war ich in Berlin
    (B) Nachdem in Berlin ich war
    (C) Nachdem ich war in Berlin
    (D) Nachdem ich in Berlin war

68. (A) habe
    (B) hatte
    (C) hätte
    (D) habte

__(69)__ Köln zu fahren.

69. (A) nach
    (B) in
    (C) zu
    (D) bei

Questions 70–71 are one sentence.

Das Fenster __(70)__ jeden Tag __(70)__ , sonst

70.   (A) wird …zugemacht

      (B) ist … zugemacht

      (C) würde … zugemacht

      (D) wurde … zumachen

__(71)__ alles __(71)__ .

71.   (A) war … kaputtgegangen

      (B) ware … kaputtgegangen

      (C) ist … kaputtgegangen

      (D) würde … kaputtgehen

PART D

DIRECTIONS: Read the following passages carefully for comprehension. Each passage is followed by a number of incomplete statements or questions. Select the completion or answer that is best according to the passage and blacken the corresponding space on the answer sheet.

Zwei junge Leute haben eine Nacht im Königspalast in Amsterdam verbracht. Gegen ein oder zwei Uhr stiegen sie über ein Baugerüst auf das Dach des Palasts. Das hatten sie schon einmal getan, aber jetzt wollten sie ins Innere des Palasts gehen. Das gelang ihnen ohne Schwierigkeiten durch ein Dachfenster. In der königlichen Küche verzehrten sie chinesische Delikatessen. Nacher nahmen sie ungestört ein Bad und schliefen selig in einem Luxusbett ein. Alles wäre wahrscheinlich gut gegangen, wenn die beiden ehemaligen Studenten an der Kunstakademie zehn Bilder als Andenken an ihr nächtliches Abenteuer nicht hätten mitnehmen wollen. Ein Hausdiener erwischte die beiden und übergab sie der Polizei. Wegen des Diebstahls mussten beide eine Strafe bezahlen. Die Übernachtung im Palast kam sie fast doppelt so teuer zu stehen wie eine Übernachtung im teuersten Hotel der Stadt.

72. Wie ist es dem jungen Paar gelungen, in den Palast zu kommen?

    (A) Sie gingen ohne Mühe durch ein Fenster im Dach.

    (B) Sie gingen durch die königliche Küche.

    (C) Sie stiegen über ein Baugerüst und fanden eine Tür.

    (D) Sie schauten durch ein Dachfenster und warteten bis niemand in der Küche war.

73. Nachdem sie im Palast waren, _____ .

    (A) hatten sie viel Angst

    (B) trauten sie sich nicht, etwas zu essen

152

(C) fühlten sie sich, als ob sie zu Hause wären

(D) wollten sie gleich wieder gehen

74.   Warum wurden sie erwischt?

(A) Weil sie ein Bad nehmen wollten.

(B) Weil sie essen wollten.

(C) Weil sie schlafen wollten.

(D) Weil sie sich für die Kunst interessierten.

75.   Die Übernachtung _____ .

(A) war teuer, weil sie eine Strafe bezahlen mussten

(B) war fast so teuer wie in einem Hotel

(C) war billiger als in einem teueren Hotel

(D) war so teuer wie im teuersten Hotel der Stadt

In Deutschland gibt es ein reichliches Angebot an Ausflugsmöglichkeiten, die von Firmen veranstaltet werden, um ihre Produkte zu verkaufen. Es gibt zweierlei solcher Fahrten: Butterfahrten und Kaffeefahrten. Butterfahrten sind immer mit einer Seefahrt verbunden und nennen sich Butterfahrten, weil man auf dem Schiff Butter und andere Produkte zu einem günstigen Preis bekommen kann. Eine typische Reklame lautet so: "Wir fahren mit dem Luxusreisebus durch das herrliche Schleswig-Holstein in die idyllische Hafenstadt Heiligenhafen. Unterwegs haben Sie die Möglichkeit an einer informativen Verkaufsveranstaltung teilzunehmen. Anschließend machen wir eine Ostsee-Kreuzfahrt. Zollfreier Einkauf an Bord von Zigaretten, Spirituosen, Kaffee, u.s.w." Diese Butterfahrt kostet nur DM 24.90 (ungefähr $14). Im Preis enthalten sind die Busfahrt, ein Mittagessen, die Ostsee-Fahrt und einige Werbegeschenke, wie Brot, Eier, Schinken, Honig und Wurst. Kaffeefahrten unterscheiden sich von Butterfahrten dadurch, dass keine Seefahrt dabei ist. Sie nennen sich Kaffeefahrten, weil die Teilnehmer unterwegs ins Cafe gehen und Kaffee trinken. Eine typische Kaffeefahrt besteht aus einer Reise im Reisebus, einer Übernachtung mit Frühstück und einer Dampferfahrt am Rhein mit einer Reiseleitung. Sie kostet nur DM 69. Alle Unkosten sind im Preis enthalten. Von den Teilnehmern an Kaffee und Butterfahrten wird es erwartet, dass sie irgendwo unterwegs an einer "informativen Verkaufsveranstaltung" teilnehmen. Das bedeutet, dass teuere Produkte vorgeführt werden, in der Hoffnung, dass die Teilnehmer möglichst viel Geld ausgeben werden. Wenn man jedoch der Versuchung, etwas zu kaufen widerstehen kann, kann man einen schönen Ausflug für wenig Geld genießen.

76. Die Veranstalter von Butter-und Kaffeefahrten wollen _____ .

   (A) Produkte verkaufen

   (B) Ausflüge zu billigen Preisen anbieten

   (C) den Teilnehmern ein Vergnügen bereiten

   (D) Butter und Kaffee verkaufen

77. Wie unterscheiden sich Butter-und Kaffeefahrten?

   (A) Auf einer Butterfahrt kauft man Butter und auf einer Kaffeefahrt kauft man Kaffee.

   (B) Eine Butterfahrt bietet immer eine Seefahrt an.

   (C) Auf einer Butterfahrt im Gegensatz zu einer Kaffeefahrt soll man vorgeführte Produkte kaufen.

   (D) Eine Butterfahrt ist teuerer als eine Kaffeefahrt.

78. Was ist ein Vorteil von Butter-und Kaffeefahrten?

   (A) Man kann viel Butter und Kaffee kaufen.

   (B) Man kann billige Ausflüge machen.

(C) Man kann immer zu günstigen Preisen Produkte kaufen.

(D) Man kann umsonst eine Reise machen.

79.   Was ist ein Nachteil von Butter-und Kaffeefahrten?

(A) Die Reisen sind lang und ermüdend.

(B) Der Kaffee schmeckt nicht.

(C) Die Butter ist teuer.

(D) Die vorgeführten Produkte sind teuer.

80.   Was für Teilnehmer können von solchen Fahrten profitieren?

(A) Diejenigen, die wenig Geld haben aber doch die teueren Produkte kaufen wollen.

(B) Diejenigen, die viel Geld haben.

(C) Diejenigen, die der Versuchung widerstehen können, die teueren Produkte zu kaufen.

(D) Diejenigen, die alles kaufen, was angeboten wird.

SAT II
SUBJECT TEST IN
GERMAN

PRACTICE TEST IV

ANSWER KEY

1.	C	21.	C	41.	B	61.	D
2.	B	22.	A	42.	A	62.	D
3.	A	23.	D	43.	B	63.	C
4.	A	24.	D	44.	D	64.	C
5.	A	25.	A	45.	A	65.	A
6.	C	26.	A	46.	C	66.	D
7.	B	27.	D	47.	B	67.	D
8.	A	28.	A	48.	B	68.	B
9.	B	29.	D	49.	C	69.	A
10.	C	30.	A	50.	A	70.	A
11.	C	31.	A	51.	B	71.	D
12.	B	32.	B	52.	B	72.	A
13.	C	33.	D	53.	D	73.	C
14.	A	34.	B	54.	D	74.	D
15.	B	35.	A	55.	B	75.	A
16.	C	36.	B	56.	A	76.	A
17.	D	37.	D	57.	A	77.	B
18.	C	38.	C	58.	A	78.	B
19.	D	39.	D	59.	B	79.	D
20.	B	40.	C	60.	A	80.	C

GERMAN PRACTICE TEST IV

DETAILED EXPLANATIONS
OF ANSWERS

1.   (C)
To state the birth date of a living person, the present tense of the verb *sein* is used. Answer (A) is incorrect because it is in the imperfect tense. Choice (B) is the imperfect tense of the verb *werden*. It would be correct if a deceased person's birth date were being discussed. One would ask, for example:

> *Wann wurde Beethoven geboren?*

Choice (D) is the present tense of the verb *werden*. It is used primarily to form the future tense and the passive. All of the answer choices are second-person singular.

2.   (B)
Dieser has the same endings as the definite article. If we were to substitute the definite article here, it would be *der*. It is nominative masculine. Choice (A) would be correct if the subject were feminine (compare to *die*). Choice (C) is the accusative masculine form (compare to *den*). (D) is both nominative and accusative neuter (compare to *das/das*).

3.   (A)
"To attend" is often expressed in German by the verb *besuchen,* which also means "to visit." Other examples:

> *Ich besuchte seine Schule.*
> (I attended his school.)
> *Gestern Abend habe ich ein Konzert besucht.*
> (Last night I attended a concert.)

Choice (B) is a form of the verb *versuchen* and means "to try." Choice (C) is derived from the verb *behandeln* and means "to treat." The last choice is derived from the verb *nehmen,* which means "to take." Although we say "to take a class" in English, this literal translation into German is not standard.

4.   (A)

In order to answer correctly, you need to know two things: The verb "sich setzen" is a verb of motion and "neben" is a two-way preposition. This means that its object is in the dative case if no motion toward a goal is involved and in the accusative, if there is. Answer (A) is the only choice in the accusative case. Choices (B) and (C) are in the dative case and would be possible if the verb were *sitzen. Er sitzt neben der Dame* means "He is sitting next to the lady." *Er setzte sich neben die Dame* means "He seated himself next to the lady." Choice (D) would not be possible with *Dame,* since *"einem"* is either a masculine or neuter form.

5.   (A)

Möchten is one of the most common subjunctive forms in German and means "would like." Choices (B), (C), and (D) are also forms of the verb *mögen* but they are in the present tense. The present tense would be possible here, but none of them agree with the subject *du.* (B) is the first- and third-person singular form. (C) is the second-person plural form and (D) is the infinitive.

6.   (C)

In German, as in all languages, prepositions are difficult. Often they simply must be learned in context. The English "at" used before an expression of time is expressed by *um* in German. *Zu* in choice (A) generally means "to," but its meaning varies with the context. Choice (B) often means "at the." Choice (D), without the definite article (*am = an dem*) also can mean "at," but not in giving the time.

7.   (B)

In order to answer this correctly, you must be familiar with the expression *sich Sorgen machen,* which means "to be worried" in

English. Furthermore, you must know the reflexive pronoun for the third-person singular subject *er. Sich* is also the reflexive for third-person plural. A quick review of reflexives:

ich: mich/mir	*wir: uns*
du: dich/dir	*ihr: euch*
er, sie, es: sich	*sie: sich*
Sie: sich	

The reflexive forms of *ich* and *du* use the accusative reflexive (*mich/dich*) if there is no other accusative object:

    Ich wasche mich.

The dative form is used, if there is:

    Ich wasche mir die Hände.

Choice (A) is simply the accusative masculine pronoun. Choice (D) could either be the infinitive of the verb "to be" or the possessive adjective "his" or "its."

8.   (A)

This is an idiom and one must know that the pronoun must be in the dative case. It means "What is wrong with you?" Choice (B) means "your" and doesn't fit, grammatically or logically. Choice (C) does not make sense, because it is in the wrong case. Choice (D) is a reflexive pronoun. It can't be used with a non-reflexive verb.

9.   (B)

This is a comparative adjective and means "bigger." Choice (A) is correct as a comparative but it has an adjectival ending and predicate adjectives (adjectives that do not come before nouns) do not have endings. Choice (C) is missing an umlaut. Most monosyllabic adjectives with the vowels *a, o,* or *u* have umlauts in their comparative forms. Choice (D) is a superlative form. However, it would have to be preceded either by the definite article (as in English: the biggest) and have an adjectival ending, or be preceded by *am.*

10.   (C)

This one is very simple if you know the idiom *weh tun,* which means "to hurt." Choice (A) uses the wrong verb. Although *"tun"* and *"machen"* are often interchangeable, they are not so in this expression. Choice (B) is plural and does not agree with the singular subject. Like choice (A), choice (D) simply uses the wrong verb.

11.   (C)

This is a relative pronoun. It means "whose." Whenever the meaning of a relative pronoun is "whose," it is in the genitive case, no matter how it is used in the relative clause. For example:

> *Das ist die Dame, in deren Tasche das Geld war.*
> (That is the woman, in whose purse the money was.)

In this sentence, *deren Tasche* is actually used as if it were dative. Choice (A) is masculine genitive and also means "whose." Answer (D) means "whose" in questions. For example:

> *"Wessen Tasche ist das?"*
> (Whose purse is that?)

A quick review of relative pronouns:

	MAS.	FEM.	N.	PL.
NOM.	*der*	*die*	*das*	*die*
ACC.	*den*	*die*	*das*	*die*
DAT.	*dem*	*der*	*dem*	*denen*
GEN.	*dessen*	*deren*	*dessen*	*deren*

Notice that they are like the definite article, except in the dative plural and all genitive forms, which are really just expanded versions of the definite article.

12.   (B)

This phrase corresponds to the English expression "love at first sight." Choice (A) might be possible, but would mean "love at first blow." Choice (C) means "view." Choice (D) means "view point."

13.   (C)

The expression *was für ein* means "what kind of a." The case of *ein* depends upon how it is used in the sentence. In this example, it is the accusative object of the verb *sehen*. Choices (A), (B), and (D) do not exist.

14.   (A)
The idiom *egal sein* always takes a dative pronoun. This sentence means "What you say is all the same to me" or "I don't care what you say." Choices (B), (C), and (D) are all in the accusative case and therefore do not fit.

15.   (B)
The idiom *Recht haben* is equivalent to the English "to be right." Choice (A) is likely to sound right to an English-speaker, since we use the verb "to be" in this expression. Choice (C) does not exist. *Richtig* used alone means "correct" or "right." Choice (D) also does not exist. *Rechnung* means "bill" or "check." If we put in an article, the sentence would make sense:
>   *Er hat die Rechnung.*
>   (He has the check/bill.)

16.   (C)
Teilnehmen an means "to participate in." The preposition *an* is used in a *"da(r)*-construction." A *"da(r)*-construction" replaces a preposition and a pronoun referring to a thing. That is the case here: Are you participating in it? Choice (A) is also a *"da(r)*-construction," but it has the wrong preposition. Choice (B) is incorrect because there must be an *"r"* inserted when the preposition begins with a vowel. Choice (D) also has the wrong preposition.

17.   (D)
The preposition used with *stolz* is *auf* and together they mean "proud of." There are many such unchangeable combinations of adjectives and prepositions that one must simply learn as they come up. The other prepositions cannot be used with *stolz*.

18.   (C)

Gern when used with a verb, means "to like" whatever the verb means.
For example:

>   *Ich trinke gern Wein.*
>   (I like to drink wine.)
>   *Er singt gern.*
>   (He likes to sing.)

Gern also has comparative and superlative forms, which are irregular.
Lieber is the comparative and the superlative is *am liebsten.* Examples:

>   *Ich trinke lieber Wein als Bier.*
>   (I prefer drinking wine to beer.)
>   *Ich trinke Bier gern, aber ich trinke Wein am liebsten.*
>   (I like drinking beer, but I prefer wine.)

19.   (D)

Bekommen means "to get" or "to receive." Its past participle, which is
what is in this sentence, looks like the infinitive. Choice (A) is the past
participle of the verb *kommen* (to come). Choice (B) is the third person
singular present tense form of *bekommen:*

>   *Er bekommt das Buch von mir.*
>   (He is getting the book from me.)

Choice (C) does not exist.

20.   (B)

The verb *aussehen* means "to look," as in "to appear." The example
says: She always looks good. Choice (A) means "to look at." An
example of its use would be:

>   *Sie sah mich komisch an.*
>   (She looked at me strangely.)

Choice (C) means "to look around." However, it is reflexive and the
reflexive participle is missing here. With the reflexive, the sentence
would make sense:

>   *Sie sieht sich immer gut um.*
>   (She always has a good look around.)

Choice (D), a form of *übersehen,* means "to overlook," and does not fit.

162

21.   (C)
This sentence uses the passive imperfect form of *anfallen* (to attack). Use of the passive voice indicates that the subject, Karl, is being acted upon. Whatever acts upon the subject (in this case, a dog) is usually preceded by *von*, which always has a dative object (*einem Hund*). The passive form of a verb consists of the proper form of *werden* and the past participle of the verb itself (*wurde angefallen*). In this case, *gestern* indicates a past occurence, so choice (A), which is in the present tense, is incorrect. Choice (B) is incorrect because an action, not a state, is being described. Karl was not "in the state of being attacked." Choice (D) is not in the third-person singular and would require the following of *angefallen* by *worden*.

22.   (A)
"For the first time" is expressed in German by *zum ersten Mal*. Choice (B) is a direct translation from English and does not exist. Choice (C) means "first of all," "for the present," or "for the time being." For example:

> *Ich möchte vorerst nichts machen.*
> (For the time being, I would like to do nothing.)

Choice (D) means "first." An example of its use:

> *Zuerst will ich etwas essen, dann schlafe ich.*
> (First I want to eat something, then I will sleep.)

23.   (D)
Before months of the year, use the preposition *"in"* and the definite article in contracted form, *im*. Since all months are masculine, *im* is always used. Choice (A) is lacking the definite article. Choice (B) could never be used in this context. Choice (C) would be correct, if the date were added:

> *Er hat am zweiten Mai Geburtstag.*

24.   (D)
Ankommen means "to arrive" and is the only logical choice here. Choice (A) might be possible, but it would be a bit drastic. *Umkommen* means "to die." Choice (B) means "to happen." A common German saying is:

Das kommt in den besten Familien vor.
(That happens in the best of families.) In English, we would
probably say, "That can happen to anyone."

Choice (C) means "to come along" and does not fit grammatically.

25.   (A)
Although it sounds strange to the ears of English-speakers, occupations
and nationalities are not preceded by articles in German. For that
reason, choices (B) and (C) are incorrect. Choice (C) is also in the
wrong case. Choice (D) is also incorrect on two counts: It has an article,
and the *-en* ending is only present in cases other than the nominative.
Further examples of the omission of the article:
Er ist Hamburger.
He is a citizen of Hamburg. (If you put in the article, it would
mean "He is a hamburger.")

26.   (A)
Although it might seem strange to have two prepositions together, it
happens here. *Zu Hause* means "at home" and "home." This example
means "He is coming directly from home."

Hause cannot be used alone, as in choice (B). Choice (C) means "(to)
home" and would make no sense in this sentence. As with choice (B),
Haus cannot stand alone here.

27.   (D)
"In my opinion" is expressed with the phrase *meiner Meinung nach* in
German. It is one of several such phrases in which the object of the
preposition comes before the preposition. For this reason, choice (B)
is not used. Choice (A) has the incorrect preposition. Choice (C) is
incomplete.

28.   (A)
Although the verb *werden* has several uses, here it means "to become."
Choice (B) is a false cognate. It looks like the English "to become," but

has a different meaning. It means "to get" or "to receive." Choice (C) is incorrect, because an infinitive is needed and choice (C) is a conjugated form. Choice (D) is incorrect for the reasons given for (B) and (C).

29.   (D)

This is an idiom that often confuses English speakers, since we simply say "I am cold." If one translates that literally into German, as in choice (A), the result is something quite different from what the speaker usually intends. It is closest to "I am frigid" in English. Choice (B) is impossible because the sentence would have no subject, stated or understood. *Mich* can only be a direct object and the verb *sein* can never have a direct object. Choice (D) would be fine without the preposition *zu*. It isn't necessary. When the blank is filled in correctly, *Mir ist kalt,* it appears to be missing a subject. However, it is not uncommon to have the understood subject *es,* which is the case here.

30.   (A)

All forms given here are interrogative forms. Only choice (A) fits. It means "whose." It is only used in questions. Choice (B) is the nominative form of "who." Choice (C) is the dative form. Choice (D) is the accusative form. Examples of their use are:

> *Wer ist das?*
> (Who is that?)
> *Wem gehört das?*
> (To whom does that belong?)
> *Wen sah er?*
> (Whom did he see?)

31.   (A)

Heute Abend corresponds to the English "this evening." Choice (B) has to do with bedtime. An example of its use is:

> *Ich hoffe, dass ich heute nacht besser schlafe.*
> (I hope that I will sleep better tonight.)

The same applies to choice (D). It has to do with bedtime and means "last night." Along the same line, one says *Guten Abend* as a greeting and *Gute Nacht* when going to bed. Choice (C) means "last night" and doesn't fit because the verb is in the present tense.

32.   (B)

There are two verbs in German meaning "to know." *Wissen* means "to know a fact." *Kennen* means "to be acquainted with" and has to do with knowing people and even books and places. The example given is concerned with knowledge of fact. If the sentence were changed slightly, choice (A) would be correct: *Er kennt mich.* Instead, the sentence has to do with the fact that "he knows my name." Therefore, (B) is correct. Other examples of the use of *kennen* and *wissen:*

> *Er weiß, wo das Buch ist.*
> (He knows where the book is.)
> *Weißt du, wer gekommen ist?*
> (Do you know who came?)
> *Er kennt Berlin sehr gut.*
> (He knows Berlin very well.)
> *Kennst du den Roman von Hesse?*
> (Are you acquainted with the novel by Hesse?)

Choice (C) is the *"du"*-form of the verb *wissen.* Choice (D) is the imperfect form of the verb *kennen.*

33.   (D)

Jeder has the same ending as the definite article. Since *Kind* is neuter and it is nominative in this sentence, the ending is *"-s"* (compare to the definite article: *das*). Choice (A) would be correct if the subject were masculine (compare to the definite article: *der*). Choice (B) is both of the wrong gender (masculine) and the wrong case (accusative). Choice (C) would be correct, if the subject were feminine (compare to the definite article: *die*).

34.   (B)

Sich lassen + infinitive means "to have___ done." The sentence given here means "He is having his hair cut." Choice (A) is from the verb *sich verlassen.* Used with the preposition *auf,* it means "to depend upon." The non-reflexive form given in choice (C) means "to leave a place or person." Choice (D), from the verb *lassen,* means "to allow."

166

Examples:

> *Er verlässt sich auf mich.*
> (He depends upon me.)
> *Er verlässt Berlin.*
> (He is leaving Berlin.)
> *Er lässt die Kinder gehen.*
> (He is letting the children go.)

35. (A)

The verb *"gehören"* takes a dative object. For this reason, choices (B), (C) and (D) are incorrect. They are all accusative forms.

36. (B)

The interrogative *welcher* has the same endings as the definite article. In order to arrive at the correct answer, you need to know that *Koffer* is masculine and that it is used here in the accusative case. Since the masculine accusative definite article is *den,* the ending here is *-en.* Choice (A) would be correct if *Koffer* were the subject of the sentence. Choice (C) would be correct if *Koffer* were neuter. Choice (D) would be correct if *Koffer* were feminine.

37. (D)

Möchten functions as a modal does. Therefore, there is no *zu* before the infinitive, as in choice (C). Choice (A) means "to lead" and doesn't fit logically. Choice (B) is a past participle and does not fit grammatically with the conjugated verb *möchte.*

38. (C)

This is an unpreceded (i.e., strong) adjective. This means that no articles are before it. Unpreceded adjective endings follow the pattern of the definite article in all cases except the genitive masculine and neuter, which have the weak ending *"-en."* To arrive at the ending for unpreceded adjectives in all other cases, ask yourself what the definite article would be if you were to substitute it for the adjective. In this case, the definite article would be *die,* since *sind* indicates that *Brötchen* is plural. Therefore, the ending is *-e.* Answer (A) would be correct, if *Brötchen* were singular. Following the logic stated above, we could substitute the definite article *das* and arrive at the *"-es"* ending. Choice (B) seems logical, since all preceded plural adjective endings are *"-en."* However, this is not the case for unpreceded adjective endings. Again, they follow the pattern of the definite article. Choice (D) might sound best to a native speaker of English, because it has no ending. However, attributive adjectives in German always have endings.

39.   (D)
The mother and daughter wanted to go shopping. Since the story states they were driving into the city, we can assume they did not live there, as stated in (A). It also states *wie sie es gewohnt waren* that they were accustomed to going shopping together. Therefore, answer (B) does not apply, since it states that they did this seldom. Since the mother was picking up the daughter, they did not live together in the city, as stated in (C).

40.   (C)
The mother sometimes picked the daughter up. She was not picked up by the daughter, as stated in (A). She did pick her up, as stated in (B), but not because it was her habit. They took turns, and this time it was the mother's turn (*Die Mutter war an der Reihe*). Therefore, she did not always (*immer*) pick her up, as stated in (D).

41.   (B)
On the way back, they saw a run-over dog in the street. They did not run over a dog in the street (A), nor did they run over a dead dog (C). They also did not see a run-over but not yet dead dog in the street (D).

42.   (A)
The man placed the dog into the trunk of the car. He did not ask if it was their dog (B). He had not accidently run over the dog (C), nor did he want to bury it (D).

43.   (B)
They became almost hysterical when they saw the dead dog. They did not cry for joy (B). They also did not believe Waldi was still at home

168

(C), nor did they want to leave the dog there (D).

44.   (D)

Waldi was still sleeping in front of the house when the two women returned. It was not Waldi who needed to be buried, but the unknown dog (A). He was not buried by the man (B). Waldi was not happy when they arrived (C). He was still sleeping.

45.   (A)

The American wanted to donate blood because she needed money. It is true that she was far away from her parents (B), but that is not the reason for her wish to donate blood. She did not want to donate blood because she was looking for a job (C), but because, as a foreigner, she was not allowed to work. She was not driven to sell her blood because her friends did not _want_ to help her (D). Perhaps they did want to, but were equally poor.

46.   (C)

She could not look for a job because foreigners are not allowed to work without permission, not because her parents were against it (A). It may be true that her friends did not work (B), but that does not explain why she could not. (D) states that she could borrow money from her friends. That is not the case.

47.   (B)

The student only understood part of what the medic said, not every-thing, as stated in choice (A). (C) states that she understood nothing. Choice (D) states that she understood exactly (_genau_) what he said.

48.   (B)

The medic did not pay attention to what she was doing because he was busy. His lack of attention had nothing to do with her need for money (B). He did not neglect her because he was trying to control himself (C) or because he was laughing (D).

49.   (C)

The student undressed because she had misunderstood, not because the doctor told her to (A). It was also not because she did not want to hesitate (B). The doctor did say it slowly and clearly (D), but only after she had undressed.

50.   (A)

The actors in the German Theater in Hamburg are looking for a runaway dog. They are not looking for a man, who is one of their main actors (B). They are also not looking for a sheepdog, who is playing the role of Aaron (C). Choice (D) states that they are looking for a dog, who could play a role in a play by Shakespeare. This is not true. They are looking for Aaron, who does play a role in a play by Shakespeare.

51.   (B)

Aaron disappeared during a walk. He did not get lost driving to Bavaria (A). He did not get lost because he wanted to run through the woods alone (C). He was chasing a female dog. He also did not get lost because he wanted to vacation in Bavaria (D).

52.   (B)

He ran away because he fell in love, not because he didn't want to work anymore (A) or because he wanted to disappear (C). It was also not because he wanted to go on (D).

53.   (D)

Not only his owner, but also the actors are hoping he will return. Therefore (A) is incorrect. It states that only his owner is interested in whether or not he returns. Choice (B) states that only a spokesperson for the theater is hoping for his return. (C) says that only a shepherd is worried.

54.   (D)

Aaron and Sissy are a strange pair, because they look different. It is not because Aaron is an actor (A) or because Sissy is not an actress (B). It also has nothing to do with the fact that Aaron is too passionate (C).

55.   (B)

Wusste is the imperfect form of the verb *wissen*. Choice (A) does not exist. It is the present tense form with a past tense ending. Choice (C) is the Subjunctive II form and does not fit the context of the sentence, since there is no contrary-to-fact condition expressed. Choice (D) is the past participle of the verb *"wissen"* and does not fit grammatically.

56.   (A)

There are three ways to say "where" in German. *Woher* means literally "from where" and must be used when that is the sense of the message. *Wo* has nothing to do with motion and is used when simply talking about location. The verb *kommen* in this sentence makes clear that that is not the case here. Therefore, choice (B) is incorrect. *Wohin* literally means "where to" and must be used when the motion is away from the speaker. Therefore, choice (C) is incorrect. Choice (D) looks as if it had to do with "where," but it means "what for." Examples of the use of *wo, wohin,* and *woher:*

   Wo bist du? (Where are you?)
   Wohin gehst du? (Where are you going?)
   Woher kommst du? (Where are you from?)

57.   (A)

Feststellen is a verb that has a separable prefix. In a main clause, as here, the prefix (*fest*) goes to the end of the main clause. This explains why choice (B) is incorrect. Choice (C) is incorrect because the *"ge-"* prefix of the past participle should be between the prefix and the rest of the verb: *festgestellt.* Choice (D) is incorrect because it does not fit into the context of the sentence. It is a passive form and the meaning of the verb *feststellen,* "to establish, to find out," makes it impossible to have a person as its subject in the passive.

58.   (A)

Because of the preposition *aus, dem gleichen Stadtteil* is in the dative case. The dative ending of all adjectives that are preceded by other adjectives (*gleichen* is preceded by *dem* in this case), whether preceded by the definite or indefinite and regardless of gender, is *"-en."* For this reason, choices (B), (C) and (D) are incorrect.

59.   (B)

A basic rule of German word order is that the verb occupies the second position in a sentence. This rule applies here. The adverb *gestern* is considered the first element in the sentence and the verb must follow. For this reason, all of the other choices are incorrect.

60.   (A)

"In" is a preposition that can have a dative object if there is no motion toward a goal, as is the case here, or an accusative object if there is motion toward a goal. One must also know that *"Bibliothek"* is feminine in order to answer the question correctly. The feminine dative definite article is *der*. Choice (B) is in the wrong case (accusative). Choice (C) is of the wrong gender (masculine or neuter) and choice (D) is the wrong case (accusative) and gender (masculine).

61.   (D)

In an indirect question, "if" is expressed by *ob*. Choice (A) is incorrect because this is an indirect question and if the speaker is trying to ask "when" I have read something by Hesse, he would have to use *wann,* and not *wenn.* Choice (B) means "although" and does not make sense in this context. The same can be said for choice (C), which means "whom."

62.   (D)

Normally the conjugated verb goes to the end of a subordinate clause. However, when there is a double infinitive in the present perfect or past perfect tense, the conjugated verb is located immediately before the double infinitive. This explains why choice (A) is incorrect. Choice (B) is incorrect for the same reason, but it also has the incorrect form of *haben* to agree with the subject *ich.* The latter is also true of choice (C), which does have the correct word order.

63.   (C)

A contrary-to-fact Subjunctive II form is used here, since "I" did <u>not</u> tell him to come again tomorrow. Since *sagen* forms its perfect tenses with *haben,* we need the Subjunctive II form of *haben.* The proper Subjunctive II form of a verb is arrived at in two ways. If a verb is a "weak" verb, that is, if *"t"* is added to the verb stem to form the imperfect and then inflections to denote the person are added (e.g.: *ich kaufe* is *ich kaufte* in the imperfect), then the Subjunctive II form of the verb becomes merely the same as the imperfect form (e.g.: *ich kaufe* becomes *ich kaufte* in the Subjunctive II). However, if a verb is a "strong" verb, that is, if it has an irregular imperfect form, then the Subjunctive II form of the verb is formed by taking the stem of the imperfect first person plural form, adding an umlaut to the stem (if possible), and then adding the endings *"-e," "-est," "-e," "-en," "-et,"* and *"-en"* (whichever is appropriate) to the modified stem. Thus, in Subjunctive II, *ich komme* is *ich käme* (*kam-käm-käme*) and *ich habe* is *ich hätte* (*hatte-hätte*) (*haben* is a rather irregular example of the formation of subjunctive).

Choice (C) is Subjunctive II, but it is from *sein*. Choice (B) is not a Subjunctive II form. Choice (D) is also not a subjunctive form.

64.   (C)
The person to whom one says something in German is in the dative case. It corresponds to English "to me, you, him," etc. Choice (A) is in the nominative and is incorrect. Choice (B) is accusative. Choice (D) can either be nominative or accusative.

65.   (A)
This is an example of the Subjunctive I, which is used in indirect discourse. The speaker is relating what he would have said. The Subjunctive I is based on the present tense of the *"wir"* form. The endings are the same as the Subjunctive II endings and are best remembered by learning the endings of the imperfect form of *arbeiten* after the -t: *ich arbeitetE, du arbeitetEST, er arbeitetE, wir arbeitetEN, ihr arbeitetET, sie arbeitetEN.*
     Wir müssen (present) → *er arbeitetE* → *er müsse.*

Choice (B) is the *ihr* present tense form of *müssen*. Choice (C) is either the infinitive or the *"wir"-*, *"sie"*- or *"Sie"*-form. Choice (D) is the *"du"*-form in the present tense.

66.   (D)
Since the conjugated verb is a modal (*müssen*), the verb at the end is an

infinitive. There is no *zu* before the infinitive when the conjugated verb is a modal. For this reason, choices (B) and (C) are wrong. Choice (A) would occur in a main clause with a plural subject, such as: *Sie kommen wieder.*

67.　　(D)

Nachdem is a subordinating conjunction, and therefore it causes the conjugated verb to go to the end of the phrase. For this reason, choice (C) is incorrect. It is immediately followed by the subject. Therefore, choices (A) and (B) are wrong. So, the word order in a *nachdem* clause is:

Nachdem　　subject . . . . conjugated verb.
　1　　　　　　2　　　　　　　　　　　　　　　　end

68.　　(B)

Since *nachdem* means "after," the following clause cannot be in the present tense. Therefore, choice (A) is wrong. Choice (C) is the present Subjunctive II and does not fit grammatically or logically. Choice (D) does not exist.

69.　　(A)

With only a few exceptions, the English preposition "to," before the name of a place, is *nach* in German. The exceptions have to do with countries having definite articles, such as *die Schweiz* (Switzerland), *die Sowjet Union, die Turkei.* For example:
　　　　　　　Er fährt in die Schweiz.
　　　　　　　(He is going to Switzerland.)

Since *Köln* has no article, choice (B) is wrong. Choices (C) and (D) would not be possible in this context. Choice (C) does mean "to" and is used before personal pronouns: *Er kommt zu mir.* (He is coming to [see] me.) Choice (D) often means "at the home of" or "at ____ house." For example: *Er wohnt bei mir.* (He lives at my house/with me.)

70.　　(A)

Wird zugemacht is the present passive. It means "is closed." There is

174

always a form of the verb *"werden"* in the passive:

> *Das Fenster wird zugemacht.*
> (The window is [being] closed.)
> *Das Fenster wurde zugemacht.*
> (The window was [being] closed.)
> *Das Fenster ist zugemacht worden.*
> (The window was [has been] closed.)
> *Das Fenster war zugemacht worden.*
> (The window had been closed.)
> *Das Fenster wird zugemacht werden.*
> (The window will be closed.)

Worden exists only to form the perfect tenses of the passive. Choice (B) is called a "false" passive. It appears to be the passive, but it isn't, since it doesn't describe an action, but a state: The window is [in the state of being] closed. *Zugemacht* in choice (B) is an adjective, not a past participle. The passive always describes an action. Choice (C) does not exist. The subjunctive form *wurde* is followed by an infinitive, not a past participle.

71.   (D)
This is an example of the subjunctive *würde* + infinitive construction. It means "would...break/be destroyed." Choice (A) is the past perfect and means "had broken." It does not fit the context of the sentence. Choice (B) would be possible if the *ware* had an umlaut. In that case, the sentence would mean: The window is closed every day; otherwise everything would be broken. Choice (C) is the present perfect tense. It means "was . . . broken" and does not fit.

72.   (A)
The young couple went through an attic window without difficulty. They did not go through the royal kitchen (B). They did climb up construction scaffolding (*"Baugerüst"*), but did not find a door (C). They did not look through an attic window until no one was in the kitchen (D).

73.   (C)

From all evidence, they felt very much at home in the palace. They were not afraid (A). They did dare to help themselves to exotic Chinese delicacies in the kitchen (B). They did not want to leave right away (D), but spent the night.

74.   (D)

The former art students were caught because they decided to take along some paintings as souvenirs, not because they wanted to take a bath (A), eat (B), or sleep (C).

75.   (A)

The night was expensive, because they had to pay a fine (*"eine Strafe bezahlen"*). It was almost twice as expensive as a night in the most expensive hotel in Amsterdam, not <u>almost</u> as expensive as a hotel (B) or cheaper than in an expensive hotel (C) or as expensive as a hotel (D).

76.   (A)

The sponsors (*Veranstalter*) of *"Butter-und-Kaffee"* trips want to sell products. They are not interested in offering excursions at low prices (A), nor do they wish to give pleasure (*ein Vergnügen bereiten*) to the participants (C). Even the sponsors of *Butter* trips are not chiefly interested in selling butter. Being able to buy butter at duty-free prices is a side attraction. *Kaffee* trips have nothing to do with buying coffee. Stopping at a cafe is usually one of the attractions, but the main purpose is to demonstrate products for sale at higher prices than those in stores (D).

77.   (B)

The difference between *Kaffee* and *Butter* trips is that a *Butter* trip always includes an ocean excursion. That explains the duty-free butter prices. A *Butter* trip is not more expensive than a *Kaffee* trip (D). Answers (A) and (C) are explained in the solution to no. 76.

78.   (B)
The advantage of such excursions is that one can have a nice trip at a low price — if one does not fall into the trap of spending a lot of money on overpriced products. One could conceivably buy lots of *Butter and Kaffee* (A), but that isn't the real advantage of such trips. It is not the case that one can always buy products at favorable prices (C). Only the duty-free products are inexpensive and they are only available on a *Butter* excursion. One cannot travel for free (*umsonst*) (D). There is a fee for both *Kaffee* and *Butter* trips, but these fees are very low.

79.   (D)
The disadvantage of *Kaffee* and *Butter* excursions is that the products shown and demonstrated are expensive. It might also be true that the trips are long and tiring (A), but that isn't discussed in this reading. It might be true as well that the coffee isn't good (B), but we aren't told that here. It probably isn't true that the butter is expensive (C), since it is duty-free.

80.   (C)
Those who can profit most from these trips are the ones who can resist the temptation (*der Versuchung widerstehen*) to purchase the expensive products. Those who have a lot of money (B) will not profit. They might unnecessarily spend their money on products they could get more inexpensively elsewhere. Those who have little money and still buy the expensive products (A) will profit least of all. The same can be said for those who buy everything offered, whether of good value (*preiswert*) or not (D).

SAT II:
SUBJECT TEST IN
GERMAN

PRACTICE
TEST V

GERMAN PRACTICE TEST V

PART A

Time: 1 Hour
80 Questions

DIRECTIONS: Each of the sentences in this part has a blank space indicating that a word or phrase has been omitted. From the four choices select the ONE that when inserted in the sentence fits grammatically and logically with the sentence as a whole. Then blacken the corresponding space on the answer sheet.

1.   Peter spricht mit der Frau, _____ er gestern getroffen hat.

   (A) wem
   (B) die
   (C) was
   (D) der

2.   Das ist die _____ Kirche, die ich je gesehen habe.

   (A) schönsten
   (B) schönster
   (C) schönste
   (D) schönstes

3.   Meine Schwester hat den Film nicht sehen _____ .

   (A) können
   (B) gekonnt
   (C) haben
   (D) worden

4. Im dritten Geschäft haben wir endlich _____ Erdbeeren gefunden.

   (A) frischen
   (B) frischer
   (C) frischen
   (D) frische

5. Von diesem Schauspieler habe ich noch nie _____ .

   (A) hören
   (B) gehören
   (C) hörte
   (D) gehört

6. Alle meine Freunde gehen nachmittags in _____ Garten.

   (A) das
   (B) dem
   (C) der
   (D) den

7. Obwohl es gefährlich war, sprang Jürgen auf den _____ Zug.

   (A) fahrend
   (B) gefahren
   (C) fahrenden
   (D) fahren

8. Inge sagte, sie _____ ihre Hausaufgaben nicht gemacht.

   (A) habe
   (B) würde
   (C) sei
   (D) hätte

9.   Warum trägst du immer die Kleider _____ Schwester?

(A) deines
(B) deinem
(C) deinen
(D) deiner

10.   _____ wurde nichts von dem Unfall gesagt.

(A) Er
(B) Ihm
(C) Ihn
(D) Sie

11.   Ich fahre lieber mit meinem eigenen Auto. Du fährst immer
        so _____ .

(A) schnellsten
(B) schnell
(C) schnelleres
(D) schnellem

12.   Im Krankenhaus habe ich viele Leute mit _____ Armen
        gesehen.

(A) brechender
(B) brechen
(C) gebrochenen
(D) bricht

13.   Vielleicht kann er es morgen noch einmal _____ .

(A) versuchen
(B) versucht
(C) versuchte
(D) zu versuchen

14.   Das Glas, aus _____ ich getrunken habe, war nicht sauber.

      (A) das
      (B) wem
      (C) der
      (D) dem

15.   Morgen _____ Dieter noch einmal kommen.

      (A) werden
      (B) wird
      (C) wurde
      (D) geworden

16.   Der Ober _____ Schnitzel mit Kartoffelsalat.

      (A) empfehlt
      (B) empfehlte
      (C) empfiehlt
      (D) empfehlen

17.   In der Loge klatschte _____ begeistert.

      (A) jemand
      (B) jemandem
      (C) jemanden
      (D) jemandes

18.   Das Geld _____ von den Einbrechern gestohlen worden.

      (A) ist
      (B) wird
      (C) sind
      (D) hat

19. Wegen _____ Regens hat die Fahrt länger gedauert.

(A) dem
(B) der
(C) die
(D) des

20. Die Zugspitze ist der _____ Berg Deutschlands.

(A) höhere
(B) hohe
(C) am höchsten
(D) höchste

PART B

DIRECTIONS: Each of the sentences in this part has a blank space indicating that a word or phrase has been omitted. From the four choices select the ONE that when inserted in the sentence fits grammatically and logically with the sentence as a whole. Then blacken the corresponding space on the answer sheet.

21. Mein Freund wohnt _____ 20 Jahren im gleichen Haus.

(A) vor
(B) nach
(C) seit
(D) für

22. Das Theaterstück von Brecht hat _____ sehr gut gefallen.

(A) unser
(B) mir
(C) mich
(D) ihre

23.   Der Lehrer wartete schon lange _____ .

(A) darauf
(B) auf es
(C) dagegen
(D) womit

24.   _____ Goethe 1794 nach Italien reiste, besuchte er auch Rom.

(A) Wenn
(B) Als
(C) Wann
(D) Ob

25.   Im November werden die Nächte immer _____ .

(A) am längsten
(B) lang
(C) länger
(D) mehr lang

26.   Das darf _____ nicht wahr sein!

(A) denn
(B) schon
(C) doch
(D) mal

27.   Wir fahren heute nicht nach München, _____ nach Salzburg.

(A) sondern
(B) weil
(C) aber
(D) denn

28.   Seit meinem letzten Besuch _____ ich Deutschland sehr gut.

(A) weiss
(B) verstehe
(C) kenne
(D) mag

29.   Nach langem Nachdenken hat er endlich eine _____ getroffen.

(A) Meinung
(B) Frage
(C) Entscheidung
(D) Antwort

30.   Bei diesem kalten Wetter kann man _____ leicht erkälten.

(A) sich
(B) mich
(C) mir
(D) uns

31.   Ich spiele manchmal Fussball, aber _____ Basketball interessiere ich mich überhaupt nicht.

(A) für
(B) über
(C) in
(D) mit

32.   Vor _____ Dingen braucht meine Schwester immer Geld.

(A) jeden
(B) ersten
(C) keinen
(D) allen

33.   Das Schillerdenkmal wurde vor 200 Jahren _____ .

(A) errichtet
(B) gelesen
(C) gekauft
(D) gefunden

34.   Meine Eltern hätten gerne ein neues Haus, aber sie können
es _____ .

(A) nicht verkaufen
(B) sich nicht leisten
(C) erst nächste Woche sehen
(D) von der Bank bekommen

35.   Weil Jürgen noch ein kleines Kind ist, soll er immer den
Mund _____ .

(A) aufmachen
(B) öffnen
(C) halten
(D) zeigen

36.   Ich gehe ins Kino. Du kannst das Essen stehen _____ .

(A) dürfen
(B) lassen
(C) mögen
(D) müssen

37.   Je früher wir aufstehen, _____ früher kommen wir an.

(A) trotz
(B) um zu
(C) aber
(D) desto

38. Meine Frau kommt immer zu früh, da ihre Uhr _____ .

    (A) vorrennt
    (B) vorläuft
    (C) vorgeht
    (D) vorkommt

39. Wenn du mir nicht geholfen hättest, _____ hätte ich es nie geschafft.

    (A) dann
    (B) wann
    (C) denn
    (D) danach

40. Eltern lieben ihre Kinder, obwohl sie _____ .

    (A) gute Noten in der Schule haben
    (B) gerne mit ihnen spielen
    (C) ihnen oft Sorgen machen
    (D) immer auf ihre Eltern hören

PART C

DIRECTIONS: The sentences below contain blank spaces indicating omissions in the text. Below each blank are four choices. Select the choice that is grammatically correct in the context and blacken the corresponding space on the answer sheet. Be sure to read the sentences first.

Questions 41–42 are one sentence.

41. Er ist nicht _____ ,

    (A) laufen
    (B) geantwortet
    (C) geblieben
    (D) fuhr

42. weil er keine _____ mehr hatte.

(A) Zeit
(B) Hunger
(C) Bier
(D) Uhr

Questions 43–45 are connected. The indefinite pronoun at the beginning of **Question 44** refers to **Question 43**.

43. _____ Sommer fahren wir immer ans Meer.

(A) Zum
(B) Im
(C) Während
(D) Auf

44. Das ist _____ für die Kinder schön,

(A) denn
(B) nie
(C) kaum
(D) besonders

45. denn sie _____ dann immer am Strand spielen.

(A) müssen
(B) können
(C) sollen
(D) werden

Questions 46–48 are connected. They all make statements about the German soccer player Franz Beckenbauer.

46. Franz Beckenbauer war ein _____ Fussballspieler.

(A) schöne
(B) bekanntes
(C) berühmter
(D) alten

47. Viele Leute sprechen noch heute über _____ .

(A) ihn
(B) sie
(C) es
(D) uns

48. Sie können ihn einfach nicht _____ .

(A) überreden
(B) versuchen
(C) vergessen
(D) unternehmen

Questions 49–51 are one sentence.

49. Ich habe den Entschluss _____ ,

(A) gefasst
(B) gemacht
(C) gehört
(D) geschrieben

50. mit dem Rauchen _____ ,

(A) aufhören
(B) aufgehört
(C) aufzuhören
(D) zu aufhören

51.   aber ich weiss, es wird _____ nicht leichtfallen.

(A) mich
(B) mir
(C) ich
(D) mein

Questions 52–54 form a single sentence. You have to understand the meaning of the whole sentence in order to answer correctly.

52.   Das Buch, das ich gestern gelesen _____ ,

(A) bin
(B) haben
(C) werde
(D) habe

53.   war sehr _____ ,

(A) romantisches
(B) romantische
(C) romantisch
(D) romantischer

54.   _____ nicht besonders spannend.

(A) denn
(B) sondern
(C) jedoch
(D) jedenfalls

Questions **55–57** are connected and **58–60** are connected.

55.   Ich freue mich immer besonders _____ Weihnachten,

    (A) zu
    (B) nach
    (C) auf
    (D) in

56.   weil _____ dann die ganze Familie versammelt,

    (A) uns
    (B) sich
    (C) euch
    (D) mich

57.   und wir uns so wenigstens einmal im Jahr unterhalten _____ .

    (A) konnten
    (B) könnten
    (C) gekonnt
    (D) können

58.   Im letzten Monat hat mein Mann _____ verdient als sonst,

    (A) am meisten
    (B) viel
    (C) mehr
    (D) meistens

59.   weil er _____ Überstunden gemacht hat,

    (A) viel
    (B) viele
    (C) vielen
    (D) vieles

60. _____ er sonst nie tut.

(A) das
(B) wie
(C) die
(D) was

PART D

DIRECTIONS: Read the following passages carefully for comprehension. Each passage is followed by a number of incomplete statements or questions. Select the completion or answer that is best according to the passage and blacken the corresponding space on the answer sheet.

Das Deutsche Reich von 1871 war Bismarcks Reich. Bismarck ist oft als einer der wichtigsten Persönlichkeiten der deutschen Geschichte bezeichnet worden. Sein Hauptinteresse galt der Außenpolitik, während die Innenpolitik mehr von den Parlamenten bestimmt wurde. Zeit seines Lebens blieb Bismarck ein Monarchist, der die Parlamente nur als notwendiges Übel ansah, und der versuchte, sie für seine Zwecke zu benutzen.

Bismarcks größte innenpolitische Erfolge waren die Gründung des deutschen Reiches, die Vermeidung der Revolution, sowie die Einführung der Sozialversicherung für Arbeiter. Seine größten innenpolitischen Probleme bestanden im sogenannten Kulturkampf zwischen Katholiken und Protestanten und dem Aufkommen der Sozialisten, die Bismarck als gefährlich für den Staat betrachtete.

Außenpolitisch muss Bismarcks Hauptleistung wohl darin gesehen werden, zuerst Preußen und dann das Deutsche Reich neben Frankreich, England und Russland zu einer Großmacht in Europa gemacht zu haben. Allerdings wird von vielen Historikern behauptet, dass Bismarcks Außenpolitik den Grundstein für den 1. Weltkrieg gelegt hat.

61. Die Absicht des Autors ist _____ .

(A) zu zeigen, dass Außen- und Innenpolitik für Bismarck gleich wichtig waren

(B) die politischen Leistungen Bismarcks kurz darzustellen

(C) Bismarck als Monarchisten zu diffamieren

(D) die Behauptung aufzustellen, dass Bismarck eine der grössten Gestalten der deutschen Geschichte war

62.   Aus dem Text kann man schließen, dass Bismarck _____ .

(A) Sozialist war

(B) den Kulturkampf entschieden hat

(C) eine Revolution wollte

(D) Parlamente nicht mochte

63.   Bismarcks Aussenpolitik hatte zum Ziel, _____ .

(A) Frankreich, England und Russland zu besiegen

(B) Deutschland mit Frankreich, England und Russland gleichzustellen

(C) den Kulturkampf in Frankreich, England und Russland zu beenden

(D) die Monarchie in Frankreich, England und Russland zu erhalten

Die Brüder Thomas und Heinrich Mann gehören beide zu den bekanntesten deutschen Dichtern des 20. Jahrhunderts. Von Thomas kennt man besonders die Romane "Buddenbrooks," "Der Zauberberg" und "Doktor Faustus"; von Heinrich die Romane "Der Untertan" und "Professor Unrat."

Das Verhältnis der Brüder zueinander war nicht immer einfach und oft von Missverständnissen und Eifersucht geprägt. Die gegenseitige Entfremdung hatte begonnen, als Thomas seinen Bruder in einem Aufsatz einen "Zivilisationsliteraten" nannte. Der Begriff war eine Anspielung auf Heinrichs Hochachtung vor der französischen Kultur und Literatur, die Thomas geringschätzte.

Während Heinrich Zeit seines Lebens ein begeisterter Demokrat war, hatte Thomas Schwierigkeiten, nach dem Zusammenbruch des Kaiserreiches 1918 die sogenannte "Weimarer Republik" zu unterstützen. Erst langsam kämpfte er sich in den zwanziger Jahren zu einer vorsichtigen Befürwortung der Demokratie durch. Heinrich hingegen liebte die Republik und wurde sogar als Präsidentschaftskandidat der Sozialdemokraten vorgeschlagen.

Nach der Machtergreifung Hitlers im Jahre 1933 mussten sowohl Thomas als auch Heinrich Mann in die USA auswandern. In der Emigration verschlechterte sich ihr Verhältnis noch mehr, weil Thomas inzwischen berühmter als Heinrich war, und Thomas deshalb in finanzieller Unabhängigkeit leben konnte, während Heinrich arm und zeitweilig auf Hilfe vom Bruder angewiesen war.

Nach 1945 kehrten die Bruder Mann nach Europa zurück. Thomas ließ sich zunächst in der Schweiz nieder, und Heinrich ging in die DDR, wo man ihn als Nationaldichter feierte. Im Alter verstanden sich die Brüder etwas besser, zu einer vollständigen Versöhnung kam es jedoch nie.

64.   Die Brüder Thomas und Heinrich Mann _____ .

(A) haben sich immer gestritten
(B) haben sich sehr geliebt
(C) hatten ein schwieriges Verhältnis zueinander
(D) haben einige Romane zusammen geschrieben

65.   Die Jahre zwischen 1933 und 1945 verbrachten Thomas und Heinrich in _____ .

(A) der Schweiz
(B) der DDR
(C) Amerika
(D) Frankreich

66.   Das Leben Heinrich Manns war _____ .

(A) typisch für einen Zivilisationsliteraten
(B) wie das vieler Präsidentschaftskandidaten
(C) eng mit dem seines Bruders verbunden
(D) durch den Zusammenbruch des Kaiserreiches im Jahre 1918 gekennzeichnet

67. Die politischen Überzeugungen der Brüder Mann waren
_____ .

(A) einander ähnlich
(B) unterschiedlich
(C) völlig dieselben
(D) reaktionär

Der deutsche Mieterbund hat in seiner Zeitschrift darauf hingewiesen, dass ein Mieter nicht haftbar gemacht werden kann, wenn er vor seinem Fernseher einschläft und daraus ein Schaden entsteht.

Die Mieter-Zeitung berichtete von einem Fall, bei dem ein Fernsehgerät in Brand geriet, nachdem sein Besitzer eingenickt war. Der Vermieter der Wohnung verlangte Schadenersatz in Höhe von 61.000 Mark, da er sich nicht hoch genug versichert hatte und in seinem Haus ein hoher Schaden durch den Brand verursacht worden war. Er behauptete, dass der Besitzer des Fernsehers für sein Gerät verantwortlich sei und keinesfalls vor ihm einschlafen dürfe.

Ein Gericht in Köln stimmte dem Argument des Vermieters jedoch nicht zu, und es vertrat die Auffassung, dass ein Fernseher beim heutigen Stand der Technik nicht besonders bewacht werden müsse. Ausserdem sei es bei der Qualität vieler Fernsehsendungen kein Wunder, dass mehr und mehr Zuschauer Schwierigkeiten hätten, wach zu bleiben, fügte der Richter in seinem Urteilsspruch hinzu.

68. In Deutschland werden offenbar _____ .

(A) einige Brände durch Fernseher verursacht
(B) Häuser oft in Brand gesteckt
(C) alle Fernseher automatisch ausgeschaltet, wenn sein Besitzer einschläft
(D) wie durch ein Wunder die Fernsehprogramme immer schlechter

69. Fernseher haben heute einen so hohen technischen Stand, dass
_____ .

(A) man nicht auf sie aufpassen muss
(B) sie keinesfalls Brände verursachen können

195

(C) sie manchmal bis zu 61.000 Mark kosten

(D) die Zuschauer oft nicht einschlafen können

70. Der Richter meint, dass manche Fernsehsendungen _____ .

(A) ausgezeichnet sind
(B) langweilig sind
(C) spannend sind
(D) qualitativ sind

71. Der deutsche Mieterbund _____ .

(A) vertritt die Ansicht, dass der Besitzer des Fernsehers für den Brand verantwortlich ist
(B) berichtet über einen interessanten Gerichtsfall
(C) findet, dass niemand vor seinem Fernseher einschlafen sollte
(D) kritisiert das Urteil des Gerichtes in Köln

72. Der Vermieter will _____ .

(A) eine neue Versicherung
(B) seine Verluste erstattet bekommen
(C) einen neuen Fernseher
(D) Schadenersatz von der Mieter-Zeitung

Ärzte der chirurgischen Universitätsklinik Münster haben in einer Untersuchung herausgefunden, dass vielleicht noch vor dem Jahr 2000 mehr Frauen an Herzinfarkten, Lungenkrebs und anderen "Männerkrankheiten" sterben werden als Männer. Diese erstaunliche Entwicklung würde dann dazu führen, dass die Lebenserwartung der Frauen unter die der Männer sinken würde.

Dr. Dittrich, der Direktor der Klinik, sagte in einem Interview: "Die Frau holt in jeder Beziehung auf. Immer mehr junge Frauen kommen mit Herzinfarkten, Bronchialkarzinomen und sogar Raucherbeinen ins Krankenhaus."

Was sind die Gründe für diesen Trend? Dr. Dittrich erläuterte, dass man fast weltweit beobachten könne, wie Frauen versuchen würden, den männlichen Lebensstil zu übernehmen. Wie dieses "verrückte" Verhalten der Frauen zu erklären sei, wisse man noch nicht genau. Einige Psychologen meinen, dass viele Frauen offenbar als Folge der Emanzipation ein so starkes seelisches Nachholbedürfnis hätten, so leben zu wollen wie Männer, dass sie ihre Gesundheit rücksichtslos gefährdeten.

73. Ärzte der Universitätsklinik Münster haben herausgefunden, dass _____ .

   (A) Männerkrankheiten eigentlich Frauenkrankheiten sind
   (B) heute mehr Frauen an Herzinfarkten sterben als Männer
   (C) bis zum Jahr 2000 Frauen kaum an Herzinfarkten sterben werden
   (D) die Zahl der Frauen, die an Herzinfarkten sterben, zunimmt

74. Dr. Dittrich stellte fest, dass _____ .

   (A) mehr junge als alte Frauen mit Herzinfarkten ins Krankenhaus kommen
   (B) mehr junge Frauen als früher Herzinfarkte bekommen
   (C) Frauen heute mehr Beziehungen als früher haben und deshalb mehr Herzinfarkte erleiden
   (D) mehr Frauen mit Raucherbeinen als mit Bronchialkarzinomen ins Krankenhaus kommen

75. Ein Grund für die in dem Artikel beschriebene Entwicklung ist möglicherweise _____ .

   (A) eine Senkung der Lebenserwartung der Frauen
   (B) die Übernahme des männlichen Lebensstiles durch Frauen
   (C) ein Anstieg der Zahl der Frauen
   (D) die immer noch nicht vollständig vollzogene Emanzipation der Frau

76.   Die Wissenschaftler halten diese Entwicklung für _____ .

(A) bemerkenswert
(B) gut
(C) unwichtig
(D) beispielhaft

In Hessen hat die Polizei Falschgeld sichergestellt, das mit Hilfe eines Farbkopierers hergestellt wurde. Es ist das erste Mal, dass es der Polizei gelungen ist, nachzuweisen, dass ein solch neuartiges Gerät zum Vervielfältigen der "Blüten," wie man Falschgeld auch oft nennt, benutzt wurde.

Das Kriminalamt in Wiesbaden war auf die Spur einer 34-jährigen Frau gekommen, als sie versuchte, mit einer zunächst täuschend echt wirkenden 500-Mark-Note ein Paar Damenstrümpfe zu kaufen. Die Kassiererin nahm den Schein zunächst an, wurde aber später unsicher und notierte sich die Autonummer der Kundin. Das Kennzeichen führte die Polizei schliesslich zu der Wohnung des 38-jährigen Freundes der Frau. Dort wurde der Farbkopierer, der zur Vervielfältigung des Falschgeldes benutzt worden war, sichergestellt.

Ob das Paar die Idee, "Blüten" mit Hilfe eines Farbkopierers in Umlauf zu bringen, alleine hatte, oder ob noch andere Täter die gleiche Methode gebrauchen, konnte von der Polizei zur Zeit noch nicht festgestellt werden.

77.   Die Herstellung von Falschgeld mit einem Farbkopierer ist _____ .

(A) schon seit längerer Zeit üblich
(B) unmöglich
(C) die neueste Methode, Falschgeld herzustellen
(D) in Hessen legalisiert worden

78.   Das Autokennzeichen der Frau war _____ .

(A) eine Spur, die der Polizei half
(B) gefälscht

(C) eine "Blüte"

(D) von der Kassiererin nicht angenommen worden

79.   Die Kassiererin hat _____ .

(A) die 500-Mark-Note mit einem Farbkopierer
      hergestellt
(B) geistesgegenwärtig das Richtige getan
(C) die 500-Mark-Note sofort als "Blüte" erkannt
(D) die Polizei zur Wohnung des Freundes der Frau geführt

80.   Die Polizei untersucht noch, _____ .

(A) wer die Kundin war
(B) wie das Falschgeld hergestellt wurde
(C) ob der 500-Mark-Schein echt war
(D) ob noch andere Personen Farbkopierer für Fälschungen
      benutzen

SAT II:
SUBJECT TEST IN GERMAN

PRACTICE TEST V

ANSWER KEY

1.	B	21.	C	41.	C	61.	B
2.	C	22.	B	42.	A	62.	D
3.	A	23.	A	43.	B	63.	B
4.	D	24.	B	44.	D	64.	C
5.	D	25.	C	45.	B	65.	C
6.	D	26.	C	46.	C	66.	C
7.	C	27.	A	47.	A	67.	B
8.	A	28.	C	48.	C	68.	A
9.	D	29.	C	49.	A	69.	A
10.	B	30.	A	50.	C	70.	B
11.	B	31.	A	51.	B	71.	B
12.	C	32.	D	52.	D	72.	B
13.	A	33.	A	53.	C	73.	D
14.	D	34.	B	54.	C	74.	B
15.	B	35.	C	55.	C	75.	B
16.	C	36.	B	56.	B	76.	A
17.	A	37.	D	57.	D	77.	C
18.	A	38.	C	58.	C	78.	A
19.	D	39.	A	59.	B	79.	B
20.	D	40.	C	60.	D	80.	D

GERMAN PRACTICE TEST V
DETAILED EXPLANATIONS
OF ANSWERS

1.   (B)
This question examines your mastery of the relative pronouns. In German, the number and gender of a relative pronoun are determined by the word the relative pronoun refers back to (here: *die Frau*) and its case is determined by the function (i.e., subject, accusative, or dative object) the relative pronoun has in the relative clause. *Die Frau* is neuter and singular and the relative pronoun is the accusative object of the relative clause. Therefore, you must choose the neuter, singular, accusative relative pronoun, which is *die* (choice (B)). Choice (A) is wrong, since German uses definite articles (i.e., *der, die, das*) as relative pronouns and not, like English, interrogative pronouns (i.e., "who," "whom"). The relative pronoun *"was"* (choice (C)) is only used when the whole main clause is referred back to. Choice (D) is incorrect because *der* is the pronoun which had to be used if the relative pronoun were the dative object of the relative clause.

2.   (C)
In this question you are asked to find the proper adjective ending. First you have to determine whether an adjective is preceded by a "*der*-word" or an "*ein*-word" or whether it is unpreceded. Here it is preceded by *die,* which is a "*der*-word." If an adjective is preceded by a "*der*-word," it always takes a weak ending. There are only two weak adjective-endings: -*e* and -*en* (choices (A) and (C)). Choices (B) and (D), -*er* and -*es,* both represent strong endings and, therefore, are incorrect. In order to choose between the two possible endings, you

201

have to recognize the gender, number, and the case of the noun, which is modified by the adjective (here: *Kirche*). *Kirche* is singular and feminine, and its case is nominative, since the verb *ist* combines a subject with a predicate noun (*die Kirche*), which is also nominative. The proper weak ending for a feminine, singular, nominative adjective is *-e* (choice (C)).

3.   (A)
You are asked to determine the proper completion for a sentence that contains *"hat"* as its auxiliary verb and an infinitive (*sehen*). The only possible construction in which this could be the case is the present perfect of a modal auxiliary verb. Neither *haben* (choice (C)) nor *worden* (choice (D)) are modals, which means that neither one is the correct answer. You have to know that German uses a double infinitive in the present perfect for modals and not, as with all other verbs, a past participle. Therefore, the past participle of the modal *können* (*gekonnt*) is wrong and the correct answer is choice (A).

4.   (D)
You have to find the proper ending for an adjective that modifies the noun *Erdbeeren*. You have to decide whether the noun is preceded by an "*ein*-word," a "*der*-word," or whether it is unpreceded. Here it is unpreceded, which means that it has to take a strong ending. The next step is to determine the case, the gender, and the number of the noun *Erdbeeren*. It is plural and accusative. The accusative plural strong adjective ending is *-e,* and the correct choice is (D).

5.   (D)
You are requested to find the proper form of the verb *hören* to complete the sentence. The auxiliary verb *habe* indicates that the tense of the verb is the present perfect. The correct verb compliment for the present perfect is a past participle. Choice (A) offers the infinitive and choice (C) the simple past, which makes them both incorrect. In order to decide between choices (B) and (D) you have to know that *hören* is a regular weak verb. These verbs form their past participle by adding a *ge-* prefix and *-t* to their stem. Therefore, choice (D) is the correct answer.

6.   (D)

The task is to find the correct definite article which is required by the preposition *in*. *In* is a two-way preposition, which means it can either take the accusative or the dative. The verb determines which case a two-way preposition takes. If the verb indicates that the activity expressed takes place within a place, the preposition takes the dative; if it indicates a change of place, it takes the accusative. The verb *gehen* expresses a change of location, and the accusative is required. Choices (B) and (C) both are dative, and therefore incorrect. To determine the gender and the number of the article, you have to look at the gender and the number of the modified noun (*Garten*), which is masculine singular. The masculine, singular, accusative definite article is *den* (choice (D)).

7.   (C)

This question requires you to determine that a present participle is needed to complete this sentence. A present participle is a verb used as an adjective and it expresses an activity that is presently performed by the noun it modifies (i.e., "the burning house"). German forms the present participle by adding -*d* to the infinitive. Choice (B) gives the past participle of *"fahren"* and (D) the infinitive.

Only choices (A) and (C) are forms of the present participles. Since it is used here as a modifying adjective, it must take an ending in addition to the -*d*. Consequently, choice (C) is the correct answer.

8.   (A)

This sentence is an example of the usage of indirect speech. German uses a special subjunctive (Subjunctive I) for indirect speech, for which English no longer has an equivalent. Its forms are derived from the present tense stem of a verb. Furthermore, this sentence is in the present perfect, which requires the past tense special subjunctive. *Machen* takes *haben* as its auxiliary verb in the present perfect, therefore you have to choose the proper special subjunctive form of *haben*. Choice (B) is the general subjunctive (Subjunctive II) of *werden*, and choice (C) the special subjunctive of *sein*. Choice (D) offers the general subjunctive of *haben*. The right answer is choice (A).

9.   (D)
You are asked to find the correct possessive adjective which corresponds with the noun *"Schwester."* The phrase indicates a possession of the phrase *"die Kleider."* Therefore, its case is genitive. *Schwester* is singular and feminine. Possessive adjectives are *"ein*-words" and the proper adjective-ending for a genitive, singular, feminine "*ein*-word" is *-er.* The correct answer is choice (D).

10.   (B)
The verb form *wurde gesagt* indicates that the sentence is in the passsive voice. Translated into English, the sentence means "He was told nothing about the accident." It appears that literally translated into German, choice (A), *er,* would be the correct answer. However, you have to recognize that the subject is based on the dative object of the active voice equivalent of this sentence ("Nothing was told to him about the accident"). Unlike English, in German such a sentence retains the dative object in the dative when transferred into the passive voice. The only personal pronoun offered in the dative is choice (B), the correct answer.

11.   (B)
You have to identify that the completion of this sentence must be an adverb. In German, only adjectives, which modify nouns, take endings. Choice (A) offers a superlative ("the fastest") with a weak ending of the adjective *schnell;* choice (C) the comparative, which is inappropriate in connection with *immer so;* and choice (D) a strong ending. Only choice (B) gives the proper adverb *schnell* without an ending.

12.   (C)
This question asks you to select the correct modifying adjective to correspond to the noun *Armen.* Choice (B) offers the infinitive of the verb *brechen,* and choice (D) the third-person singular present tense. Both forms can never be used as adjectives, and should not be considered. Choice (A) is the present participle ("breaking") used as an adjective, and choice (C) a past participle ("broken"). However, only choice (C) has the correct ending (*-en*) for an unpreceded adjective in the dative plural, and is therefore the right choice.

13.   (A)

You are requested to find the proper verb completion for a sentence, in which the conjugated verb is a modal auxiliary verb (i.e., *müssen, sollen, können*). A sentence can only contain one conjugated verb form (here: *kann*). Therefore, choices (B) and (C) have to be eliminated, since both are conjugated forms. Choice (B) is the present tense, and choice (C) the simple past. In order to determine whether to use choice (A) or choice (D), you have to know that the proper verb complement for a modal is the infinitive without *zu*. The infinitive with *zu* would have to be used if the conjugated verb would be a full verb, and not a modal auxiliary verb.

14.   (D)

You are requested to insert the proper relative pronoun to complete this sentence. If a relative pronoun is the object of a preposition, it has to be in the case which this preposition requires. *Aus* requires the dative. Choice (A) can only be a nominative or an accusative relative pronoun, and is therefore not possible. Choice (B) is an interrogative pronoun, which can never be used as a relative pronoun. Choice (C) is the feminine dative relative pronoun and choice (D) the masculine and neuter relative pronoun. The gender of a relative pronoun is determined by the word it refers back to (here: *Glas*), which is neuter. The correct choice is (D).

15.   (B)

The task is to determine the auxiliary verb that would fit with the infinitive *kommen* and with the subject *Dieter*. Furthermore, the time expression *Morgen* indicates that the whole sentence is in the future tense. The subject *Dieter* is singular, which makes choice (A) incorrect because *werden* is plural. Choice (C) is the simple past form of *werden* and is used only when *werden* is a full verb ("to become") and in the passive voice, which would require the past participle of *kommen* at the end of the sentence (*gekommen*). Choice (D) offers the past participle of *werden,* which cannot be the conjugated part of the verb. The correct answer is choice (B), in which the third-person singular form of *werden* is used as the auxiliary for the future tense.

16.   (C)

You have to identify the correct form of the verb *empfehlen*. In order to do so, you have to be familiar with all forms of this particular verb. *Empfehlen* has, as many verbs do, a vowel change in the present tense. Vowel changes take effect only in the second- and third-person singular. Choice (A) is incorrect, since the vowel is not changed. Furthermore, you have to know that all verbs with a vowel change in the present tense are strong n-verbs, which means that they again change their vowel in the simple past. Therefore, choice (B) is impossible, since it offers the simple past of a weak t-verb. Choice (D) does not correspond with the subject (*der Ober*) and is also wrong. The correct choice is (C).

17.   (A)

This question deals with the proper use of indefinite pronouns (i.e., "no one, someone, everyone"). Indefinite pronouns in German behave like unpreceded adjectives: they take the ending of the definite article, if it was used. The exception is the nominative, in which indefinite pronouns do not take any ending. In order to find the correct answer, you have to determine whether the indefinite pronoun is the subject, the accusative object, or the dative object. Since the sentence only contains a verb (*klatschte*), a prepositional phrase (*in der Loge*), and an adverb (*begeistert*), the missing element must be the subject. Choice (B) offers the dative ending, choice (C) the accusative ending, and choice (D) the genitive ending. The correct answer is choice (A).

18.   (A)

The verb form *"gestohlen worden"* indicates that this sentence is in the passive voice, which means the subject of the sentence is acted upon and not acting itself. The second element *worden* shows that the tense of the sentence is either present perfect or past perfect. Although the verb *stehlen* takes *haben* as its auxiliary verb (choice (D)), the auxiliary verb for passive perfect tenses is always *sein*. Choice (B) is wrong because a form of *werden* is used as the auxiliary verb in the passive voice only in the present, simple past, and future tenses. In a passive sentence, the thing or the person acting is not the subject of the sentence but a prepositional phrase (*"von den Einbrechern"*). The subject of this sentence is *das Geld,* which is singular. Therefore, choice (C) is incorrect and choice (A) is the correct answer.

19.   (D)

This question requires that you know the proper use of the preposition *wegen* and that you know the gender of the noun *Regen*. *Wegen* is one of the few German prepositions which takes the genitive (the other most common ones are *trotz, während,* and *anstatt*). Only choices (B) and (D) are genitive forms of the definite article. Therefore, choices (A) and (C) are incorrect. Choice (B), however, is the feminine form of the definite article, and since *Regen* is masculine, the correct answer is choice (D), *des.*

20.   (D)

In order to find the correct answer to this question, you have to know that the superlative form of an adjective is required to complete this sentence. All choices are forms of the adjective *hoch,* except choice (C), which is the superlative of *hoch* as an adverb. Choice (A) is a comparative form and consequently incorrect. Choice (B) offers a positive form of *hoch* and is also wrong. The correct answer is choice (D).

21.   (C)

You are asked to find the proper preposition to complete this sentence. The tense of the sentence is the present tense. German uses the present tense with a prepositional phrase in the dative to express an activity that began in the past and is continuing in the present (i.e., "He has been living here for two years"). Choice (A) is wrong because the preposition *vor* is used to indicate an event which happened in the past and is not continuing ("20 years ago"). *Nach* (choice (B)) would be used in order to express the equivalent of the English phrase "after 20 years." Choice (D) would be a literal translation of the intended meaning ("for 20 years"). The correct answer is choice (C).

22.   (B)

The question deals with the German verb *gefallen,* which is used in order to express that someone likes something. The thing or the person who is liked is the subject of the sentence and the person who likes that thing or that person is a dative object of *gefallen.* In the example the dative object is missing. There is no noun phrase offered as a possible choice, therefore, the missing element must be a personal pronoun.

Choices (A) and (D), however, are possessive pronouns, which are very similar to personal pronouns, but they have a different function in a sentence. Choice (B) *mir* and choice (C) *mich* are both personal pronouns (first-person singular), but *mich* is the accusative form. The correct choice is (B).

23.   (A)
The task is to find the proper preposition to complement the verb *warten.* The English phrase "to wait for" is translated into German as *warten auf.* Furthermore, German uses a "*da*-compound" if the object of a preposition is a pronoun, and the pronoun replaces a thing or an idea and not a person. Therefore, choices (B) (preposition and personal pronoun), and (D) ("*wo*-compound") are wrong. Choice (C) is incorrect, since it offers the "*da*-compound" of the wrong preposition (*gegen*) for the verb *warten.* The only possible choice is (A).

24.   (B)
You are asked to select the proper conjunction to complete this sentence. The two German conjunctions, *wenn* and *als,* and the interrogative pronoun, *wann,* mean "when" in English. *Als* is used if the sentence is referring to a single event in the past, *wann* for an indirect question of time, and *wenn* covers all other instances. The conjunction *ob* also means "if," but only when it is used in the sense of "whether" (indirect yes/no-question). Since this sentence refers to a single event in the past, and is not an indirect question, the correct Choice is (B).

25.   (C)
You are asked to find the logical completion for the time adverb *immer.* German uses *immer* and a comparative of an adverb for something that becomes stronger and stronger. Choice (A) gives the superlative form of the adverb *lang,* and may not be used. Choice (B) is the positive form of the adverb and, therefore, also improper. Choice (D) (*mehr lang*) is a construction which German does not have, but which English uses for the comparative of adverbs of more than two syllables (i.e., "more beautiful"). The correct choice is (C).

208

26.   (C)

German uses certain adverbs in order to express doubt, anger, surprise or delight. The proper use of these adverbs, or "gesture-words" is very idiomatic, and requires a lot of practice. The sentence here expresses that the speaker is very upset about something and wishes that the event had not occurred. ("My god, that cannot be true.") The only adverb that is idiomatically correct and emphasizes his anger is *doch* (choice (C)).

27.   (A)

You have to find the correct coordinating conjunction to complete the sentence. It has to be a coordinating conjunction, since the verb in the second clause is in second position. Choice (B), *weil,* is a subordinating conjunction, which would require that the verb goes to the end of the clause. Choice (D) means "then" and must not be confused with the coordinating conjunction *denn.* Choices (A) and (C) both mean "but"; however, *sondern* is used only if the first clause is a negative clause, and the second clause implies "but on the contrary." Since both these conditions are fulfilled, choice (A) is correct.

28.   (C)

You have to determine the proper verb form. Choice (B) *verstehe* is incorrect because in German you can understand a sentence or a book but not a country. Choice (D), *mag,* is also improper, since the adverbial construction *sehr gut* ("very well") does not make sense with *mag.* (You can like a country "very much," but not "very well.") The German verbs *wissen* and *kennen* both mean "to know," but *wissen* means "to know a fact," whereas *kennen* means "to be acquainted with." It is possible to be acquainted with a country but not to know a country as a fact. Choice (C) is the correct answer.

29.   (C)

This question examines your mastery of vocabulary. You have to know that "to make a decision" means *eine Entscheidung treffen* (choice (C)). All choices offered have something to do with an act you could perform after a long deliberation (*"Nach langem Nachdenken"*), but only *Entscheidung* can be used with the verb *treffen,* of which *getroffen* is the past participle.

30. (A)

This question tests whether you can use the reflexive verb *sich erkälten* ("to catch a cold") properly. A reflexive verb is a verb that always needs a reflexive pronoun to be complete. In sentences with a reflexive pronoun, the subject and the object of the sentence are identical. The subject of the sentence here is *man*, an impersonal pronoun. Therefore, you have to choose the third-person singular reflexive pronoun *sich*.

31. (A)

This question tests your mastery of vocabulary. In order to answer correctly, you have to know that you cannot translate the English phrase "to be interested in" literally into German (choice (C)). Choices (B) and (D) are also idiomatically improper. The correct choice is (A).

32. (D)

In order to determine the correct answer you have to know what the phrase "above all" means in German. All choices come close to the intended meaning, but only choice (D) can be used with the preposition *vor* and the noun *Dingen*. Choice (A) *jeden* is idiomatically used as *In jedem Fall* ("in any case"), Choice (B) as *Beim ersten Mal* ("at the first time"), and choice (C) as *In keinem Fall* ("under no circumstances").

33. (A)

This question again examines your mastery of vocabulary. You have to know that *Denkmal* means "Monument" and that *errichten* means "to erect." If you know these two words, which are frequently used in combination, you arrive at the correct answer by determining that monuments are usually not "read" (choice (B)), "bought" (choice (C)), or "found" (choice (D)).

34. (B)

All four possible choices have something to do with what could happen if someone wants to buy a new house. In order to come to the correct conclusion, you have to realize that the first clause is in the subjunctive. It indicates that your parents would like to have a new house, but are, for some reason, unable to get one. The only choice which would logically conclude the sentence is choice (B). You have to know that *sich etwas leisten können* means "to be able to afford something."

35. (C)
The meaning of this sentence is that Jürgen, since he is only a little child, is always expected to do something with his mouth. You have to know that the phrase *den Mund halten* means "to shut up" or "to be quiet." If you know that, you arrive at the conclusion that only choice (C) *halten* is a logically meaningful completion, which expresses something that Jürgen is supposed to do <u>because</u> he is a little child.

36. (B)
This question deals with the idiomatic use of the verb *lassen* ("to let"). As in English, this verb is sometimes used as a modal auxiliary verb, which means that it modifies the meaning of the main verb. In this sentence here the main verb is *stehen.* If *lassen* is used in combination with *können,* it expresses that the speaker wants someone else to initiate the activity expressed in the main verb, but not to perform it himself. Choices (A), (C) and (D) offer modal auxiliary verbs, which cannot be used with another modal. The only possible choice is (B).

37. (D)
In order to determine the correct answer, you have to know the meaning of the two German conjunctions *Je...desto. Desto* is used only in combination with *je.* They correspond to the English "The ... the" as in "the more he practices, the more he learns." You can eliminate choices (A) and (B) immediately, because this sentence requires a conjunction and neither *trotz* nor *um zu* are conjunctions. Choice (C) *aber* is a conjunction; however, it does not complete a sentence whose first clause starts with *Je.*

38. (C)
This question requires that you know which idiomatic phrase German uses in order to express that someone's watch or clock is fast. Although all four choices present verbs that have something to do with movement, only choice (C) *vorgeht* is correct in this context.

39. (A)

This question asks you to identify a construction that German very often employs to express a hypothetical situation. Above all, you have to see that this sentence is in the subjunctive mood and that the first clause is a "*Wenn*-clause," which means that the second clause is the main clause of the whole sentence. This conclusion eliminates choices (B), an interrogative pronoun, and (C), a coordinating conjunction. Choice (D) is logically impossible. The correct choice is (A).

40. (C)

The most important thing you have to know to determine the correct answer is the meaning of the conjunction *obwohl* ("although"). In this sentence this conjunction indicates that parents love their children, although they do something parents do not like. Choices (A), (B) and (D) describe something positive and they would only make sense if the conjunctions *weil* ("because"), or *wenn* ("if," "when") were used. The correct and logical answer is choice (C).

41. (C)

In question 41 you are asked to find the logical verb completion for *"ist"* as the auxiliary verb. A form of the verb *sein* is often used as the auxiliary verb for the present perfect tense. The only possible form for the main verb is a past participle. (Past participles usually have a ge-prefix and can easily be recognized, i.e., *gefahren, gekommen.*) Choice (A) offers an infinitive and not a past participle, which would only make sense if the auxiliary verb was *wird* (future tense) or a modal verb (i.e., *sollen, können*). Choice (D) gives the simple past of the verb *fahren.* The only two past participles offered are *geantwortet* (choice (B)), and *geblieben* (choice (C)). However, *antworten* takes *haben* as its auxiliary verb for the present perfect. The correct answer is choice (C).

42. (A)

Question 42 asks you to find the correct accusative object to complement the verb *hatte.* You have to know that *haben* is a verb that requires an accusative object. The adjective ending *"-e"* added to *kein* can only be accusative feminine singular (i.e., *keine Frau*), or

212

accusative plural (i.e., *keine Kinder*). Choice (B), *Hunger,* is masculine, and choice (C), *Bier,* is neuter. Choice (D), *Uhr,* is idiomatically awkward, since this noun refers only to the object telling the time (watch or clock; i.e., *Ich habe eine neue Uhr*) and not to a time span. The correct choice is (A).

43.　(B)

Choice (B) is the best answer for this question. You are asked which preposition would complete this sentence. Many German conjunctions have a basic meaning and a second meaning, when they are used in time expressions. Two of these conjunctions are *während* and *in. Zu* and *auf* are not used in time expressions and can therefore never be used with the noun *Sommer* ("summer"). The preposition *während,* however, would require that *"Sommer"* be preceded by a definite article.

44.　(D)

In order to determine the proper answer for this question you have to connect this sentence with sentence 43. Sentence 43 states that someone goes to the sea every summer. The definite pronoun *das* at the beginning of sentence 44 refers back to the previous clause and it expresses that the fact that someone goes to the sea every summer is nice for the children. The most appropriate completion is choice (D) *besonders.* Choices (A) – (C) are grammatically possible, but would not make much sense.

45.　(B)

This sentence gives the cause for the fact indicated in sentence 44; in other words, it tells you by using the coordinating conjunction *denn* why it is especially nice for the children to go to the sea. The infinitive at the end of the clause tells you that the reason is that the children play at the beach. You are asked to find the proper modal auxiliary verb to complement the infinitive *spielen* ("to play"). If you put the sentence in context with sentences 43 and 44, only choice (B), which indicates that the children <u>can</u> play at the beach, provides a sensible completion.

46.   (C)

You are asked to find the most meaningful and grammatically correct adjective that modifies the noun *Fussballspieler* ("soccer player"). Choices (A) and (D) are both grammatically incorrect and not meaningful in connection with this noun. Choices (B) and (C) are both meaningful options, but since *Fussballspieler* is masculine and its function is a predicate noun, only choice (C) *berühmter* carries the proper strong adjective-ending.

47.   (A)

You are requested to find the proper personal pronoun to complete this sentence. Again, you have to connect this sentence with the previous one. It is clear that the pronoun you have to insert refers back to *"Franz Beckenbauer."* Since he is male, you have to find the masculine accusative singular personal pronoun, which is *ihn*. Consequently, choice (A) is the correct answer.

48.   (C)

This sentence contains two personal pronouns which refer back to sentences 46 and 47. *Sie* refers back to *"viele Leute"* in sentence 47 and *ihn* to *"Franz Beckenbauer"* in sentence 46. Sentence 46 says that Beckenbauer was a famous soccer player and sentence 47 expresses that people still talk about him. If you consider this information, only choice (C) *vergessen* ("to forget") is a logical completion for this sentence.

49.   (A)

The most important thing you have to know in order to answer this question is that the phrase *einen Entschluss fassen* means "to make a decision." Furthermore, you have to recognize that the sentence is in the present perfect, and therefore the missing element is a past participle. All choices have something to do with what a person can do with his senses, but only choice (A) is used with the direct object, *Entschluss*.

50. (C)

You have to realize that the phrase following the main clause is not a complete clause, since there is no element which could be the subject of this clause. Therefore, the missing element must be an infinitive with *zu,* on which the prepositional phrase *mit dem Rauchen* is depending. For that reason choices (A) and (B) can be eliminated, since choice (A) offers an infinitive without *zu* and choice (B) offers a past participle. In order to decide between choices (C) and (D) you have to know that the verb *aufhören* is a separable prefix verb and that this group of verbs inserts *zu* between the prefix and the main verb in an infinitive construction. The correct choice is (C).

51. (B)

You have to know that the verb *leicht fallen* means that something is easy for someone, and that the person for whom it is easy is in the dative. Since choice (A) offers the accusative first-person singular personal pronoun, choice (C) the nominative first-person singular personal pronoun, and choice (D) a possessive adjective which requires a noun to complement it, the correct choice is (B).

52. (D)

Above all, you have to know that the verb *lesen* takes *haben* as its auxiliary verb in the present perfect. Choice (C) is incorrect because *werden* is the auxiliary for the future tense, the adverb *gestern* refers to the past, and because *lesen* would be in the infinitive and not in the past participle. Since the auxiliary has to be in agreement with the subject of the clause (*ich*), choice (D) is the correct answer.

53. (C)

All four choices offer forms of the word *romantisch.* However, if an adjective follows a form of the verb *sein,* and if it is not modifying a noun, it is used as a predicate adjective. Predicate adjectives do not take endings in German, and consequently choice (C) is the correct answer to this question.

54.   (C)

The clause does not have a verb which immediately eliminates choice (A), because the coordinating conjunction *denn* can only be used in complete clauses. Choice (B) *sondern* is wrong since it means "but, on the contrary," and is only used if the preceding clause is a negative statement. In order to determine between choices (C) and (D) you have to know that the adverb *jedenfalls* means "at any rate," which would not make sense. The correct answer is choice (C).

55.   (C)

First of all, you have to know that the reflexive verb *sich freuen* always takes *auf* plus accusative (choice (C)) as its prepositional complement. Choice (A) is a literal translation of the English equivalent "to look forward to" and would be inappropriate in German. The preposition *nach* (choice (B)) is only used in time expression to indicate a specific time of day (i.e., *viertel nach eins*).

56.   (B)

The verb *versammeln* means in this context "to gather" and in German it is always used reflexively, when it has this particular meaning. Therefore, the missing element in this clause is the proper reflexive pronoun. You have to know that a reflexive pronoun is used when the subject and the object of a sentence are identical. Here, the subject is *die ganze Familie,* which is feminine singular. The correct third-person feminine singular reflexive pronoun is *"sich"* (choice (B)).

57.   (D)

In order to arrive at the correct answer, you must realize that the whole clause (Questions 55–57) is in the present tense, since the adverb *immer* in clause 55 indicates that everything which is said is referring to a recurring event. Therefore, you have to choose the proper present tense form of the modal verb *können,* which is choice (D).

58.   (C)

This question deals with different adverbs indicating quantities. To arrive at the correct answer you have to know that *mehr ... als* means "more... than". Choice (A) (*am meisten*) is the superlative adverb "the most"; choice (B) (*viel*) means in this context "a lot"; choice (D) (*meistens*) is a time expression meaning "mostly." The correct answer is choice (C) (*mehr*), which is the comparative of *viel* and the only one of the offered choices which can idiomatically be used with *als*.

59. (B)

This question asks you to find the correct adjective ending for *viel* when it modifies the noun *Überstunden*. First of all, you have to realize that *Überstunden* is in the plural. *Viel* only takes on endings when it modifies a noun in the plural, and it is unpreceded when it modifies a noun in the singular (choice (A)). In order to determine which of the three remaining choices offers the correct ending, you have to realize that *Überstunden* is the direct object of the sentence. Therefore, you have to choose the accusative plural ending, which is -*e*. The correct answer is choice (B).

60. (D)

You have to insert the proper relative pronoun to complete this sentence. Usually, the number and the gender of a German relative pronoun are determined by its antecedent, and its case is determined by its function in the relative clause. The only exceptions to this rule are if the antecedent is unknown, or if the whole main clause is the antecedent. The latter is the case in this sentence. The relative clause does not refer back to *Überstunden,* but to the whole clause. Therefore, the relative pronoun *was* (choice (D)) has to be used. The relative pronouns *das* and *die* (choices (A) and (C)) are used only when the antecedent is known and *wie* (choice (B)) can never be used as a relative pronoun.

61. (B)

Question 61 asks you to identify the attitude of the author towards his text. In order to come to the correct conclusion, you have to understand that the author tries to summarize Bismarck's achievements (choice (B)). He does not give his own evaluation of these achievements, nor does he assess Bismarck's politics. You must recognize that the author only wants to give a brief overview of Bismarck's domestic and foreign policies, without mentioning whether one or the other was more important to him (choice (A)) without passing a value judgement on Bismarck's ideas (choice (C)); and without making an assumption about his overall significance for German history (choice (D)). He merely quotes other people who have said that Bismarck was "one of the most important figures in German history."

62.   (D)
Question 62 wants you to deduce one of Bismarck's characteristics. In order to come to the logical conclusion you have to collect carefully the information provided in the text. Choice (A) should immediately be dismissed, since the text states that Bismarck saw Socialism as a danger, and for that reason it is safe to say that he definitely was not a Socialist and did not want a revolution (choice (C)). Choice (B) is wrong, because the past participle *entschieden* means "decided" and the text does not mention the outcome of the *Kulturkampf* but only that it was a severe problem for Bismarck. The correct answer is (D), because the text does say that Bismarck saw parliaments as something "evil," and it is correct to deduce that he did not like them.

63.   (B)
This question tests your comprehension of a specific sentence of the text. In order to answer correctly (choice (B)), you have to understand that the first sentence of the last paragraph says that Bismarck's major accomplishment in foreign politics was that he established Germany beside France, England, and Russia as a superpower in Europe. The only choice which expresses the equivalent to this statement is choice (B). The terms used for the other choices are mentioned in the text but not in connection with Bismarck's foreign policies.

64.   (C)
Question 64 asks you to evaluate the relationship of Thomas and Heinrich Mann based on the information provided in the text. It is obvious that they did not love each other very much (choice (B)) and the text does not mention that they ever wrote anything together (choice

(D)). Choice (A) claims that the brothers always argued. The text, however, states that their relationship was a problematic one, but that they had a reconciliation after their return from the United States after the end of World War II. If you consider all the information, only choice (C) is fully supported by the text.

65.　　(C)

This question tests whether you have understood a certain paragraph of the text. You have to comprehend what the brothers did between 1933 and 1945. The text says that Thomas and Heinrich had to emigrate to the United States due to Hitler's rise to power. Since German uses the terms "USA" and "Amerika" often synonymously, choice (C) is the correct answer. The other countries (France, the DDR, Switzerland) are mentioned somewhere in the text, but not in the context of the time period between 1933 and 1945.

66.　　(C)

Question 66 asks you to make a general assumption about Heinrich Mann's life. Choice (A) claims that it was typical for a *Zivilisationsliterat,* which cannot be derived from the text, because all that is said about a *Zivilisationsliterat* is that Thomas used this term to describe his brother. Choice (B) offers a comparison between the fact that Heinrich was at one time a presidential candidate and the lives of presidential candidates in general. This assertion is not supported by the text, either. The contention of choice (D) that Heinrich's life was characterized by the fall of the German Empire in 1918 can also not be verified with the text, since it only mentions Thomas' reluctance to embrace the Republic after the fall of the Empire. Choice (C), which says that Thomas' and Heinrich's lives were very closely connected, is the only logical answer.

67.　　(B)

This question attempts to compare the political convictions of Thomas and Heinrich Mann. Throughout the text it becomes clear that the friction between the brothers was partially caused by different political views. Therefore, they cannot have been either similar (*ähnlich,* choice

(A)) or identical (*gleich,* choice (C)). Choice (D) (*reaktionär,* "reactionary") also finds no support in the text, since only Thomas' political views were at a certain point in his life reactionary. The correct choice is (B), which says that their views were different (*unterschiedlich*).

68.   (A)
In this question you have to make an inference based on statements made in the text. The correct answer is (A). Nowhere in the text is it directly said that TV sets cause fires, but it is obvious from the context that some fires are caused by TV sets. For any of the statements made in choices (B) – (D), no proof can be found in the text.

69.   (A)
In order to answer this question correctly you have to understand how the judge substantiates his decision in this case. He reasons that TV sets today are of such a high quality technologically that they do not need to be monitored all the time. Therefore, choice (A) is the correct answer. Choice (B) runs counter to all the facts given in the article; the statement of choice (C) is ridiculous; and choice (D) is not logical.

70.   (B)
To answer this question you have to comprehend what statement the judge makes when he refers to the quality of TV shows. He says that it is not surprising that due to the quality of TV shows people fall asleep, and in this context it is clear that he means due to their bad quality. The correct choice is (B), which infers that TV shows are boring (*langweilig*) and consequently people fall asleep.

71.   (B)
This question asks you to assess what the tenants' association does. It neither states that the owner of the TV set is responsible for the fire (choice (A)), nor does it claim that nobody is allowed to fall asleep in front of his TV set (choice (C)), nor does it criticize the judge's decision (choice (D)). The tenants' association only objectively reports what has happened in this particular case (choice (B)).

72. (B)

Question 72 tests your comprehension of what the landlord's intentions were for suing his tenant. Choice (B) is the correct answer. In order to come to that conclusion you have to know that *seine Verluste erstattet bekommen* means "to get reimbursed for one's losses," which is precisely what the landlord wants to accomplish. He does not necessarily want a new insurance policy (choice (A)), although he might consider it, nor is he suing the tenants' association's newspaper (choice (D)), nor does he want a new TV set (choice (C)).

73. (D)

You have to understand the findings of the study conducted by the doctors at the hospital in Münster. The text says the results suggested the possibility that before the year 2000 more women than men will die of heart attacks, lung cancer, and carcinomas. The doctors support their claim by citing the increasing numbers of women dying of these illnesses (stated in choice (D)). It is essential to know that the German verb *zunehmen* means "to increase." Choice (A) is incorrect because the text does not suggest that "men-diseases" should from now on be called "women-diseases." Choice (B) is wrong, since the absolute number of men dying of heart attacks today still outnumbers that of women. Choice (C) should not be considered because the adverb *kaum* means "hardly" and the text does not say that in the year 2000 women will hardly die of heart attacks.

74. (B)

In order to make the right choice you have to fully comprehend the meaning of the direct quote in the second paragraph. You have to know that *aufholen* means "to catch up" and that *immer mehr* means "more and more." Consequently, Dr. Dittrich says that women are catching up in every respect, and that more and more young women are coming to the hospital with typical "male" diseases. The only choice which partially concurs with this statement is (B).

75. (B)

You are asked to identify one possible reason for the development that women suffer more and more heart attacks. Since the doctors who conducted the study are uncertain about it, some psychologists contend that one of the reasons is that women, as a result of emancipation, want to lead a "male" life and that as a consequence women also acquire "male" diseases. The correct choice is (B). Choice (A) offers one of the effects (and not one of the causes) of the development under consideration, namely that life expectancy of women will decrease, and choices (C) and (D) would misrepresent the statements made in the text.

76.   (A)

In order to arrive at the correct solution to this question, you have to realize that it becomes evident throughout the text that the doctors are more than anything baffled by the fact that the number of women dying of "male" diseases is increasing, and that they have no positive explanation to offer. Therefore, choice (A) *bemerkenswert* ("astonishing") is the correct answer.

77.   (C)

Question 77 wants you to make the proper conclusion why the incidents described in the text are newsworthy. Choice (A) says that it is common practice for a considerable amount of time to duplicate counterfeit money with a color copier, a statement which is not made in the text. Choices (B) and (D), namely that it is impossible to reproduce bogus money with a color copier (B) and that it is now legal in the state of Hessen to copy money with that particular device (D), would certainly be newsworthy if they were true, but they are not supported by the text. The correct answer is choice (C).

78.   (A)

The task of this question is to determine which role the license plate of the car plays in the story. The correct answer is (A). You have to understand that the cashier of the store where the woman tried to buy stockings did not initially suspect that anything was wrong with the bill. After a while she became suspicious, ran out of the store and was able to write down the license plate number. Choices (B) – (D) all refer to the counterfeit money and not to the plate.

79.   (B)

This question also deals with the second paragraph in which the events that took place in the store are described. You are asked to evaluate what the cashier did. Obviously she did not fabricate the counterfeit money (choice (A)), but helped to catch a criminal. She neither immediately (*sofort*) realized that something was wrong with the bill (choice (C)), nor personally led the police to the apartment of the woman's friend (choice (D)). The correct answer is (B), which says that she alertly (*geistesgegenwärtig*) did the right thing after she became suspicious.

80.   (D)

In order to answer this question correctly you have to understand the last paragraph. This paragraph puts the whole story into a broader context by stating that the police as of now do not know whether the couple alone had the idea to copy the money with the help of a color copier, or whether other criminals use the same method. Since the police have already determined who the woman is (choice (A)), how the money was fabricated (choice (B)), and whether the 500-Mark bill was genuine or not (choice (C)), the correct answer is choice (D).

SAT II:
SUBJECT TEST IN
GERMAN

PRACTICE
TEST VI

GERMAN PRACTICE TEST VI

PART A

Time: 1 Hour
80 Questions

DIRECTIONS: Each of the sentences in this part has a blank space indicating that a word or phrase has been omitted. From the four choices select the ONE that when inserted in the sentence fits grammatically and logically with the sentence as a whole. Then blacken the corresponding space on the answer sheet.

1.   Ich bin ihm zufällig auf der Straße _____ .

    (A) begegnet
    (B) getroffen
    (C) kennengelernt
    (D) entgegengegangen

2.   Das Land hat Schulden in Höhe von DM 1.000.000.000, also eine _____ Mark.

    (A) Million
    (B) Milliarde
    (C) Billion
    (D) Trillion

3.   Der Satz "Das hätte ich machen können" besteht aus fünf _____ .

    (A) Worten
    (B) Wörten
    (C) Wortern
    (D) Wörtern

4.   Die Stadt Konstanz in Süddeutschland liegt _____ .

       (A) an der Bodensee
       (B) am Bodensee
       (C) auf der Bodensee
       (D) an den Bodensee

5.   In diesem Semester habe ich an der Universität fünf _____
       belegt.

       (A) Klassen
       (B) Stunden
       (C) Kurse
       (D) Stände

6.   Gestern abend haben wir drei Stunden lang Deutsch _____ .

       (A) studiert
       (B) gelernt
       (C) gestudiert
       (D) studieren

7.   Meine Schwester weiß es schon lange, aber ich habe es
       _____ heute gehört.

       (A) nur
       (B) allein
       (C) erst
       (D) einzig

8.   Jeden Abend sendet das erste Programm _____ .

       (A) die Neuen
       (B) die Neuigkeiten
       (C) die Nachrichten
       (D) das Neue

9. Was halten Sie vom neuen Präsidenten? Ich _____ .

   (A) halte ihn intelligent
   (B) halte von ihm intelligent
   (C) halte ihm für intelligent
   (D) halte ihn für intelligent

10. Wir _____ uns ein neues Haus bauen.

    (A) lassen
    (B) machen
    (C) haben
    (D) gehen

11. Sie sagte, sie würde das machen, und _____ .

    (A) es ist ihr gelungen
    (B) sie hat gelungen
    (C) sie ist gelungen
    (D) es hat ihr gelungen

12. Das ist mein Privatzimmer. Du _____ nicht in das Zimmer hineingehen!

    (A) musst
    (B) darfst
    (C) magst
    (D) kannst

13. "Guten Abend, Herr Generaldirektor. Dürfte ich Ihnen meine Frau _____ ?" "Ich freue mich, Ihre Bekanntschaft zu machen, gnädige Frau."

    (A) einführen
    (B) einleiten
    (C) vorstellen
    (D) einbringen

14. Ich _____ nicht, wie die Frau heißt.

    (A) kenne
    (B) kann
    (C) weiß
    (D) wisse

15. Er hat seine Frau und seine Kinder _____ und ist nach
    Australien gegangen.

    (A) abgefahren
    (B) liegenlassen
    (C) hinterlassen
    (D) verlassen

16. Ich _____ , es wird bald regnen.

    (A) denke daran
    (B) halte
    (C) glaube
    (D) danke

17. Das ist ein interessantes Ehepaar; die Frau ist Amerikanerin
    und der _____ ist Japaner.

    (A) man
    (B) Mann
    (C) Mensch
    (D) Man

18. Mein Vater trinkt gern Bier, aber noch _____ trinkt er Wein.

    (A) lieber
    (B) gerner
    (C) vielmehr
    (D) sondern

19. "Dürfte ich Herrn Schmidt sprechen, bitte?" "Hier gibt es keinen Schmidt. Welche _____ haben Sie gewählt?"

   (A) Zahl
   (B) Anzahl
   (C) Ziffer
   (D) Nummer

20. Herr Ober, ich habe vor einer halben Stunde eine Bratwurst _____ . Wie lange muss ich noch warten?

   (A) bestellt
   (B) befohlen
   (C) geordnet
   (D) verlangt

PART B

DIRECTIONS: Each of the sentences in this part has a blank space indicating that a word or phrase has been omitted. From the four choices select the ONE that when inserted in the sentence fits grammatically and logically with the sentence as a whole. Then blacken the corresponding space on the answer sheet.

21. Ich gehe heute in die Stadt, _____ .

   (A) weil ich einkaufen muss
   (B) denn ich einkaufen muss
   (C) weil ich muss einkaufen
   (D) damit ich einkaufen muss

22. _____ , und fühle mich jetzt hier zu Hause.

   (A) Ich habe seit drei Jahren in Berlin gewohnt
   (B) Ich habe für drei Jahre in Berlin gewohnt
   (C) Ich wohne für drei Jahre in Berlin
   (D) Ich wohne seit drei Jahren in Berlin

23. Ich habe _____ geschenkt.

   (A) eine Uhr dem Mann
   (B) dem Mann eine Uhr
   (C) die Uhr ihm
   (D) dem Mann sie

24. Unser Lehrer _____ .

   (A) will uns fleißig zu arbeiten
   (B) will uns fleißig arbeiten
   (C) will, dass wir fleißig arbeiten
   (D) will, dass wir arbeiten fleißig

25. Weil ich kein Geld hatte, habe ich _____ .

   (A) arbeiten gemusst
   (B) gearbeitet müssen
   (C) arbeiten müssen
   (D) müssen arbeiten

26. Das Buch _____ auf dem Tisch.

   (A) legte
   (B) liegte
   (C) lag
   (D) lagte

27. Maria, _____ den Schulaufsatz schon geschrieben?

   (A) haben Sie
   (B) habt ihr
   (C) hast du
   (D) habst du

28.   _____ ins Kino.

(A) Nach dem Essen wir gehen
(B) Nach dem Essen gehen wir
(C) Wir nach dem Essen gehen
(D) Gehen nach dem Essen wir

29.   Wenn es morgen _____ , arbeiten wir nicht.

(A) regnen würde
(B) regnete
(C) regnet
(D) geregnet hätte

30.   Wenn ich mehr Geld _____ , hätte ich einen Urlaub machen
       können.

(A) verdient hätte
(B) verdient habe
(C) verdiene
(D) verdienen würde

31.   Meine Schwester sagte, sie _____ keinen Kuchen mehr, aber
       ich glaube ihr nicht.

(A) hatte
(B) habe
(C) hat
(D) wäre

32.   Die Kinder sind immer _____ zur Schule gegangen.

(A) während der Tag
(B) während des Tages
(C) während dem Tag
(D) während den Tag

33. Ich warte _____ .

(A) auf dich zu kommen
(B) für dich zu kommen
(C) darauf, dass du kommst
(D) auf dass du kommst

34. Sie ist gestern nach Hause gefahren, _____ .

(A) ohne besuchend mich
(B) ohne mich besuchen
(C) ohne mich zu besuchen
(D) ohne sie mich besucht hat

35. Ich arbeite, um mir ein Auto zu kaufen, aber mein Vater hat gearbeitet, _____ .

(A) damit seine Kinder studieren könnten
(B) um seine Kinder zu studieren
(C) um seine Kinder studieren könnten
(D) damit seine Kinder zu studieren

36. Es gibt hier _____ , die das verstehen können.

(A) keinen Studenten
(B) keine Studenten
(C) kein Student
(D) kein Studenten

37. Er hat die Polizei angerufen, und sie _____ sofort gekommen.

(A) ist
(B) sind
(C) hat
(D) haben

38.   Meine Freunde _____ klassische Musik.

        (A) sind interessiert in
        (B) interessieren sich in
        (C) interessieren sich für
        (D) interessieren sich an

39.   Haben Sie den neuen Tenor _____ ?

        (A) hören singen
        (B) singen gehört
        (C) gesungen hören
        (D) singen hören

40.   _____ älter ich werde, _____ langsamer ich arbeite.

        (A) Das mehr ... das mehr
        (B) So ... so
        (C) Je ... desto
        (D) Desto ... je

PART C

DIRECTIONS: The sentences below contain blank spaces indicating omissions in the text. Below each blank are four choices. Select the choice that is grammatically correct in the context and blacken the corresponding space on the answer sheet. Be sure to read the sentences first.

41.   _(41)_ ich meine Großmutter besuchte, gab sie mir immer Kuchen.

        (A) Als
        (B) Wenn
        (C) Wann
        (D) Wahrend

233

Questions 42–44 are connected.

Gibt es __(42)__ Wein mehr? __(43)__ , er steht __(44)__ Tisch.

42. (A) kein   43. (A) Ja
     (B) keinen   (B) Nein
     (C) nicht   (C) Doch
     (D) keiner   (D) Nicht

44. (A) am
     (B) an der
     (C) auf dem
     (D) auf den

Questions 45–46 are connected.

Ihr Wagen ist alt, aber __(45)__ ist neu. Er __(46)__ mir letzte Woche
von meinem Vater geschenkt.

45. (A) mein   46. (A) war
     (B) meiner   (B) wird
     (C) meins   (C) wurde
     (D) meinen   (D) hat

Questions 47–48 form one sentence.

Ich weiß, __(47)__ er jetzt wohnt, aber ich weiß nicht, __(48)__ seine
Familie auch dort wohnt.

47. (A) wohin   48. (A) wenn
     (B) woher   (B) ob
     (C) wo   (C) weder
     (D) wer   (D) Wetter

Questions 49–50 form one sentence.

Der __(49)__ Mann hat der __(50)__ Frau geholfen.

234

49.   (A) alter   50.   (A) junger
       (B) alte   (B) junge
       (C) alten   (C) jungen
       (D) älter   (D) jünger

51.   _(51)_ , der das Kind gerettet hatte, wurde von den Eltern herzlich gedankt.

(A) Dem Studenten
(B) Dem Student
(C) Der Student
(D) Den Studenten

52.   Mein Freund hat mir eine schöne Blume gegeben, _(52)_ mir sehr gefiel.

(A) der
(B) das
(C) was
(D) dass

53.   Seine Familie wohnt in einem schönen Haus _(53)_ Schillerstraße.

(A) auf
(B) an der
(C) in
(D) in der

54.   Ich habe _(54)_ die Frage nicht geantwortet.

(A) - - - (no preposition necessary)
(B) auf
(C) zu
(D) an

Ich habe (55) gewaschen.

55. (A) meine Hände
     (B) mich die Hände
     (C) mir den Händen
     (D) mir die Hände

Answer choices for nos. 56–57 must be selected as pairs, i.e, (A)–(A), (B)–(B), …, etc.

Beethoven wurde (56)   (57) geboren.

56. (A) 1770   57. (A) in Bonn
     (B) in 1770   (B) in Bonn
     (C) in Bonn   (C) im Jahre 1770
     (D) in Bonn   (D) 1770

Ich habe ihn (58) noch einmal gesehen, aber er kannte mich nicht.

58. (A) einen Abend
     (B) einem Abend
     (C) eines Abends
     (D) ein Abend

Das Wetter war schlecht, (59) haben wir gearbeitet.

59. (A) aber
     (B) aber trotzdem
     (C) obwohl
     (D) aber trotzdem gestern

Sie drehte (60) um und schaute mich an.

60. (A) – – –
     (B) ihr
     (C) sich
     (D) langsam

PART D

DIRECTIONS: Read the following passages carefully for comprehension. Each passage is followed by a number of incomplete statements or questions. Select the completion or answer that is best according to the passage and blacken the corresponding space on the answer sheet.

Um 1300 hatten damalige Großstädte wie Wien, Hamburg, Nürnberg und Danzig über 20.000 Einwohner und Köln hatte sogar nahezu 30.000. Venedig, Rom, und Paris waren noch größer. In den deutschen Städten erlebte der Kaufmannsstand im 14. Jahrhundert einen großen Aufstieg. Die Einwohner der Städte, die "Bürger," wurden immer reicher und traten deswegen mit dem Adel in Wettstreit, weil sie sich nicht nur wirtschaftlich, sondern auch politisch durchsetzen wollten. Manche Städte wurden von der Macht der Grafen und Herzöge befreit und durften sich selbst verwalten. Sie konnten sich direkt dem König unterstellen und hießen daher "freie Städte." Hamburg und Bremen, die auch Mitglieder der Hansa waren, nennen sich noch heute stolz "freie Hansestädte."

61.   In Deutschland gab es vor 1300 _____ .

   (A) keine großen Städte
   (B) mehrere große Städte
   (C) nur im Süden Großstädte
   (D) Städte mit mehr als 50.000 Einwohnern

62.   Die deutschen Städte im Spätmittelalter _____ .

   (A) waren wirtschaftlich schwach
   (B) hatten kein Interesse an Politik
   (C) wollten vom Adel abhängig sein
   (D) wurden wirtschaftlich immer stärker

63.   Einige Städte hießen "freie Städte," weil sie _____ .

   (A) Mitglieder der Hansa waren
   (B) von Grafen und Herzögen regiert wurden
   (C) nur dem König unterstellt waren
   (D) kein Geld zahlen mussten

237

Vor dem zweiten Weltkrieg hatten fast alle Deutschen zwei Muttersprachen: das erst in der Schule erlernte Hochdeutsch und den zu Hause gesprochenen Dialekt. Manche Kinder glaubten sogar, eine Geheimsprache mit den Eltern zu haben, weil andere Hochdeutsch sprachen. Da die Bevölkerung ziemlich seßhaft war, blieben die Dialekte verhältnismäßig rein. Nach 1945 kam es aber in Deutschland zu große Wanderungen. Viele Leute mussten ihre Heimat verlassen und in neue Gebiete übersiedeln. Diese Leute behielten ihre Dialekte aber sie fanden häufig Ehepartner, die einen anderen Dialekt sprachen. Weil sie dann zu Hause keinen Dialekt sprechen konnten, wuchsen ihre Kinder ohne Dialekt auf. Deswegen gibt es heute in Deutschland viele Menschen, die keinen Dialekt sprechen können.

64. Vor dem zweiten Weltkrieg haben deutsche Kinder ihren Dialekt _____ .

(A) zu Hause gesprochen
(B) nur in der Schule gesprochen
(C) in der Schule gelernt
(D) nicht mit den Eltern gesprochen

65. Viele Ehepaare haben nach 1945 zu Hause keinen Dialekt gesprochen, weil _____ .

(A) sie keinen Dialekt konnten
(B) sie eine Geheimsprache haben wollten
(C) sie keinen Dialekt gemeinsam hatten
(D) sie ihre Heimat vergessen wollten

66. Viele Deutsche sprechen heute keinen Dialekt, weil _____ .

(A) ihre Eltern früh gestorben sind
(B) ihre Eltern zu Hause keinen Dialekt gesprochen haben
(C) sie in der Schule Hochdeutsch gelernt haben
(D) sie als Kinder häufig übersiedelt sind

In seinem Roman *Die Blechtrommel* erzählt Günter Grass die Geschichte von Oskar Matzerath, der vom Moment seiner Geburt an alles versteht, was um ihn vorgeht, und an seinem dritten Geburtstag beschließt, nicht weiter zu wachsen. Weil er dann nachher immer so aussieht, als wäre er erst drei Jahre alt, kann er ohne Bestrafung manches machen, was einem größeren Kind oder einem Erwachsenen nicht erlaubt wäre. Oskar hat zwei große Gaben: er kann mit seiner Stimme nicht nur Glas zerbrechen, sondern es auch kunstvoll schneiden; und er kann durch sein Trommeln die Gedanken und Gemüter der Menschen beeinflussen. In dieser grotesken Figur will Grass den Deutschen ihre eigenen Schwächen und Probleme vor Augen führen.

67. Oskar Matzerath ist _____ .

(A) ein normales Kind
(B) ein sehr ungewöhnliches Kind
(C) der Verfasser des Romans *Die Blechtrommel*
(D) ein ungewöhnlich großes Kind

68. Wenn Oskar etwas Unanständiges macht, wird er wegen seiner Größe _____ .

(A) immer erwischt und bestraft
(B) von einem größerem Kind begleitet
(C) nie gesehen
(D) selten bestraft

69. Oskar Matzerath kann _____ .

(A) mit den richtigen Werkzeugen kunstvoll Glas schneiden
(B) durch Trommeln Glas zerbrechen
(C) Menschen durch Trommeln verführen
(D) Menschen durch seine Stimme stören

70. Der Romanschriftsteller Günter Grass glaubt, _____ .

(A) die Deutschen haben weder Schwächen noch Probleme
(B) die Literatur kann die Schwächen und Probleme eines Volkes verdeutlichen
(C) die Deutschen sollten Oskar nachahmen

(D) es wäre gut, wenn alle Deutschen Kinder bleiben würden

Es ist fast dunkel und das Auto rast schnell durch die Stadt. Ein Polizist, der sieht, wie gefährlich das sein könnte, hält es an. Er fragt den Fahrer: "Brennt es vielleicht irgendwo?" Der Fahrer sagt ganz höflich, "Nein." Weil er sieht, dass jemand neben dem Fahrer sitzt, fragt der Polizist weiter: "Fahren Sie so schnell, weil Sie Ihren Freund ins Krankenhaus bringen?" Noch einmal sagt der Fahrer "Nein," aber es ist klar, dass er ungeduldig wird. Da sagt der Polizist, "Wenn Sie keinen guten Grund dafür haben, sollten Sie eigentlich nicht so schnell durch die Stadt fahren, mein Herr." Darauf sagt der Fahrer: "Sehen Sie, Herr Wachtmeister, es wird jetzt dunkel. Ich will nach Hause kommen, bevor es ganz dunkel ist, weil meine Scheinwerfer kaputt sind. Und ich will nicht ohne Scheinwerfer fahren, weil meine Bremsen nicht funktionieren. Deswegen muss ich so schnell fahren. Gestatten Sie bitte, dass ich jetzt losfahre."

71.   Der Polizist hält das Auto an, weil er glaubt, _____ .

(A) der Fahrer ist wahrscheinlich betrunken
(B) es ist gefährlich, so durch die Stadt zu rasen
(C) es muss irgendwo brennen
(D) es wird bald dunkel sein

72.   Der Fahrer antwortet dem Polizisten höflich, aber er ist ungeduldig, weil _____ .

(A) der Polizist ihn beschimpft
(B) er weiß, warum er bald zu Hause sein muss
(C) er seinen Freund schnell ins Krankenhaus bringen will
(D) er dem Polizisten nicht erklären will, warum er so schnell fährt

73.   Das Erstaunliche bei dieser Geschichte ist, dass _____ .

(A) der Fahrer nicht zu verstehen scheint, warum er nicht so schnell fahren sollte
(B) der Polizist den Fahrer nicht beschimpft

(C) der Fahrer so schnell fährt

(D) der Passagier nichts zu sagen hat

Erst mit der Veröffentlichung von Lavoisiers *Elemente der Chemie* im Jahre 1789 befreite sich die Chemie endgültig von der Herrschaft der Alchimie und wurde eine Naturwissenschaft im modernen Sinn, obwohl der Anfang der Chemie viel weiter zurückliegt. Für die Alchimisten waren die Naturwissenschaften Teile der Philosophie gewesen, aber Lavoisier befürwortete die Anwendung von quantitativen Methoden bei naturwissenschaftlichen Untersuchungen und führte dabei das Prinzip der Stofferhaltung ein. Er stellte fest, dass bei einer chemischen Reaktion nichts verloren geht oder gewonnen wird, da das Gesamtgewicht der Produkte dem Gesamtgewicht der an der Reaktion beteiligten Stoffe gleicht. Er erkannte auch das Wesen der Elemente: dass sie Stoffe sind, die sich durch chemische Mittel nicht abbauen lassen. Er kannte nur 23 Elemente, aber er glaubte, durch weitere Untersuchungen würden sich bestimmt andere finden.

74.   Lavoisier war _____ .

(A) ein berühmter Alchimist

(B) ein Mitbegründer der Chemie als Naturwissenschaft

(C) der erste, der die Ideen der Chemie vertreten hat

(D) Verlenger des Romans *Elemente der Chemie*

75.   Lavoisier glaubte, der Naturwissenschaftler sollte _____ .

(A) bei einer Untersuchung alles sorgfältig messen

(B) die philosophische Bedeutung seiner Wissenschaft untersuchen

(C) die Methoden der Alchimisten anwenden

(D) Stoffe in gewissen Quantitäten untersuchen

76.   Unter "Prinzip der Stofferhaltung" versteht man: _____ .

(A) alle Stoffe, die in wissenschaftlichen Untersuchungen verwendet werden, sollten vorher sorgfältig erhalten werden

241

(B) bei einer chemischen Reaktion ändert sich gar nichts

(C) bei einer chemischen Reaktion wird das Gesamtgewicht der beteiligten Stoffe weder größer noch kleiner

(D) mit Hilfe der Chemie kann man Stoffe länger erhalten

77. Lavoisier kannte nur 23 Elemente, weil _____ .

(A) es nur 23 Elemente gibt

(B) es damals nur 23 Elemente gab

(C) er nicht daran interessiert war, neue Elemente zu finden

(D) die Wissenschaft seiner Zeit nur 23 Elemente identifizieren konnte

Obwohl der zweite Weltkrieg eine große Katastrophe für die ganze Welt war, ging es der amerikanischen Volkswirtschaft während des Krieges glänzend. Es gab keine Arbeitslosigkeit und alles, was die Fabriken und Werkstätten herstellen konnten, wurde sofort gekauft. Als dann der Krieg zu Ende war, stand die amerikanische Regierung vor zwei großen Problemen: die ausländischen Märkte, auf denen vor dem Krieg amerikanische Waren verkauft worden waren, existierten nicht mehr und Millionen von Soldaten würden bald nach Hause kommen und Arbeitsplätze verlangen. Da die Vereinigten Staaten jetzt keine Waffen mehr produzieren mussten und fast nichts im Ausland verkaufen konnten, würde es sehr schwer sein, Arbeit für alle zu finden. Wie sollte man neue Märkte schaffen und gleichzeitig die Suche nach Arbeitsplätzen so lange verschieben, bis es solche Arbeitsplätze geben würde? Die Lösung bestand aus zwei Teilen: dem Marshall-Plan, durch den die im Krieg zerstörten ausländischen Wirtschaften wiederhergestellt wurden, und dem sogenannten "G.I. Bill," durch das viele der ehemaligen Soldaten, die sonst vergeblich Arbeit hätten suchen müssen, an die Universitäten gelockt wurden.

78. Die Vereinigten Staaten konnten nach dem Krieg nur wenig exportieren, weil _____ .

(A) die Soldaten bald nach Hause kommen würden

(B) die Länder Europas und Asiens fast nichts kaufen konnten

(C) die amerikanischen Arbeiter nur Waffen produzieren konnten

(D) es nicht genug Arbeiter gab

79. Diesem Text nach war der Hauptzweck des Marshall-Plans, _____ .

(A) den Opfern des Krieges zu helfen
(B) die Abhängigkeit Europas von Amerika zu sichern
(C) ausländische Märkte für amerikanische Waren zu schaffen
(D) sofort Arbeitsplätze für heimkehrende Soldaten zu schaffen

80. Durch das "G.I. Bill" hat die amerikanische Regierung _____ .

(A) neue Arbeitsplätze für Soldaten geschaffen
(B) den armen Europäern geholfen
(C) neue Märkte für amerikanische Waren gefunden
(D) viele Soldaten studieren lassen, damit sie zunächst keine Arbeitsplätze nötig hatten

SAT II:
SUBJECT TEST IN GERMAN

PRACTICE TEST VI

ANSWER KEY

1.	A	21.	A	41.	B	61.	B
2.	B	22.	D	42.	B	62.	D
3.	A	23.	B	43.	C	63.	C
4.	B	24.	C	44.	C	64.	A
5.	C	25.	C	45.	B	65.	C
6.	B	26.	C	46.	C	66.	B
7.	C	27.	C	47.	C	67.	B
8.	C	28.	B	48.	B	68.	D
9.	D	29.	C	49.	B	69.	C
10.	A	30.	A	50.	C	70.	B
11.	A	31.	B	51.	A	71.	B
12.	B	32.	B	52.	C	72.	B
13.	C	33.	C	53.	D	73.	A
14.	C	34.	C	54.	B	74.	B
15.	D	35.	A	55.	D	75.	A
16.	C	36.	B	56.	A	76.	C
17.	B	37.	A	57.	A	77.	D
18.	A	38.	C	58.	C	78.	B
19.	D	39.	D	59.	B	79.	C
20.	A	40.	C	60.	C	80.	D

GERMAN PRACTICE TEST VI

DETAILED EXPLANATIONS OF ANSWERS

1.   (A)
Only (A) is correct. *Begegnen* uses the auxiliary verb *sein* and a dative object, and is often used with *zufällig*. *Treffen* and *kennenlernen* both translate into the English "meet," but both require *haben* as auxiliary verb and an accusative object. Furthermore, *treffen* means "to meet by appointment" and *kennenlernen* means "make the acquaintance of"; neither fits here. *Entgegengehen* has the auxiliary verb *sein* and a dative object, but it means "go to meet" and would not be used with *zufällig*.

2.   (B)
In English the number written 1,000,000,000 is called a billion, but in German the same number is called *eine Milliarde*. *Eine Billion* in German is one million millions (one trillion in English). Thus, (B) is the correct choice.

3.   (A)
The German word *das Wort* has two plurals. *Wörter* is used when the words are unconnected; thus *gestern, sieben, Mutter, nach,* and *schlafen* would be five *Wörter*. A *Wörterbuch*, "dictionary," is a list of single words in alphabetical order. But if the words are connected in such a way as to make sense together, then the plural is *Worte*. The sentence in this question is such a group of words, so the correct choice is (A). This question is complicated somewhat by the fact that the choices are all in the dative plural (after *aus*), and therefore all end in *–n*. (B) and (C) are impossible forms; they can never occur. (D) would be correct for unrelated words.

4.   (B)

To answer this question correctly you must first of all know that the word *See* can be either masculine or femine, and that the meaning varies with the gender. *Der See* means "lake," but *die See* means "ocean" or "sea," as in *die Nordsee,* the North Sea. It is assumed that you know enough geography to realize that if the city of Konstanz is in South Germany it is not on any ocean, so the correct choice will be a masculine form. This eliminates (A) and (C), since *der* after the prepositions *an* or *auf* can only be feminine. (C) is also wrong because *auf* is the wrong preposition for this usage. A ship might be *auf dem See,* but a town is *am See.* Finally, since the reference is to location rather than to motion, the dative is the correct case. Thus, (D) cannot be correct, and (B) is the right answer.

5.   (C)

This sentence means "This semester I have enrolled in five classes at the university." One must be very careful in choosing a German equivalent for the English "class." *Die Klasse* (A) refers to a group of people or things as a group; thus the members of a school class (e.g. fourth grade) would be called *eine Klasse. Die Stunde* (B) refers to the actual meetings of the class (*Ich habe jeden Morgen um neun Uhr eine Deutschstunde*). *Der Kurs* (C) refers to the class as course of study; this is the correct choice here, the only appropriate object for the verb *belegen*, which means "enroll in." "Class" can also have a socio-political meaning, as in an expression like "the middle class." German also expresses this concept with *die Klasse.*

6.   (B)

(B) is the correct choice. *Studieren* means "be a student." It refers to a status rather than to an activity as such. Thus, one might say *Wir haben drei Jahre studiert,* but one would not use the verb *studieren* in reference to an activity that lasted only three hours. Thus, (A), though a correct grammatical form, is the wrong word. (C) and (D) are not only the wrong word choice, but are also grammatically incorrect; (C) is wrong because *studieren* (like all verbs ending in *"-ieren"*) has no ge- in the past participle, and (D) is wrong because the infinitive form *studieren* is not correct here.

7.   (C)

We are looking here for the correct German equivalent of "only." All four choices are possible equivalents, but all have different meanings, and each is correct only in its proper context. The correct choice here is (C); *erst* means "only" in the sense of "not until" and the sentence means "I only heard it today," i.e., "I did not hear it until today." *Nur* (A) has a limiting meaning; in this sentence it would mean "today is the only day on which I heard it," which obviously is not the correct meaning. *Allein* (B) and *einzig* (D) can mean "only" but cannot fit grammatically into the sentence given here. *Ich allein habe es gehört* or *Ich habe es als Einziger gehört* would both mean "I was the only one who heard it."

8.   (C)

The correct German equivalent of "news," in the sense of "a report on the day's events or a broadcast on television or radio," is *die Nachrichten* (C). The other words given here have different meanings. *Die Neuen* (A) could mean "the new people" or "the new things." *Die Neuigkeiten* (B) does mean "news" in the sense of "recent developments," but it does not refer to a television or radio broadcast. *Das Neue* (D) means "that which is new" in a sentence like *Das Neue ist nicht immer das Beste.*

9.   (D)

This question asks for knowledge of a specific idiom. The correct choice is (D). "To think that ... is ... " expressed in German as ... (accusative object) "*für* ... (adjective) *halten.*" Thus, (A) is wrong because it lacks the preposition *für;* (B) is wrong because it has the wrong preposition, the wrong case and the wrong word order; (C) is wrong because it has a dative instead of an accusative object.

10.   (A)

German expresses the idea "to cause something to be done" by the verb *lassen,* followed by an infinitive. Thus, (A) is the correct choice here; the sentence means "We are having a new house built (for ourselves)." Though the English may imply "making" someone do something, *machen* is not used with this meaning; the German equivalent of "He made the students read the book" would be *Er hat die Studenten gezwungen, das Buch zu lesen.* So (B) is also wrong. English also frequently uses "have" ("We are having a house built"), but the German *haben* is never correct in this context, so (C) is also wrong. Finally, German has no equivalent of the English "We are going to build a house." The German equivalent of such a sentence would simply use the main verb (*bauen*) in the present or future (*Wir bauen uns ein neues Haus* or *Wir werden uns ein neues Haus bauen*).

11.　(A)

The English expression "to succeed" has no exact equivalent in German; English expresses the idea personally (someone succeeds), while German expresses it impersonally, with the subject *"es"* and the person expressed as a dative object. The verb used in German is *gelingen/gelang/ist gelungen.* Thus, (A) is the correct choice here. (B) and (C) both try to make *sie* the subject, which is wrong, and (D) uses the auxiliary *haben* instead of the correct form of *sein.*

12.　(B)

The modal verbs in German have some similarities with the English modal verbs, but differ in many significant ways. To answer this question correctly you must know the range of meanings of four modal verbs. (C) and (D) are fairly easy to eliminate. *Magst* (from *mögen*) indicates either "liking" or "possibility" and has no meaning that makes sense in this context. Just as speakers of English sometimes use "can" for "may" ("Can I have another cookie?"), speakers of German sometimes use forms of *können* when they should use forms of *dürfen;* but proper usage in both languages is clearly opposed to such substitutions. To choose between (A) and (B) you must know that German *müssen* and English "must" are not always used in the same way. The two verbs do have approximately the same meaning in positive statements; "I must do that" and *Ich muss das tun* both mean "I am obliged to do that." But in negative statements the meanings are different. "I must not do that" usually means "I am obliged not to do that," while *Ich muss das nicht tun* means "I am not obliged to do that." Thus, the English sentence expresses a negative obligation, while the German sentence indicates an absence of obligation. The idea of negative obligation is expressed in German by *nicht dürfen*. Thus, (B) (*darfst*) is the correct choice here, since the sentence clearly implies a negative obligation: "You must not enter that room." If (A) (*musst*) were used here, the sentence would mean "You are not obliged to enter that room."

13.   (C)

In this question a choice must be made from four words, all of which are German equivalents of the English "introduce." The correct choice is (C); *vorstellen* is used in formally introducing one person to another. *Einführen* (A), when it refers to people, has no connotation of a formal presentation (*Sie führte uns in diese Gruppe ein*). *Einleiten* (B) refers to the initial part of any process, as in *Der Professor leitete das Buch mit einem Vorwort ein*. *Einbringen* (D) means "introduce a bill in a legislative body."

14.   (C)

The correct choice here is *weiß* (C). You must first distinguish between the various words that mean "know" in German. *Kennen* (A) refers to some specific person, place, or thing: *Ich kenne Hans Schmidt; Ich kenne Berlin; Ich kenne das Haus an der Ecke*. *Können* (B) means "know" only in the sense of "know how to do something"; *Sie kann gut Deutsch* means "She knows how to speak German well" or "She knows German well." *Wissen* means "know" in reference to something abstract. Further, *wissen* is always used if the object (the thing known) is expressed as a subordinate clause: *Ich weiß, was er macht; Wir wissen, wo du wohnst; Sie weiß, dass es bald regnet*. To distinguish between (C) and (D) here, you must also know that *wissen*, like the modal verbs, is one of the so-called "preterite-present" verbs. The present tense forms of these verbs are actually old past tense forms that have taken on present meaning. As in the past tense of strong verbs, there is no ending in the first and third person singular; *ich weiß* and *er weiß* correspond to *ich kam* and *er kam*. So *wisse* (D) is incorrect.

15.   (D)

All four of the possible answers are equivalents of "leave" but each of them has a different meaning. The correct choice is (D), *verlassen*, which means "abandon." *Abfahren* (A) simply means "depart;" it uses the auxiliary verb *sein* and cannot be used with a direct object. *Liegenlassen* (B) means "leave lying"; one might say *Er hat das Buch auf dem Tisch liegenlassen,* but one would hardly use this word in reference to people. *Hinterlassen* (C) usually means "leave behind at death"; one might say *Er hat seinen Kindern viel Geld hinterlassen.* Note that (B), (C), and (D), though they are past participles, do not have *"ge-."* In general, any verb whose infinitive form is not stressed on the first syllable will not have *"ge-"* in the past participle. Here the absence of stress on the first syllable is due to the presence of an unstressed prefix. In no. 6, we noted that some verbs, notably those that are formed with *"-ieren,"* are never stressed on the first syllable; they too have no initial *"ge-"* in the past participle.

16.   (C)
German has several words that mean "think" but the correct choice here is *glaube* (C). *Glauben* has the basic meaning "believe" but in this context it means "to be of the opinion." Thus, the sentence means "I think it will rain soon." *Denken an* (A) means something like "give thought to" and is usually used with some sort of subordinate clause, e.g., *Ich denke daran, nach Italien zu reisen,* "I am thinking of traveling to Italy." *Halten* (B) is used in the expression "to think that ... is ... "; *"Ich halte ihn für intelligent"* means "I think he is intelligent." (See the discussion after no. 9). Finally, it is important to distinguish *denken* (think) from *danken* (thank) (D).

17.   (B)
The correct choice here is (B). *Mann* means both "husband" and "adult human male." (A) (*"man"*) is an indefinite pronoun, meaning something like "one" (*Das hört man oft* means "One often hears that"). Actually, *"man"* is often best translated as a passive; *Man macht die Tür auf* is the equivalent of "The door is opened." (C) (*Mensch*) means simply "human being" and would be used in a sentence like *Der Mensch ist intelligenter als der Hund.* (D) (*Man*) is wrong because of its form. *Mann,* the noun, is written with a capital *M* and double *n; "man,"* the pronoun, has only one *n* and is capitalized only if it is the first word of a sentence.

18.   (A)

Except for *gerner* (B), which is an impossible form, all these words express somehow the idea of "rather." *Lieber* (A) is indeed the comparative form of *gern* and is the correct answer here. The sentence means "My father likes to drink beer, but he would rather drink wine." *Vielmehr* (C) is used to indicate that the speaker has changed his/her mind: *Er kommt morgen, oder vielmehr übermorgen* would mean "He'll come tomorrow, or rather, I mean the day after tomorrow." *Sondern* (D) can be used only after a negative expression, to indicate that that expression is not correct, but something else is correct: *Er ist nicht ins Kino gegangen, sondern zu Hause geblieben* means "He did not go to the movies, but rather he stayed home."

19.   (D)

All four choices are equivalents of the English word "number" but again all have different meanings. The correct choice is (D) *Nummer;* this word refers to numbers in series, such as house numbers, telephone numbers or identification numbers. *Zahl* (A) usually refers to "number" as an abstract or mathematical concept, as in *eine gerade Zahl*, "an even number." *Anzahl* (B) means an indefinite number, as in *eine große Anzahl von Studenten,* "a large number of students." *Ziffer* (C) refers to the number as a written or concrete object, as in *Diese Ziffer ist eine Fünf* or *Er konnte die römischen Ziffern nicht lesen.*

20.   (A)

The correct choice here is (A) *bestellt. Bestellen* means "order" in the sense of "ask someone to bring or send something" and is the correct term for use in a restaurant. *Befehlen* (B) means "order" in the sense of "command." *Ordnen* (C) means "arrange, put in order." *Verlangen* (D) means "demand" and implies that what is demanded is one's due; it might be used to refer indirectly to a restaurant order, but it would not be used in speaking directly to the waiter. Thus, all these words can be equivalents of English "order," but only (A) is correct in this sentence.

21.   (A)

Only (A) is correct. The verb in a subordinate clause must be at the end, which makes (C) wrong. (B) is introduced by *denn,* which is not a "subordinating" but a "coordinating" conjunction and does not affect word order. (B) would be correct if it were *denn ich muss einkaufen*. (D) might be correct with a different modal verb (e.g., *damit ich einkaufen kann*) but is not appropriate here.

22.   (D)

German normally uses the present tense with the preposition *seit* to express an action that began in the past and continues into the present. Thus, (D) is the correct answer here. (A) is wrong because it uses the perfect tense. (B) and (C) are wrong because the preposition *für* is used in time expressions only if the time of the time expression is not the same as the time implied by the verb:

> *Ich fahre drei Tage nach Italien.*   = Driving to Italy takes me three days.
> *Ich fahre für drei Tage nach Italien.* = I'll drive to Italy and stay there three days.

23.   (B)

The challenge here is to determine the proper order of objects in the inner field of a sentence (i.e., between the parts of the verb). This order is determined by "news value." Something that has already been mentioned has little news value, while something that has not yet been mentioned has more news value. Where there are two objects, the one with more news value comes later. A pronoun will therefore always precede a noun, since a pronoun by definition always refers to something that has already been mentioned. Thus, (C) and (D) are both wrong because in them the pronoun comes after the noun. But if two nouns are used in a sentence like this, with no context, how can one tell whether or not either of them has already been mentioned? The answer is in the use of articles. If something has already been mentioned, it will have a definite article the next time it is mentioned, whereas something not yet mentioned will have an indefinite article when first mentioned. English uses the very same clues.

> What did you do with that watch?   I gave **the** watch to a man.
> What did you give the man?   I gave the man **a** watch.

252

In the first pair of sentences, "watch" occurs in the question, so it comes first, preceded by **the**, in the answer; in the second pair, "watch" is first mentioned in the answer, so it comes second, preceded by **a**. Applying this structure to German, we see that (B) is the correct choice among those given here. (A) is wrong because *"eine Uhr,"* with an indefinite article, should come second.

24.   (C)
The sentence "Our teacher wants us to work diligently" is perfectly normal in English, but German does not permit the literal equivalent. If the sentence has two different subjects, German requires a subordinate clause. This produces the literal equivalent of the rather awkward English sentence "Our teacher wants that we work diligently." The main verb in the subordinate clause must agree with the subject of that clause. Thus, the correct choice here is (C).

Both (A) and (B) are wrong because they try to use the infinitive complement, with or without *zu*. (D) is wrong because the verb in the subordinate clause must come at the end.

25.   (C)
When a modal verb is used in a compound tense with a complementary verb, the construction is called a "double infinitive." In such cases the infinitive is substituted for the normal past participle of the modal, resulting in what looks like two infinitives together at the end of the clause. The modal always comes after the complementary verb. Thus, the correct choice here is (C), the only choice with two infinitives, the latter of which is the modal. (A) tries to use the regular past participle of the modal; (B) tries to use the past participle of the complementary verb instead of the infinitive; and (D) has the modal before the complement instead of after it.

It is worth noting that nothing can come after a double infinitive in the same clause. This leads to some problems. If, for instance, a double infinitive occurs in a subordinate clause, a conflict arises, because the main verb in the subordinate clause is also supposed to come last. Here the double infinitive wins: the main verb is displaced.

Er sagte, dass er kommen wollte.
but
Er sagte, dass er hat kommen wollen.

It is also worth noting that if there is no complementary verb, the normal past participle of the modal is used: *Das habe ich nicht gewollt.*

26.   (C)
German and English both have pairs of verbs in which one of the verbs indicates an action and the only other means "to cause that action." The former are always strong verbs and the latter are weak verbs derived from the strong verbs. Thus:

Action	Cause
sitzen/saß/gesessen (sit/sat/sat)	*setzen/setzte/gesetzt* (set/set/set)
liegen/lag/gelegen (lie/lay/lain)	*legen/legte/gelegt* (lay/laid/laid)

The strong verb in such a pair is intransitive and the weak verb is transitive (i.e., it has a direct object). Furthermore, the strong verb always refers to a "continuous state" rather than to an action. If these verbs are followed by one of the prepositions that can take a dative object (referring to location) or an accusative object (referring to motion), the strong verb will always refer to location and the weak verb will always refer to motion.

The correct choice here is (C). (B) and (D) can be eliminated easily as impossible forms: *liegte* has the vowel of the present tense of the strong verb with a past tense weak verb ending; *lagte* has the past tense strong form with a weak ending. To choose between *legte* (A) and *lag* (C), note that there is no direct object and the prepositional phrase is *auf dem Tisch*. Both the absence of a direct object and the dative object of the preposition *auf* indicate that the correct verb is *lag*.

27.   (C)
Except for archaic uses of words like "thou," English has lost its former distinction between formal and familiar address. But like most other European languages, German has kept this distinction. Today the distinction is no longer between social inferiors and superiors; instead

254

the use of *du/ihr* and *Sie* is determined primarily by the degree of intimacy between the speaker and the one spoken to. The familiar form is used when addressing relatives, close friends, children, animals, and in prayers. The formal form is used with others. As a rule of thumb, you use *du* with anyone whom you address by their first name, and you use *Sie* with anyone whom you address with a title, such as *Herr, Frau, Doktor,* etc.

The *Sie* form is actually the third-person plural form; in former times it was felt that this form was especially deferential. *Ihr* is of course the plural of *du.*

Since the person addressed in this question is called by her first name and is only one person, the correct choice is (C). (A) would be correct if you called her "Frau Schmidt" instead of Maria. (B) would be correct if several people were being addressed. (D), however, would never be correct, because it contains an impossible form of *haben*; the "*-b-*" in the stem of *haben* is lost in the second and third person singular forms: *hast* and *hat.*

28.   (B)

In English it is quite natural to put two grammatical elements (normally the subject and an adverbial expression) before the verb in a statement: "(After dinner) (we) go to the movies." German, however, requires that the main verb in a normal statement be the second grammatical element, so only one thing can precede it. This one thing may be the subject (*Ich besuche dich morgen*), an object (*Dich besuche ich morgen*), or an adverb (*Morgen besuche ich dich*). So in the sentence given here, the correct choice is (B), the only choice that has one grammatical element before the verb. (A) and (C) both have two elements before the verb and (D) has the verb first.

Actually, it is quite possible to begin a German sentence with a verb, but such sentences are not simple statements. An "exhortation," sometimes called a "first-person imperative," begins with a verb, but the subject always follows immediately. Thus, it would be possible to rearrange (D) to read *Gehen wir nach dem Essen ins Kino,* meaning "Let's go to the movies after dinner." But (D) as it stands here cannot begin a grammatically correct sentence.

29.   (C)

There are two kinds of conditional sentences: those that have not been, or will not be, fulfilled, and those that may or may not be, or have been, fulfilled. The former are called "closed" conditions or "contrary-to-fact" conditions and use the subjunctive; the latter are called "open" conditions and use the indicative.

Contrary to fact:
Present:
Wenn sie hier wäre, würde ich sie sehen.
If she were here, I would see her. (Since I don't see her, she is not here.)

Past:
Wenn sie hier gewesen wäre, hätte ich sie gesehen.
If she had been here, I would have seen her. (Since I did not see her, she was not here.)

Open:
Present:
Wenn ich Geld habe, mache ich Urlaub.
If I have money I take a vacation. (I may or may not have money.)

Past:
Wenn ich Geld hatte, machte ich Urlaub.
If I had money, I took a vacation. (Sometimes I did not have money, so I had no vacation.)

In this question the use of the indicative form in the second part of the sentence indicates that it is an open condition, one that may or may not be fulfilled; "If it rains tomorrow we will not work (but if it does not rain we will work)." So the indicative is called for in the first part as well. Thus, the correct choice is (C), the only indicative form. (A) and (B) are subjunctive forms that would be correct if there were also a subjunctive form in the second part of the sentence. (D) is also a subjunctive form, but is a past subjunctive, so it is wrong because the verb in the second part of the sentence is present indicative.

30.   (A)

This illustrates the other kind of conditional sentence, the "contrary-to-fact" condition, in the past. The sentence means: "If I had earned more money I would have been able to take a vacation." The correct choice is (A), the only past subjunctive form. (B) is a perfect indicative; (C) is a present indicative and (D) is a variant form of the present subjunctive.

For the use of the double infinitive *hätte ... machen können,* see the explanation of no. 25.

31.   (B)
Although contemporary colloquial German does use indicative verbs in some indirect statements, the need for the subjunctive is emphasized in this sentence by the statement of disbelief; the subjunctive is commonly used to indicate that the speaker doubts what is being indirectly reported. Thus, choices (A) and (C) here can be eliminated at once because they are indicative forms. *Wäre* (D) is a subjunctive form, but it is not the right word; it makes no sense in this sentence. That leaves (B) as the only possible correct choice.

There are two subjunctive conjugations in German, one based on the present stem of the verb and one based on the past stem. The latter, called variously the "general subjunctive" or "Subjunctive II" is used anywhere a subjunctive is called for. The former, called the "special subjunctive," the "indirect discourse subjunctive" or "Subjunctive I" is used today primarily in indirect quotations. Even in indirect quotations, its use is usually limited to the third person singular, since its other forms look and sound too much like indicative forms. The third-person singular, where the indicative ends in "–t" and the subjunctive ends in "–e," is clearly distinct. The form *habe,* appearing here as choice (C), is the third-person singular form of the "indirect discourse subjunctive."

32.   (B)
Während is one of the prepositions that takes a genitive object; the only correct choice here is (B). (A) is wrong because the nominative form (*der Tag*) can never be used as the object of a preposition. (C) and (D) have dative and accusative objects respectively; other prepositions use these cases, but *während* does not. Other common prepositions that have genitive objects are *wegen, trotz,* and *(an) statt.*

33.   (C)

Warten is usually followed by a prepositional phrase consisting of *auf* and an accusative object (*Ich warte auf dich*), or by a dependent clause. If a dependent clause is used, it differs significantly from the corresponding English idiom. In English we say "I am waiting for you to come" using an infinitive construction, but German does not allow this. Hence (A) and (B) are both wrong here. "To wait for something or someone" is expressed in German with *warten auf* ..., but German does not permit a dependent clause to be the immediate object of a preposition, so we may not say *Ich warte auf dass du kommst.* Instead, the dependent clause is anticipated by a *"da-"* preceding the preposition, and we say *Ich warte darauf, dass du kommst,* as in (C), the correct choice. The literal equivalent in English would be "I am waiting for this, that you come," and the clause *dass du kommst* really functions as an "expansion" or "explanation" of *darauf.*

34.   (C)

The German equivalent of "without ... verb + ing" usually requires *ohne* and an infinitive with *zu.* Thus, the correct choice here is (C). (A) is a literal translation, unintelligible to a German, of the English idiom "without visiting me." (B) lacks the necessary *zu.* Another way to express this idiom in German is with *ohne dass;* the addition of *dass* would make (D) acceptable (*ohne dass sie mich besucht hat*), but without *dass* it is wrong.

35.   (A)

The idea of "purpose" can be expressed in German in several ways. If the subject of both clauses is the same, as in the first part of this sentence ("I" am both the one who works and the one who studies), then the normal way is with *um* and an infinitive with *zu.* However, if the subjects are not the same, the idea is expressed with *damit* and a finite verb. Thus, the correct choice here is (A), and the second part of the sentence means "but my father worked so that his children could study." (B) is wrong because the *um ... zu* construction cannot be used if the subjects are different. (C) is wrong because *um* cannot be combined with a finite verb in this context. (D) is wrong because *damit* requires a finite verb, not an infinitive.

36.   (B)
Since *es gibt* always has an accusative object, only an accusative form can be the correct choice here. The word *"student"* has the ending *-en* in all forms except the nominative singular. Thus, (C), which can only be nominative, is wrong. Since *"student"* is masculine, the accusative form of the preceding *kein* must be either *keinen* (singular) or *keine* (plural). Thus, (D) must also be wrong. (A) and (B) are both acceptable accusative forms, but (A) is singular and (B) is plural. To choose between them you must realize that the relative pronoun in the next clause is plural. Since the relative clause depends on its antecedent for number and gender, a plural relative pronoun means that the antecedent must also be plural. Thus, (B), the plural form, is the correct choice.

37.   (A)
Most intransitive verbs that indicate motion or change require *sein* as their auxiliary verb in the perfect and *kommen* is no exception; therefore, (C) and (D) can be eliminated at once. To choose between (A) and (B), however, you must be careful to use the German rather than the English idiom. In English, a word like "police" is usually thought of as plural. We say "The police are coming" rather than "The police is coming." But in German *die Polizei* is singular and the verb used with it must also be singular. Thus, the correct choice here is (A).

38.   (C)
(A) is the literal translation of the English idiom "are interested in" and is impossible in German. The other three choices are the same except for the preposition used; the only correct choice is (C). It is worth noting that there is a related idiom that uses *an;* we can say *Ich bin an der klassischen Musik interessiert.*

39.   (D)
This sentence means "Have you heard the new tenor sing?" The verbs *helfen, hören, sehen* and *lassen* function like modal verbs, in that they make use of the "double infinitive" construction when used in compound tenses with another verb. Thus, the correct choice here is (D). (A) has two infinitives, but they are in the wrong order. Just as the

modal verb must be the second infinitive (see explanation no. 35), so these verbs must also come after the complementary verb. (B) and (C) are not double infinitives. To illustrate further the use of these verbs:

Wir haben den Arzt kommen lassen.	We sent for the doctor.
Ich habe ihnen arbeiten helfen.	I helped them work.
Sie hat uns kommen sehen.	She saw us coming.

40.　　(C)

To express the idea that one thing varies as a function of something else, German uses *je ... desto* (or *je ... um so*). They must be used in a definite order: the "independent" variable is preceded by *je,* and the "dependent" variable is preceded by *desto.* Thus, the sentence given here means "The older I get, the more slowly I work." The placement of *je* and *desto* has to indicate that working more slowly is a function of aging. Thus, the correct choice here is (C). (A) is an attempt to bring over from English the idiom "the more ... the more." (B) is meaningless. (D) uses the right words, but in the wrong order.

41.　　(B)

Only (B) is correct. *Als, wenn,* and *wann* all translate the English "when," but with different meanings. *Wann* is used only in questions, direct or indirect (*Wann kommt der Zug an?* or *Weißt du, wann der Zug ankommt?*). *Als* is used to refer to a single action in the past, no matter how long that action may have lasted (*Als ich ankam, hatten sie schon gegessen* or *Als ich jung war, wohnte ich in Berlin*). *Wenn* is used for all present and future actions, and (as here) for repeated action in the past. Repeated action is indicated here by *immer. Während* means "while," but is not appropriate here because the action described is repeated.

42.　　(B)

Es gibt must be followed by an accusative, and *Wein* is masculine, so the correct answer is (B), the only word that can be masculine accusative. (A) *kein* could be masculine nominative or neuter nominative/accusative. (C) *nicht* is wrong because *nicht* is not used to negate a noun; it negates verbs: *Er kommt nicht.* (D) *keiner* cannot possibly be accusative, but it could be the nominative masculine singular if the word were used as a pronoun, i.e., not as a modifier: *Keiner von meinen Brüdern studiert in Heidelberg.*

43.   (C)

When a question or statement is phrased negatively, *doch* is used in the response to indicate that the contrary is true. In this case the question ("Is there no more wine?") is expressed negatively and the answer is clearly that there is wine and that it is on the table. Thus, (C) is the correct choice. (A) (*Ja*) is never used to respond to a negative question. (B) (*Nein*) means that the answer is also negative: there is no more wine. Since the only possible responses to such a negatively phrased question are *nein* and *doch,* (D) (*Nicht*) is also wrong.

44.   (C)

Both *a* and *auf* are prepositions that can have dative or accusative objects, depending on whether the verb with which they are used indicates motion (accusative) or location (dative). This verb indicates location, so the preposition, whichever one is used, will have a dative object. Some speakers of English might be tempted to choose the preposition *an* because it sounds like English "on," but this is deceptive; *auf* corresponds to English "on," while *an* corresponds to English "at." The correct preposition here is *auf* and since *Tisch* is masculine, the correct answer is (C). (A) and (B) are wrong because *an* is the wrong preposition and (D) is wrong because *den* is either accusative singular or dative plural, neither of which is correct here.

45.   (B)

The possessives normally modify nouns: *mein Haus, mein Freund, meine Mutter.* In this usage, the masculine and neuter forms of the nominative singular and the neuter accusative singular have no endings. But when one of these forms is used as a pronoun instead of modifying a noun, endings are required and they are the endings normally associated with these cases: *meiner* in the nominative masculine singular and *mein(e)s* in the nominative and accusative neuter singular. Therefore, the correct choice in question 45 is (B); the word has to refer to *Wagen* (masculine) and be the subject of its clause and (B) is the only form given that can be nominative masculine. (A) (*mein*), having no ending, can only be a modifier; (C) (*meins*) is neuter and (D) (*meinen*) is accusative.

46.   (C)

This sentence requires a passive verb in the past tense and only (C) is correct. The passive in German is constructed with forms of *werden* and the past participle of the verb used. (B) and (C) both offer forms of *werden,* but the context demands a past tense and (B) is present. In English the passive is made with forms of "to be" ("The door is opened every day at nine." "The criminal was seen in Chicago.") Hence speakers of English sometimes try to make the passive in German using forms of *sein.* (A) is wrong because the verb *war* is the too-literal translation of English "was." (D) (*hat*) is wrong because it cannot be passive. A sentence like *Er hat mir den Wagen geschenkt* is grammatically correct, but it is not passive and the sentence to be completed here requires a passive.

47.   (C)

English uses the word "where" in several different ways, while German has a different word for each of these usages. *Wo* refers only to location: "Where is he?"; *wohin* refers to motion toward a destination: "Where is he going?"; *woher* refers to motion away from some other place: "Where is he coming from?" Since the verb here, *wohnen,* refers to location, the correct choice is (C). Some speakers of English are confused by the fact that the German word *wer* (D) looks and sounds similar to the English "where." This is unfortunate, since *wer* means "who."

48.   (B)

German has two possible ways to express the English "if": the conditional "if" ("If it rains we can't go.") is expressed by *wenn,* but the "if" that is the equivalent of "whether" is expressed by *ob.* This sentence is of the latter sort, so (A) is wrong and (B) is the correct choice. *Weder* (C) and *Wetter* (D) both sound something like "whether" but have entirely different meanings; *weder* means "neither" and *Wetter* means "weather."

49.   (B)   See explanation for no. 50.

50.   (C)
Both these questions are concerned with the proper endings for adjectives used after definite articles and other "*der*-words" (e.g., *dieser, jeder, jener*), the so-called "weak" endings. The ending "*-e*" is used in five cases: the nominative singular in all three genders and the accusative singular feminine and neuter. The ending "*-en*" is used in all other cases. In question 49, *der Mann* is masculine nominative and the correct ending on a following adjective is "*-e,*" so the correct choice is (B). (A) *alter* is the nominative masculine singular "strong" ending, to be used when there is no preceding determiner or when the preceding determiner is *ein*. (B) *alten* has the wrong ending and (D) *älter* can only be the comparative form; the "*-er*" is not an ending here at all, but a suffix indicating "comparative."

In question 50, the form *der* can only be the feminine dative singular, since the verb *helfen* requires a dative object and *Frau* is feminine. The correct adjective ending is therefore "*-en,*" and the correct choice is (C). (A) *junger* would be correct if there were no preceding article, since it has the dative feminine "strong" ending "*-er.*" (D) *jünger* is like *älter* in question 49, a comparative form with no ending.

51.   (A)
This question shows a fundamental difference between English and German grammar: it is possible in German to have a sentence with no subject. The correct choice is (A), a dative expression. When an active sentence is transformed into the corresponding passive sentence, the normal transformation process is as follows: the accusative object (if any) of the active sentence becomes the subject of the passive sentence and the subject of the active sentence becomes the agent in the passive sentence. This is true for both English and German. Thus:

263

| I see him. | *Ich sehe ihn.* |
| He is seen by me. | *Er wird von mir gesehen.* |

But if the verb in the active sentence requires a dative object in German, there is no accusative object and hence there is nothing that can become the subject of the passive sentence. The dative object remains dative and the passive sentence simply has no subject. In English we no longer make any distinction between dative and accusative; any object in the active sentence can become the subject of the passive sentence. So when a German verb has a dative object, the sentence structure is quite different from English.

| I help him. | *Ich helfe ihm.* |
| He is helped by me. | *Ihm wird von mir geholfen.* |

The sentence in question 51 is a bit more complex, but its basic structure is: *Dem Studenten wurde von den Eltern gedankt,* which corresponds to *Ihm wird von mir geholfen.*

Many speakers of English would choose (C) because *Der Student* is the nominative form, which is what English would use. (B) is wrong because *Student* must have the ending *"-en"* in all forms except the nominative singular. And (D) is wrong because it is either accusative (the wrong case) or dative plural; the dative form might be correct, but if it were, the relative pronoun and the verb in the following relative clause would have to be plural as well.

52.　(C)

A relative pronoun can refer back to a specific word as antecendent or it can refer to the whole preceding clause. If it refers to a specific word, it must have the same gender and number as that word, but its case is determined by its use in its own clause. If it refers to the whole preceding clause and functions as subject or direct object in its own clause, it takes the form *was.* In this sentence the relative pronoun must be nominative, since it functions as the subject in its own clause. The only plausible specific antecedent is *eine Blume,* which is feminine, but there is no feminine nominative among the choices. So (C) *was* is the only correct choice. (A) and (B) could both be relative pronouns, but they are wrong because they are not nominative feminine singular.

Because English uses "that" as an all-purpose relative pronoun ("the man that I met," "the ball that hit me"), some English speakers assume that *dass* functions the same way in German; unfortunately, this is not true, so (D) is also wrong.

53.   (D)
Street addresses are almost always given with the article preceding the name of the street, so (A) and (C) are wrong because they lack an article. There remains the question of which preposition to choose; German usually prefers *in,* so (D) is the correct choice.

54.   (B)
If (A) (no preposition) were correct, *die Frage* would be the direct object of *antworten.* Since *antworten* cannot have a direct object, (A) must be wrong. As in question 53, there remains the problem of which preposition to choose. The correct choice is (B) *auf.*

55.   (D)
In referring to parts of the body and articles of clothing, German prefers a "dative of reference" instead of a possessive. Thus, such references often have two objects, one in the accusative, indicating the actual body part of article of clothing, and one in the dative indicating the person to whom the body part or piece of clothing belongs. In question 55, (A) is grammatically correct, but is idiomatically doubtful. (B) is wrong because both objects are accusative. (C) is wrong because both objects are dative. Thus, (D), with a dative object of the person and accusative object of the thing, is the correct choice. Other sentences of this type are:

Er gab es mir in die Hand.	He put it into my hand.
Sie kämmte dem Kind die Haare.	She combed the child's hair.
Ich muss mir die Schuhe anziehen.	I have to put on my shoes.

Note, however, that if the person is the only object, it will often be in the accusative:

Ich muss mich anziehen.	I have to get dressed.
Ich habe mich gewaschen.	I washed (myself).

56. (A) See explanation no. 57.

57. (A)
Two things are being illustrated here (nos. 56 and 57): the placement of adverbs in the inner field of a sentence and the proper way to express dates. In general, when there are several adverbial expressions in a sentence (i.e., expressions that answer questions like "where?," "when?," "how?"), they occur in a certain order. Time-expressions usually come first and place-expressions usually come last. Other kinds of expressions, such as "means" or "accompaniment" come after time-expressions and before place-expressions. In this sentence, therefore, the date must precede the place; *in Bonn* must be the second of the two adverbial expressions, so (C) and (D) are both wrong.

In German there are two legitimate ways to express a date: either with no preposition at all, as in (A) (no. 56) and (D) (no. 57), or with the expression *im Jahre,* as in (C) (no. 57). But since (C) has the adverbial expressions in the wrong order, (A) must be the correct choice. Note that German does not use the preposition *in* to express dates.

58. (C)
German uses the genitive case to express indefinite time, so the correct choice here is (C). Expressions of definite time are in the accusative, as in (A), or in a sentence like *Ich habe ihn letzten Dienstag gesehen.* However, here the indefinite article is used, and therefore there is no indication of definite time. Neither the dative alone (B) nor the nominative alone (D) is ever used in time expressions.

59. (B)
Aber (A) is a coordinating conjunction; it stands between two clauses and belongs to neither, so used alone it has no effect on the word order of a following clause. If *aber* were the correct word here, there would be something in front of the verb *haben* to keep it from being the first element in the clause; since there is no such thing here, (A) must be wrong. *Obwohl* (C) is a subordinating conjunction; any clause it introduces will have its finite verb at the end. Since the finite verb here *haben* is not at the end, (C) must be wrong. If there are too few words

before the verb in (A), there are too many in (D). The verb must be the second grammatical element in the clause, but (D) has two separate adverbs (*trotzdem* and *gestern*) before the verb. So (D) is also wrong. That leaves (B) as the only possible correct choice. In (B), *aber* has no effect on word order and *trotzdem,* "nevertheless," is the single grammatical element before the verb.

60.   (C)

Some verbs in German must have an accusative object. In English we can say "She turned around and looked at me," but in German the subject of a verb like *drehen, bewegen,* or *entwickeln* must act upon some object or upon itself. Thus, if there is no other object, such a verb will have reflexive object.

Sie drehte den Stuhl um.	She turned the chair around.
Sie drehte sich um.	She turned (herself) around.

Thus, (A) is wrong because there must be some object after this verb. (D) is wrong because *langsam* is an adverb, not an object. (B) is wrong because *ihr* cannot be an accusative object. (C) is the correct choice.

Note that although the reflexive pronouns for the first and second persons are identical with the personal pronouns, the third person has only one "all-purpose" reflexive pronoun, *sich.* It is singular and plural, dative and accusative, masculine, feminine, and neuter.

61.   (B)

This text deals with the political and economic development of cities in late medieval Europe. As the cities became more powerful economically, they demanded more political independence and got it by escaping the authority of local nobles.

For question 61, (B) is the only correct answer that can be obtained from the text. The main point of the first sentence is that there were some large cities, so (A) is wrong. Among the cities listed are three in the north; hence (C) cannot be correct. No cities with more than 50,000 people are mentioned and the text implies that Cologne, with almost 30,000, was the largest city in Germany, so (D) is not correct.

62.   (D)

(D) is the only correct answer to question 62. (A) says that the cities were economically weak; (B) says that they had no interest in politics and (C) states that they wanted to be dependent on the nobility. The text, however, states that the growing economic power of the cities was associated with a desire for political power, and that made the people in the cities want to be free of the rule of the nobility.

63.   (C)

To answer question 63 you must understand that the text defines a "free city" as one that is subject only to the king. Thus, (C) is correct. Some cities were members of the Hanseatic League (A), but that was not what made them "free cities." Free cities were those that had escaped the rule of the lesser nobility (B) ("counts and dukes") and were subject directly to the king. (D) is wrong for several reasons, but mainly because the German word *frei* is not the equivalent of English "free" in the sense of "without cost."

64.   (A)

(A) is the only correct answer to question 64. The text states that before World War II most German children spoke dialect at home and learned Hochdeutsch in school. So (B), which states that they only spoke dialect in school and (C), which states that they learned dialect in school, are both clearly wrong. The text further makes it clear that they did speak dialect with their parents: it says that they spoke it at home. It also says that some thought the dialect was a secret language, which they shared with their parents, so (D) is also wrong.

65.   (C)

Question 65 asks why many couples who married in the time after World War II did not speak dialect at home. The reason given is that many people in that period married people who came from different regions and hence spoke different dialects. Thus, only (C) is correct; most Germans could speak a dialect, but many couples had no common dialect. (A) is wrong because each could speak a dialect, even though they had no dialect in common. (B) states that they wanted to have a secret language; the text uses this term, but in reference to a different pair of generations. (D) is wrong because the text nowhere says that they wanted to forget their home regions.

66.   (B)
The whole text leads up to the final sentence and explains why many Germans today do not speak any dialect. The only answer to question 66 that can be justified from the text is (B). (A) and (D) are possible reasons why Germans might not speak dialect today, but neither is mentioned in the text. (C) is irrelevant; dialects were normally learned at home.

67.   (B)
This text is concerned with the main character in the novel *The Tin Drum*, by Günter Grass. Oskar Matzerath is a most unusual child; from the moment of his birth he is totally aware of what is happening around him and on his third birthday he stops growing by an an act of his own will. He also has two most unusual talents: he cannot only shatter glass with his voice, but can cut glass in specific forms as well, and he can influence people's thoughts and moods with his drumming. Grass uses Oskar to show Germans their weaknesses and problems.

The correct answer to question 67 is (B): the text makes it clear that Oskar is a very unusual child, so (A) is obviously wrong. (C) is wrong because Oskar is not the author, but the main character in the novel. And (D) is wrong because the text implies that he grew normally until his third birthday, then stopped growing entirely. Thus, he was an unusually small child from the age of three on.

68.   (D)
(D) is the correct answer to question 68: the text states that because he looks like a three-year-old, Oskar is often not punished for doing things for which a bigger child or an adult would be punished. (A) is wrong because it says that he is always caught and punished when he does something bad and (C) is wrong because the text does not say that he is not seen because of his size. (B) is simply irrelevant.

69.   (C)

The answer to question 69 is (C): Oscar can influence the thoughts and moods of people by means of his drumming. (A) is wrong because it implies that he needs tools to break glass, whereas the text states that he does it with his voice. (B) is wrong for the same reason; he breaks glass with his voice, not by drumming. And (D) is wrong because the text does not say that his voice disturbs people, only that it breaks or cuts glass.

70.   (B)

For question 70 only (B) is correct: the text states clearly that Grass intends this novel to show the Germans their weaknesses and problems. Thus, (A), that the Germans have no weaknesses or problems, is clearly false. (C) is wrong because the text does not say that Germans should imitate Oskar and (D) is wrong because neither Grass nor this text says that all Germans should remain children.

71.   (B)

A policeman stops a motorist who is driving too fast for safety. When he asks why the man is driving so fast, he gets an outrageous answer: it is almost dark, and the motorist does not want to drive after dark because his headlights are broken; furthermore, he does not want to drive without headlights because his brakes do not function.

Question 71 asks why the policeman stops the motorist. The only correct answer is (B) ("it is dangerous to drive so fast in the city"). The text does not imply that the driver is drunk (A) and the policeman does not suspect that the driver is rushing because it is getting dark (D). (C) is a conventional question, asked of anyone in a hurry, but seldom taken seriously: "Where's the fire?"

72.   (B)

Question 72 requires that you draw an inference. The text does not state explicitly why the driver is impatient but it is nevertheless clear that it is because he knows, as the policeman does not, why he is driving so fast and how important it is that he get home before dark. Thus, the correct answer is (B). (A) is wrong because the policeman does not scold the driver. (C) is wrong because, as the policeman's question brings out, they are not heading for the hospital. And (D) is wrong because the man seems not at all reluctant to explain why he is driving so fast; he only wants to do it quickly so he can continue on his way.

73.   (A)
Question 73 gets to the point of the story. To the reader's astonishment, the driver seems to think that his reasons for driving so fast are perfectly valid and he expects to be allowed to continue. Thus, (A) is the correct answer. It is not really surprising that the policeman does not scold the driver; the policeman does not yet know what the driver is thinking. So (B) is wrong. (C) (that the driver is driving so fast) and (D) (that the passenger has nothing to say) are not surprising.

74.   (B)
This text is concerned with the origins of the science of chemistry. Chemistry began as alchemy but sometime before the 18th century new ideas were proposed, which led to the release of chemistry from bondage to alchemy. The process was completed with the publication in 1789 of Lavoisier's book *Elements of Chemistry*. He emphasized the importance of quantitative methods and introduced several important ideas, among them a) the conservation of matter (in any chemical reaction no matter is lost or gained, since careful measurement reveals that the total weight of the products of that reaction is equal to the total weight of the original matter) and b) the nature of a chemical element, a substance that cannot be further broken down by chemical means.

The text makes it clear that although Lavoisier played an important role in the foundation of the science of chemistry, the beginnings of that science predated his work. Thus, in question 74, (B) is correct, and (C) (that he was the first to propose the ideas of modern chemistry) is wrong. (A) is wrong because Lavoisier was not an alchemist and (D) is wrong because, though Lavoisier was indeed the author of *Elements of Chemistry*, we are not told that he was a publisher.

75.   (A)
Using quantitative methods means, among other things, paying close

attention to measurements in all scientific experiments. Therefore, the correct answer to question 75 is (A). The text states that the alchemists saw natural science as part of philosophy and that Lavoisier rejected that idea. Thus, (B) (that the scientist should be searching for the philosophical meaning of science) and (C) (that the scientist should use the methods of the alchemist) are both wrong. Finally, (D) is wrong because the text says nothing about the quantities of matter to be investigated.

76.   (C)
To answer question 76 you must recognize the correct definition of the term "Principle of Conservation of Matter." It means that in a chemical reaction no matter is gained or lost; careful measurement shows that the total weight of the matter involved is the same before and after the reaction. Thus, the correct answer to question 76 is (C). (A) says that all matter to be used in scientific experiments should be carefully stored (conserved) beforehand; (B) says that in a chemical reaction nothing at all changes, which is obviously not true, and (D) says that materials can be kept for a longer time by means of chemical preservatives.

77.   (D)
Question 77 asks how it was that Lavoisier knew only 23 chemical elements. The answer, both from history and from the text, is that the people of his time had managed to identify only that many elements. So (D) is correct. (A) says that only 23 elements exist, which is of course wrong and (B) implies that the nature of the universe has changed since then: there are more elements now than there were then. (C) says that Lavoisier was not interested in finding more elements, but the text implies that he was quite interested in this question, and expected that more elements would be identified in time.

78.   (B)
This text provides economic justification for two measures taken by the American Government after WWII: the Marshall Plan and the G.I. Bill. During the war there was no unemployment (most of the workers were in the armed services) and the war produced a market for everything the country could produce. After the war, however, the domestic market

was much smaller and the old foreign markets no longer existed, since much of Europe and Asia had been reduced to rubble. Furthermore, the returning soldiers would be seeking work, and there would not be enough work for all of them until foreign markets could be restored. So the government tried a two-pronged solution to the problem: the Marshall Plan was intended to enable foreign countries to rebuild their economies, and the G.I. Bill sent the veterans back to school, thus, keeping them out of the job market for a while.

Question 78 asks why the U.S. could not export very much after the war. The correct answer is (B) (that the countries of Europe and Asia were not able to buy). (A) (that the soldiers were coming home) is irrelevant; (C) (that American workers could only produce munitions) is not true and (D) (that there were not enough workers) is precisely the opposite of the truth; there would soon be too many workers.

79.   (C)
Although the Marshall Plan did have several purposes, only one of which was the rebuilding of foreign markets, question 79 specifically asks you to answer with reference to this text, which states that the main purpose of the Marshall Plan was to rebuild foreign markets. Thus, the correct answer is (C). (A) (to help the victims of the war) is actually true. It was one of the purposes of the Marshall Plan, but it is not the correct answer to this question because it is not the main purpose as given in this text. (B) (to emphasize Europe's dependence on America) is not supported by the text, and (D) (to provide immediate jobs for returning soldiers) is simply wrong.

80.   (D)
Question 80 asks what the G.I. Bill accomplished. It did not create new jobs at once (A), it did not help the poor Europeans (B), and it did not find new markets for American goods (C). But it did enable many soliders to go to college, thus keeping them out of the job market temporarily, so (D) is the correct answer.

SAT II:
SUBJECT TEST IN

GERMAN
TEST I
ANSWER SHEET

1. Ⓐ Ⓑ Ⓒ Ⓓ Ⓔ
2. Ⓐ Ⓑ Ⓒ Ⓓ Ⓔ
3. Ⓐ Ⓑ Ⓒ Ⓓ Ⓔ
4. Ⓐ Ⓑ Ⓒ Ⓓ Ⓔ
5. Ⓐ Ⓑ Ⓒ Ⓓ Ⓔ
6. Ⓐ Ⓑ Ⓒ Ⓓ Ⓔ
7. Ⓐ Ⓑ Ⓒ Ⓓ Ⓔ
8. Ⓐ Ⓑ Ⓒ Ⓓ Ⓔ
9. Ⓐ Ⓑ Ⓒ Ⓓ Ⓔ
10. Ⓐ Ⓑ Ⓒ Ⓓ Ⓔ
11. Ⓐ Ⓑ Ⓒ Ⓓ Ⓔ
12. Ⓐ Ⓑ Ⓒ Ⓓ Ⓔ
13. Ⓐ Ⓑ Ⓒ Ⓓ Ⓔ
14. Ⓐ Ⓑ Ⓒ Ⓓ Ⓔ
15. Ⓐ Ⓑ Ⓒ Ⓓ Ⓔ
16. Ⓐ Ⓑ Ⓒ Ⓓ Ⓔ
17. Ⓐ Ⓑ Ⓒ Ⓓ Ⓔ
18. Ⓐ Ⓑ Ⓒ Ⓓ Ⓔ
19. Ⓐ Ⓑ Ⓒ Ⓓ Ⓔ
20. Ⓐ Ⓑ Ⓒ Ⓓ Ⓔ
21. Ⓐ Ⓑ Ⓒ Ⓓ Ⓔ
22. Ⓐ Ⓑ Ⓒ Ⓓ Ⓔ
23. Ⓐ Ⓑ Ⓒ Ⓓ Ⓔ
24. Ⓐ Ⓑ Ⓒ Ⓓ Ⓔ
25. Ⓐ Ⓑ Ⓒ Ⓓ Ⓔ
26. Ⓐ Ⓑ Ⓒ Ⓓ Ⓔ
27. Ⓐ Ⓑ Ⓒ Ⓓ Ⓔ

28. Ⓐ Ⓑ Ⓒ Ⓓ Ⓔ
29. Ⓐ Ⓑ Ⓒ Ⓓ Ⓔ
30. Ⓐ Ⓑ Ⓒ Ⓓ Ⓔ
31. Ⓐ Ⓑ Ⓒ Ⓓ Ⓔ
32. Ⓐ Ⓑ Ⓒ Ⓓ Ⓔ
33. Ⓐ Ⓑ Ⓒ Ⓓ Ⓔ
34. Ⓐ Ⓑ Ⓒ Ⓓ Ⓔ
35. Ⓐ Ⓑ Ⓒ Ⓓ Ⓔ
36. Ⓐ Ⓑ Ⓒ Ⓓ Ⓔ
37. Ⓐ Ⓑ Ⓒ Ⓓ Ⓔ
38. Ⓐ Ⓑ Ⓒ Ⓓ Ⓔ
39. Ⓐ Ⓑ Ⓒ Ⓓ Ⓔ
40. Ⓐ Ⓑ Ⓒ Ⓓ Ⓔ
41. Ⓐ Ⓑ Ⓒ Ⓓ Ⓔ
42. Ⓐ Ⓑ Ⓒ Ⓓ Ⓔ
43. Ⓐ Ⓑ Ⓒ Ⓓ Ⓔ
44. Ⓐ Ⓑ Ⓒ Ⓓ Ⓔ
45. Ⓐ Ⓑ Ⓒ Ⓓ Ⓔ
46. Ⓐ Ⓑ Ⓒ Ⓓ Ⓔ
47. Ⓐ Ⓑ Ⓒ Ⓓ Ⓔ
48. Ⓐ Ⓑ Ⓒ Ⓓ Ⓔ
49. Ⓐ Ⓑ Ⓒ Ⓓ Ⓔ
50. Ⓐ Ⓑ Ⓒ Ⓓ Ⓔ
51. Ⓐ Ⓑ Ⓒ Ⓓ Ⓔ
52. Ⓐ Ⓑ Ⓒ Ⓓ Ⓔ
53. Ⓐ Ⓑ Ⓒ Ⓓ Ⓔ
54. Ⓐ Ⓑ Ⓒ Ⓓ Ⓔ

55. Ⓐ Ⓑ Ⓒ Ⓓ Ⓔ
56. Ⓐ Ⓑ Ⓒ Ⓓ Ⓔ
57. Ⓐ Ⓑ Ⓒ Ⓓ Ⓔ
58. Ⓐ Ⓑ Ⓒ Ⓓ Ⓔ
59. Ⓐ Ⓑ Ⓒ Ⓓ Ⓔ
60. Ⓐ Ⓑ Ⓒ Ⓓ Ⓔ
61. Ⓐ Ⓑ Ⓒ Ⓓ Ⓔ
62. Ⓐ Ⓑ Ⓒ Ⓓ Ⓔ
63. Ⓐ Ⓑ Ⓒ Ⓓ Ⓔ
64. Ⓐ Ⓑ Ⓒ Ⓓ Ⓔ
65. Ⓐ Ⓑ Ⓒ Ⓓ Ⓔ
66. Ⓐ Ⓑ Ⓒ Ⓓ Ⓔ
67. Ⓐ Ⓑ Ⓒ Ⓓ Ⓔ
68. Ⓐ Ⓑ Ⓒ Ⓓ Ⓔ
69. Ⓐ Ⓑ Ⓒ Ⓓ Ⓔ
70. Ⓐ Ⓑ Ⓒ Ⓓ Ⓔ
71. Ⓐ Ⓑ Ⓒ Ⓓ Ⓔ
72. Ⓐ Ⓑ Ⓒ Ⓓ Ⓔ
73. Ⓐ Ⓑ Ⓒ Ⓓ Ⓔ
74. Ⓐ Ⓑ Ⓒ Ⓓ Ⓔ
75. Ⓐ Ⓑ Ⓒ Ⓓ Ⓔ
76. Ⓐ Ⓑ Ⓒ Ⓓ Ⓔ
77. Ⓐ Ⓑ Ⓒ Ⓓ Ⓔ
78. Ⓐ Ⓑ Ⓒ Ⓓ Ⓔ
79. Ⓐ Ⓑ Ⓒ Ⓓ Ⓔ
80. Ⓐ Ⓑ Ⓒ Ⓓ Ⓔ

SAT II:
SUBJECT TEST IN

GERMAN
TEST II
ANSWER SHEET

1. (A) (B) (C) (D) (E)
2. (A) (B) (C) (D) (E)
3. (A) (B) (C) (D) (E)
4. (A) (B) (C) (D) (E)
5. (A) (B) (C) (D) (E)
6. (A) (B) (C) (D) (E)
7. (A) (B) (C) (D) (E)
8. (A) (B) (C) (D) (E)
9. (A) (B) (C) (D) (E)
10. (A) (B) (C) (D) (E)
11. (A) (B) (C) (D) (E)
12. (A) (B) (C) (D) (E)
13. (A) (B) (C) (D) (E)
14. (A) (B) (C) (D) (E)
15. (A) (B) (C) (D) (E)
16. (A) (B) (C) (D) (E)
17. (A) (B) (C) (D) (E)
18. (A) (B) (C) (D) (E)
19. (A) (B) (C) (D) (E)
20. (A) (B) (C) (D) (E)
21. (A) (B) (C) (D) (E)
22. (A) (B) (C) (D) (E)
23. (A) (B) (C) (D) (E)
24. (A) (B) (C) (D) (E)
25. (A) (B) (C) (D) (E)
26. (A) (B) (C) (D) (E)
27. (A) (B) (C) (D) (E)

28. (A) (B) (C) (D) (E)
29. (A) (B) (C) (D) (E)
30. (A) (B) (C) (D) (E)
31. (A) (B) (C) (D) (E)
32. (A) (B) (C) (D) (E)
33. (A) (B) (C) (D) (E)
34. (A) (B) (C) (D) (E)
35. (A) (B) (C) (D) (E)
36. (A) (B) (C) (D) (E)
37. (A) (B) (C) (D) (E)
38. (A) (B) (C) (D) (E)
39. (A) (B) (C) (D) (E)
40. (A) (B) (C) (D) (E)
41. (A) (B) (C) (D) (E)
42. (A) (B) (C) (D) (E)
43. (A) (B) (C) (D) (E)
44. (A) (B) (C) (D) (E)
45. (A) (B) (C) (D) (E)
46. (A) (B) (C) (D) (E)
47. (A) (B) (C) (D) (E)
48. (A) (B) (C) (D) (E)
49. (A) (B) (C) (D) (E)
50. (A) (B) (C) (D) (E)
51. (A) (B) (C) (D) (E)
52. (A) (B) (C) (D) (E)
53. (A) (B) (C) (D) (E)
54. (A) (B) (C) (D) (E)

55. (A) (B) (C) (D) (E)
56. (A) (B) (C) (D) (E)
57. (A) (B) (C) (D) (E)
58. (A) (B) (C) (D) (E)
59. (A) (B) (C) (D) (E)
60. (A) (B) (C) (D) (E)
61. (A) (B) (C) (D) (E)
62. (A) (B) (C) (D) (E)
63. (A) (B) (C) (D) (E)
64. (A) (B) (C) (D) (E)
65. (A) (B) (C) (D) (E)
66. (A) (B) (C) (D) (E)
67. (A) (B) (C) (D) (E)
68. (A) (B) (C) (D) (E)
69. (A) (B) (C) (D) (E)
70. (A) (B) (C) (D) (E)
71. (A) (B) (C) (D) (E)
72. (A) (B) (C) (D) (E)
73. (A) (B) (C) (D) (E)
74. (A) (B) (C) (D) (E)
75. (A) (B) (C) (D) (E)
76. (A) (B) (C) (D) (E)
77. (A) (B) (C) (D) (E)
78. (A) (B) (C) (D) (E)
79. (A) (B) (C) (D) (E)
80. (A) (B) (C) (D) (E)

SAT II:
SUBJECT TEST IN
GERMAN
TEST III
ANSWER SHEET

1. (A) (B) (C) (D) (E)
2. (A) (B) (C) (D) (E)
3. (A) (B) (C) (D) (E)
4. (A) (B) (C) (D) (E)
5. (A) (B) (C) (D) (E)
6. (A) (B) (C) (D) (E)
7. (A) (B) (C) (D) (E)
8. (A) (B) (C) (D) (E)
9. (A) (B) (C) (D) (E)
10. (A) (B) (C) (D) (E)
11. (A) (B) (C) (D) (E)
12. (A) (B) (C) (D) (E)
13. (A) (B) (C) (D) (E)
14. (A) (B) (C) (D) (E)
15. (A) (B) (C) (D) (E)
16. (A) (B) (C) (D) (E)
17. (A) (B) (C) (D) (E)
18. (A) (B) (C) (D) (E)
19. (A) (B) (C) (D) (E)
20. (A) (B) (C) (D) (E)
21. (A) (B) (C) (D) (E)
22. (A) (B) (C) (D) (E)
23. (A) (B) (C) (D) (E)
24. (A) (B) (C) (D) (E)
25. (A) (B) (C) (D) (E)
26. (A) (B) (C) (D) (E)
27. (A) (B) (C) (D) (E)

28. (A) (B) (C) (D) (E)
29. (A) (B) (C) (D) (E)
30. (A) (B) (C) (D) (E)
31. (A) (B) (C) (D) (E)
32. (A) (B) (C) (D) (E)
33. (A) (B) (C) (D) (E)
34. (A) (B) (C) (D) (E)
35. (A) (B) (C) (D) (E)
36. (A) (B) (C) (D) (E)
37. (A) (B) (C) (D) (E)
38. (A) (B) (C) (D) (E)
39. (A) (B) (C) (D) (E)
40. (A) (B) (C) (D) (E)
41. (A) (B) (C) (D) (E)
42. (A) (B) (C) (D) (E)
43. (A) (B) (C) (D) (E)
44. (A) (B) (C) (D) (E)
45. (A) (B) (C) (D) (E)
46. (A) (B) (C) (D) (E)
47. (A) (B) (C) (D) (E)
48. (A) (B) (C) (D) (E)
49. (A) (B) (C) (D) (E)
50. (A) (B) (C) (D) (E)
51. (A) (B) (C) (D) (E)
52. (A) (B) (C) (D) (E)
53. (A) (B) (C) (D) (E)
54. (A) (B) (C) (D) (E)

55. (A) (B) (C) (D) (E)
56. (A) (B) (C) (D) (E)
57. (A) (B) (C) (D) (E)
58. (A) (B) (C) (D) (E)
59. (A) (B) (C) (D) (E)
60. (A) (B) (C) (D) (E)
61. (A) (B) (C) (D) (E)
62. (A) (B) (C) (D) (E)
63. (A) (B) (C) (D) (E)
64. (A) (B) (C) (D) (E)
65. (A) (B) (C) (D) (E)
66. (A) (B) (C) (D) (E)
67. (A) (B) (C) (D) (E)
68. (A) (B) (C) (D) (E)
69. (A) (B) (C) (D) (E)
70. (A) (B) (C) (D) (E)
71. (A) (B) (C) (D) (E)
72. (A) (B) (C) (D) (E)
73. (A) (B) (C) (D) (E)
74. (A) (B) (C) (D) (E)
75. (A) (B) (C) (D) (E)
76. (A) (B) (C) (D) (E)
77. (A) (B) (C) (D) (E)
78. (A) (B) (C) (D) (E)
79. (A) (B) (C) (D) (E)
80. (A) (B) (C) (D) (E)

SAT II:
SUBJECT TEST IN
GERMAN
TEST IV
ANSWER SHEET

1. Ⓐ Ⓑ Ⓒ Ⓓ Ⓔ
2. Ⓐ Ⓑ Ⓒ Ⓓ Ⓔ
3. Ⓐ Ⓑ Ⓒ Ⓓ Ⓔ
4. Ⓐ Ⓑ Ⓒ Ⓓ Ⓔ
5. Ⓐ Ⓑ Ⓒ Ⓓ Ⓔ
6. Ⓐ Ⓑ Ⓒ Ⓓ Ⓔ
7. Ⓐ Ⓑ Ⓒ Ⓓ Ⓔ
8. Ⓐ Ⓑ Ⓒ Ⓓ Ⓔ
9. Ⓐ Ⓑ Ⓒ Ⓓ Ⓔ
10. Ⓐ Ⓑ Ⓒ Ⓓ Ⓔ
11. Ⓐ Ⓑ Ⓒ Ⓓ Ⓔ
12. Ⓐ Ⓑ Ⓒ Ⓓ Ⓔ
13. Ⓐ Ⓑ Ⓒ Ⓓ Ⓔ
14. Ⓐ Ⓑ Ⓒ Ⓓ Ⓔ
15. Ⓐ Ⓑ Ⓒ Ⓓ Ⓔ
16. Ⓐ Ⓑ Ⓒ Ⓓ Ⓔ
17. Ⓐ Ⓑ Ⓒ Ⓓ Ⓔ
18. Ⓐ Ⓑ Ⓒ Ⓓ Ⓔ
19. Ⓐ Ⓑ Ⓒ Ⓓ Ⓔ
20. Ⓐ Ⓑ Ⓒ Ⓓ Ⓔ
21. Ⓐ Ⓑ Ⓒ Ⓓ Ⓔ
22. Ⓐ Ⓑ Ⓒ Ⓓ Ⓔ
23. Ⓐ Ⓑ Ⓒ Ⓓ Ⓔ
24. Ⓐ Ⓑ Ⓒ Ⓓ Ⓔ
25. Ⓐ Ⓑ Ⓒ Ⓓ Ⓔ
26. Ⓐ Ⓑ Ⓒ Ⓓ Ⓔ
27. Ⓐ Ⓑ Ⓒ Ⓓ Ⓔ

28. Ⓐ Ⓑ Ⓒ Ⓓ Ⓔ
29. Ⓐ Ⓑ Ⓒ Ⓓ Ⓔ
30. Ⓐ Ⓑ Ⓒ Ⓓ Ⓔ
31. Ⓐ Ⓑ Ⓒ Ⓓ Ⓔ
32. Ⓐ Ⓑ Ⓒ Ⓓ Ⓔ
33. Ⓐ Ⓑ Ⓒ Ⓓ Ⓔ
34. Ⓐ Ⓑ Ⓒ Ⓓ Ⓔ
35. Ⓐ Ⓑ Ⓒ Ⓓ Ⓔ
36. Ⓐ Ⓑ Ⓒ Ⓓ Ⓔ
37. Ⓐ Ⓑ Ⓒ Ⓓ Ⓔ
38. Ⓐ Ⓑ Ⓒ Ⓓ Ⓔ
39. Ⓐ Ⓑ Ⓒ Ⓓ Ⓔ
40. Ⓐ Ⓑ Ⓒ Ⓓ Ⓔ
41. Ⓐ Ⓑ Ⓒ Ⓓ Ⓔ
42. Ⓐ Ⓑ Ⓒ Ⓓ Ⓔ
43. Ⓐ Ⓑ Ⓒ Ⓓ Ⓔ
44. Ⓐ Ⓑ Ⓒ Ⓓ Ⓔ
45. Ⓐ Ⓑ Ⓒ Ⓓ Ⓔ
46. Ⓐ Ⓑ Ⓒ Ⓓ Ⓔ
47. Ⓐ Ⓑ Ⓒ Ⓓ Ⓔ
48. Ⓐ Ⓑ Ⓒ Ⓓ Ⓔ
49. Ⓐ Ⓑ Ⓒ Ⓓ Ⓔ
50. Ⓐ Ⓑ Ⓒ Ⓓ Ⓔ
51. Ⓐ Ⓑ Ⓒ Ⓓ Ⓔ
52. Ⓐ Ⓑ Ⓒ Ⓓ Ⓔ
53. Ⓐ Ⓑ Ⓒ Ⓓ Ⓔ
54. Ⓐ Ⓑ Ⓒ Ⓓ Ⓔ

55. Ⓐ Ⓑ Ⓒ Ⓓ Ⓔ
56. Ⓐ Ⓑ Ⓒ Ⓓ Ⓔ
57. Ⓐ Ⓑ Ⓒ Ⓓ Ⓔ
58. Ⓐ Ⓑ Ⓒ Ⓓ Ⓔ
59. Ⓐ Ⓑ Ⓒ Ⓓ Ⓔ
60. Ⓐ Ⓑ Ⓒ Ⓓ Ⓔ
61. Ⓐ Ⓑ Ⓒ Ⓓ Ⓔ
62. Ⓐ Ⓑ Ⓒ Ⓓ Ⓔ
63. Ⓐ Ⓑ Ⓒ Ⓓ Ⓔ
64. Ⓐ Ⓑ Ⓒ Ⓓ Ⓔ
65. Ⓐ Ⓑ Ⓒ Ⓓ Ⓔ
66. Ⓐ Ⓑ Ⓒ Ⓓ Ⓔ
67. Ⓐ Ⓑ Ⓒ Ⓓ Ⓔ
68. Ⓐ Ⓑ Ⓒ Ⓓ Ⓔ
69. Ⓐ Ⓑ Ⓒ Ⓓ Ⓔ
70. Ⓐ Ⓑ Ⓒ Ⓓ Ⓔ
71. Ⓐ Ⓑ Ⓒ Ⓓ Ⓔ
72. Ⓐ Ⓑ Ⓒ Ⓓ Ⓔ
73. Ⓐ Ⓑ Ⓒ Ⓓ Ⓔ
74. Ⓐ Ⓑ Ⓒ Ⓓ Ⓔ
75. Ⓐ Ⓑ Ⓒ Ⓓ Ⓔ
76. Ⓐ Ⓑ Ⓒ Ⓓ Ⓔ
77. Ⓐ Ⓑ Ⓒ Ⓓ Ⓔ
78. Ⓐ Ⓑ Ⓒ Ⓓ Ⓔ
79. Ⓐ Ⓑ Ⓒ Ⓓ Ⓔ
80. Ⓐ Ⓑ Ⓒ Ⓓ Ⓔ

SAT II:
SUBJECT TEST IN
GERMAN
TEST V
ANSWER SHEET

1. Ⓐ Ⓑ Ⓒ Ⓓ Ⓔ
2. Ⓐ Ⓑ Ⓒ Ⓓ Ⓔ
3. Ⓐ Ⓑ Ⓒ Ⓓ Ⓔ
4. Ⓐ Ⓑ Ⓒ Ⓓ Ⓔ
5. Ⓐ Ⓑ Ⓒ Ⓓ Ⓔ
6. Ⓐ Ⓑ Ⓒ Ⓓ Ⓔ
7. Ⓐ Ⓑ Ⓒ Ⓓ Ⓔ
8. Ⓐ Ⓑ Ⓒ Ⓓ Ⓔ
9. Ⓐ Ⓑ Ⓒ Ⓓ Ⓔ
10. Ⓐ Ⓑ Ⓒ Ⓓ Ⓔ
11. Ⓐ Ⓑ Ⓒ Ⓓ Ⓔ
12. Ⓐ Ⓑ Ⓒ Ⓓ Ⓔ
13. Ⓐ Ⓑ Ⓒ Ⓓ Ⓔ
14. Ⓐ Ⓑ Ⓒ Ⓓ Ⓔ
15. Ⓐ Ⓑ Ⓒ Ⓓ Ⓔ
16. Ⓐ Ⓑ Ⓒ Ⓓ Ⓔ
17. Ⓐ Ⓑ Ⓒ Ⓓ Ⓔ
18. Ⓐ Ⓑ Ⓒ Ⓓ Ⓔ
19. Ⓐ Ⓑ Ⓒ Ⓓ Ⓔ
20. Ⓐ Ⓑ Ⓒ Ⓓ Ⓔ
21. Ⓐ Ⓑ Ⓒ Ⓓ Ⓔ
22. Ⓐ Ⓑ Ⓒ Ⓓ Ⓔ
23. Ⓐ Ⓑ Ⓒ Ⓓ Ⓔ
24. Ⓐ Ⓑ Ⓒ Ⓓ Ⓔ
25. Ⓐ Ⓑ Ⓒ Ⓓ Ⓔ
26. Ⓐ Ⓑ Ⓒ Ⓓ Ⓔ
27. Ⓐ Ⓑ Ⓒ Ⓓ Ⓔ

28. Ⓐ Ⓑ Ⓒ Ⓓ Ⓔ
29. Ⓐ Ⓑ Ⓒ Ⓓ Ⓔ
30. Ⓐ Ⓑ Ⓒ Ⓓ Ⓔ
31. Ⓐ Ⓑ Ⓒ Ⓓ Ⓔ
32. Ⓐ Ⓑ Ⓒ Ⓓ Ⓔ
33. Ⓐ Ⓑ Ⓒ Ⓓ Ⓔ
34. Ⓐ Ⓑ Ⓒ Ⓓ Ⓔ
35. Ⓐ Ⓑ Ⓒ Ⓓ Ⓔ
36. Ⓐ Ⓑ Ⓒ Ⓓ Ⓔ
37. Ⓐ Ⓑ Ⓒ Ⓓ Ⓔ
38. Ⓐ Ⓑ Ⓒ Ⓓ Ⓔ
39. Ⓐ Ⓑ Ⓒ Ⓓ Ⓔ
40. Ⓐ Ⓑ Ⓒ Ⓓ Ⓔ
41. Ⓐ Ⓑ Ⓒ Ⓓ Ⓔ
42. Ⓐ Ⓑ Ⓒ Ⓓ Ⓔ
43. Ⓐ Ⓑ Ⓒ Ⓓ Ⓔ
44. Ⓐ Ⓑ Ⓒ Ⓓ Ⓔ
45. Ⓐ Ⓑ Ⓒ Ⓓ Ⓔ
46. Ⓐ Ⓑ Ⓒ Ⓓ Ⓔ
47. Ⓐ Ⓑ Ⓒ Ⓓ Ⓔ
48. Ⓐ Ⓑ Ⓒ Ⓓ Ⓔ
49. Ⓐ Ⓑ Ⓒ Ⓓ Ⓔ
50. Ⓐ Ⓑ Ⓒ Ⓓ Ⓔ
51. Ⓐ Ⓑ Ⓒ Ⓓ Ⓔ
52. Ⓐ Ⓑ Ⓒ Ⓓ Ⓔ
53. Ⓐ Ⓑ Ⓒ Ⓓ Ⓔ
54. Ⓐ Ⓑ Ⓒ Ⓓ Ⓔ

55. Ⓐ Ⓑ Ⓒ Ⓓ Ⓔ
56. Ⓐ Ⓑ Ⓒ Ⓓ Ⓔ
57. Ⓐ Ⓑ Ⓒ Ⓓ Ⓔ
58. Ⓐ Ⓑ Ⓒ Ⓓ Ⓔ
59. Ⓐ Ⓑ Ⓒ Ⓓ Ⓔ
60. Ⓐ Ⓑ Ⓒ Ⓓ Ⓔ
61. Ⓐ Ⓑ Ⓒ Ⓓ Ⓔ
62. Ⓐ Ⓑ Ⓒ Ⓓ Ⓔ
63. Ⓐ Ⓑ Ⓒ Ⓓ Ⓔ
64. Ⓐ Ⓑ Ⓒ Ⓓ Ⓔ
65. Ⓐ Ⓑ Ⓒ Ⓓ Ⓔ
66. Ⓐ Ⓑ Ⓒ Ⓓ Ⓔ
67. Ⓐ Ⓑ Ⓒ Ⓓ Ⓔ
68. Ⓐ Ⓑ Ⓒ Ⓓ Ⓔ
69. Ⓐ Ⓑ Ⓒ Ⓓ Ⓔ
70. Ⓐ Ⓑ Ⓒ Ⓓ Ⓔ
71. Ⓐ Ⓑ Ⓒ Ⓓ Ⓔ
72. Ⓐ Ⓑ Ⓒ Ⓓ Ⓔ
73. Ⓐ Ⓑ Ⓒ Ⓓ Ⓔ
74. Ⓐ Ⓑ Ⓒ Ⓓ Ⓔ
75. Ⓐ Ⓑ Ⓒ Ⓓ Ⓔ
76. Ⓐ Ⓑ Ⓒ Ⓓ Ⓔ
77. Ⓐ Ⓑ Ⓒ Ⓓ Ⓔ
78. Ⓐ Ⓑ Ⓒ Ⓓ Ⓔ
79. Ⓐ Ⓑ Ⓒ Ⓓ Ⓔ
80. Ⓐ Ⓑ Ⓒ Ⓓ Ⓔ

SAT II:
SUBJECT TEST IN

GERMAN
TEST VI
ANSWER SHEET

1. Ⓐ Ⓑ Ⓒ Ⓓ Ⓔ
2. Ⓐ Ⓑ Ⓒ Ⓓ Ⓔ
3. Ⓐ Ⓑ Ⓒ Ⓓ Ⓔ
4. Ⓐ Ⓑ Ⓒ Ⓓ Ⓔ
5. Ⓐ Ⓑ Ⓒ Ⓓ Ⓔ
6. Ⓐ Ⓑ Ⓒ Ⓓ Ⓔ
7. Ⓐ Ⓑ Ⓒ Ⓓ Ⓔ
8. Ⓐ Ⓑ Ⓒ Ⓓ Ⓔ
9. Ⓐ Ⓑ Ⓒ Ⓓ Ⓔ
10. Ⓐ Ⓑ Ⓒ Ⓓ Ⓔ
11. Ⓐ Ⓑ Ⓒ Ⓓ Ⓔ
12. Ⓐ Ⓑ Ⓒ Ⓓ Ⓔ
13. Ⓐ Ⓑ Ⓒ Ⓓ Ⓔ
14. Ⓐ Ⓑ Ⓒ Ⓓ Ⓔ
15. Ⓐ Ⓑ Ⓒ Ⓓ Ⓔ
16. Ⓐ Ⓑ Ⓒ Ⓓ Ⓔ
17. Ⓐ Ⓑ Ⓒ Ⓓ Ⓔ
18. Ⓐ Ⓑ Ⓒ Ⓓ Ⓔ
19. Ⓐ Ⓑ Ⓒ Ⓓ Ⓕ
20. Ⓐ Ⓑ Ⓒ Ⓓ Ⓔ
21. Ⓐ Ⓑ Ⓒ Ⓓ Ⓔ
22. Ⓐ Ⓑ Ⓒ Ⓓ Ⓔ
23. Ⓐ Ⓑ Ⓒ Ⓓ Ⓔ
24. Ⓐ Ⓑ Ⓒ Ⓓ Ⓔ
25. Ⓐ Ⓑ Ⓒ Ⓓ Ⓔ
26. Ⓐ Ⓑ Ⓒ Ⓓ Ⓔ
27. Ⓐ Ⓑ Ⓒ Ⓓ Ⓔ

28. Ⓐ Ⓑ Ⓒ Ⓓ Ⓔ
29. Ⓐ Ⓑ Ⓒ Ⓓ Ⓔ
30. Ⓐ Ⓑ Ⓒ Ⓓ Ⓔ
31. Ⓐ Ⓑ Ⓒ Ⓓ Ⓔ
32. Ⓐ Ⓑ Ⓒ Ⓓ Ⓔ
33. Ⓐ Ⓑ Ⓒ Ⓓ Ⓔ
34. Ⓐ Ⓑ Ⓒ Ⓓ Ⓔ
35. Ⓐ Ⓑ Ⓒ Ⓓ Ⓔ
36. Ⓐ Ⓑ Ⓒ Ⓓ Ⓔ
37. Ⓐ Ⓑ Ⓒ Ⓓ Ⓔ
38. Ⓐ Ⓑ Ⓒ Ⓓ Ⓔ
39. Ⓐ Ⓑ Ⓒ Ⓓ Ⓔ
40. Ⓐ Ⓑ Ⓒ Ⓓ Ⓔ
41. Ⓐ Ⓑ Ⓒ Ⓓ Ⓔ
42. Ⓐ Ⓑ Ⓒ Ⓓ Ⓔ
43. Ⓐ Ⓑ Ⓒ Ⓓ Ⓔ
44. Ⓐ Ⓑ Ⓒ Ⓓ Ⓔ
45. Ⓐ Ⓑ Ⓒ Ⓓ Ⓔ
46. Ⓐ Ⓑ Ⓒ Ⓓ Ⓔ
47. Ⓐ Ⓑ Ⓒ Ⓓ Ⓔ
48. Ⓐ Ⓑ Ⓒ Ⓓ Ⓔ
49. Ⓐ Ⓑ Ⓒ Ⓓ Ⓔ
50. Ⓐ Ⓑ Ⓒ Ⓓ Ⓔ
51. Ⓐ Ⓑ Ⓒ Ⓓ Ⓔ
52. Ⓐ Ⓑ Ⓒ Ⓓ Ⓔ
53. Ⓐ Ⓑ Ⓒ Ⓓ Ⓔ
54. Ⓐ Ⓑ Ⓒ Ⓓ Ⓔ

55. Ⓐ Ⓑ Ⓒ Ⓓ Ⓔ
56. Ⓐ Ⓑ Ⓒ Ⓓ Ⓔ
57. Ⓐ Ⓑ Ⓒ Ⓓ Ⓔ
58. Ⓐ Ⓑ Ⓒ Ⓓ Ⓔ
59. Ⓐ Ⓑ Ⓒ Ⓓ Ⓔ
60. Ⓐ Ⓑ Ⓒ Ⓓ Ⓔ
61. Ⓐ Ⓑ Ⓒ Ⓓ Ⓔ
62. Ⓐ Ⓑ Ⓒ Ⓓ Ⓔ
63. Ⓐ Ⓑ Ⓒ Ⓓ Ⓔ
64. Ⓐ Ⓑ Ⓒ Ⓓ Ⓔ
65. Ⓐ Ⓑ Ⓒ Ⓓ Ⓔ
66. Ⓐ Ⓑ Ⓒ Ⓓ Ⓔ
67. Ⓐ Ⓑ Ⓒ Ⓓ Ⓔ
68. Ⓐ Ⓑ Ⓒ Ⓓ Ⓔ
69. Ⓐ Ⓑ Ⓒ Ⓓ Ⓔ
70. Ⓐ Ⓑ Ⓒ Ⓓ Ⓔ
71. Ⓐ Ⓑ Ⓒ Ⓓ Ⓔ
72. Ⓐ Ⓑ Ⓒ Ⓓ Ⓔ
73. Ⓐ Ⓑ Ⓒ Ⓓ Ⓔ
74. Ⓐ Ⓑ Ⓒ Ⓓ Ⓔ
75. Ⓐ Ⓑ Ⓒ Ⓓ Ⓔ
76. Ⓐ Ⓑ Ⓒ Ⓓ Ⓔ
77. Ⓐ Ⓑ Ⓒ Ⓓ Ⓔ
78. Ⓐ Ⓑ Ⓒ Ⓓ Ⓔ
79. Ⓐ Ⓑ Ⓒ Ⓓ Ⓔ
80. Ⓐ Ⓑ Ⓒ Ⓓ Ⓔ

SAT II:
SUBJECT TEST IN
GERMAN

ANSWER SHEET

1. Ⓐ Ⓑ Ⓒ Ⓓ Ⓔ
2. Ⓐ Ⓑ Ⓒ Ⓓ Ⓔ
3. Ⓐ Ⓑ Ⓒ Ⓓ Ⓔ
4. Ⓐ Ⓑ Ⓒ Ⓓ Ⓔ
5. Ⓐ Ⓑ Ⓒ Ⓓ Ⓔ
6. Ⓐ Ⓑ Ⓒ Ⓓ Ⓔ
7. Ⓐ Ⓑ Ⓒ Ⓓ Ⓔ
8. Ⓐ Ⓑ Ⓒ Ⓓ Ⓔ
9. Ⓐ Ⓑ Ⓒ Ⓓ Ⓔ
10. Ⓐ Ⓑ Ⓒ Ⓓ Ⓔ
11. Ⓐ Ⓑ Ⓒ Ⓓ Ⓔ
12. Ⓐ Ⓑ Ⓒ Ⓓ Ⓔ
13. Ⓐ Ⓑ Ⓒ Ⓓ Ⓔ
14. Ⓐ Ⓑ Ⓒ Ⓓ Ⓔ
15. Ⓐ Ⓑ Ⓒ Ⓓ Ⓔ
16. Ⓐ Ⓑ Ⓒ Ⓓ Ⓔ
17. Ⓐ Ⓑ Ⓒ Ⓓ Ⓔ
18. Ⓐ Ⓑ Ⓒ Ⓓ Ⓔ
19. Ⓐ Ⓑ Ⓒ Ⓓ Ⓔ
20. Ⓐ Ⓑ Ⓒ Ⓓ Ⓔ
21. Ⓐ Ⓑ Ⓒ Ⓓ Ⓔ
22. Ⓐ Ⓑ Ⓒ Ⓓ Ⓔ
23. Ⓐ Ⓑ Ⓒ Ⓓ Ⓔ
24. Ⓐ Ⓑ Ⓒ Ⓓ Ⓔ
25. Ⓐ Ⓑ Ⓒ Ⓓ Ⓔ
26. Ⓐ Ⓑ Ⓒ Ⓓ Ⓔ
27. Ⓐ Ⓑ Ⓒ Ⓓ Ⓔ

28. Ⓐ Ⓑ Ⓒ Ⓓ Ⓔ
29. Ⓐ Ⓑ Ⓒ Ⓓ Ⓔ
30. Ⓐ Ⓑ Ⓒ Ⓓ Ⓔ
31. Ⓐ Ⓑ Ⓒ Ⓓ Ⓔ
32. Ⓐ Ⓑ Ⓒ Ⓓ Ⓔ
33. Ⓐ Ⓑ Ⓒ Ⓓ Ⓔ
34. Ⓐ Ⓑ Ⓒ Ⓓ Ⓔ
35. Ⓐ Ⓑ Ⓒ Ⓓ Ⓔ
36. Ⓐ Ⓑ Ⓒ Ⓓ Ⓔ
37. Ⓐ Ⓑ Ⓒ Ⓓ Ⓔ
38. Ⓐ Ⓑ Ⓒ Ⓓ Ⓔ
39. Ⓐ Ⓑ Ⓒ Ⓓ Ⓔ
40. Ⓐ Ⓑ Ⓒ Ⓓ Ⓔ
41. Ⓐ Ⓑ Ⓒ Ⓓ Ⓔ
42. Ⓐ Ⓑ Ⓒ Ⓓ Ⓔ
43. Ⓐ Ⓑ Ⓒ Ⓓ Ⓔ
44. Ⓐ Ⓑ Ⓒ Ⓓ Ⓔ
45. Ⓐ Ⓑ Ⓒ Ⓓ Ⓔ
46. Ⓐ Ⓑ Ⓒ Ⓓ Ⓔ
47. Ⓐ Ⓑ Ⓒ Ⓓ Ⓔ
48. Ⓐ Ⓑ Ⓒ Ⓓ Ⓔ
49. Ⓐ Ⓑ Ⓒ Ⓓ Ⓔ
50. Ⓐ Ⓑ Ⓒ Ⓓ Ⓔ
51. Ⓐ Ⓑ Ⓒ Ⓓ Ⓔ
52. Ⓐ Ⓑ Ⓒ Ⓓ Ⓔ
53. Ⓐ Ⓑ Ⓒ Ⓓ Ⓔ
54. Ⓐ Ⓑ Ⓒ Ⓓ Ⓔ

55. Ⓐ Ⓑ Ⓒ Ⓓ Ⓔ
56. Ⓐ Ⓑ Ⓒ Ⓓ Ⓔ
57. Ⓐ Ⓑ Ⓒ Ⓓ Ⓔ
58. Ⓐ Ⓑ Ⓒ Ⓓ Ⓔ
59. Ⓐ Ⓑ Ⓒ Ⓓ Ⓔ
60. Ⓐ Ⓑ Ⓒ Ⓓ Ⓔ
61. Ⓐ Ⓑ Ⓒ Ⓓ Ⓔ
62. Ⓐ Ⓑ Ⓒ Ⓓ Ⓔ
63. Ⓐ Ⓑ Ⓒ Ⓓ Ⓔ
64. Ⓐ Ⓑ Ⓒ Ⓓ Ⓔ
65. Ⓐ Ⓑ Ⓒ Ⓓ Ⓔ
66. Ⓐ Ⓑ Ⓒ Ⓓ Ⓔ
67. Ⓐ Ⓑ Ⓒ Ⓓ Ⓔ
68. Ⓐ Ⓑ Ⓒ Ⓓ Ⓔ
69. Ⓐ Ⓑ Ⓒ Ⓓ Ⓔ
70. Ⓐ Ⓑ Ⓒ Ⓓ Ⓔ
71. Ⓐ Ⓑ Ⓒ Ⓓ Ⓔ
72. Ⓐ Ⓑ Ⓒ Ⓓ Ⓔ
73. Ⓐ Ⓑ Ⓒ Ⓓ Ⓔ
74. Ⓐ Ⓑ Ⓒ Ⓓ Ⓔ
75. Ⓐ Ⓑ Ⓒ Ⓓ Ⓔ
76. Ⓐ Ⓑ Ⓒ Ⓓ Ⓔ
77. Ⓐ Ⓑ Ⓒ Ⓓ Ⓔ
78. Ⓐ Ⓑ Ⓒ Ⓓ Ⓔ
79. Ⓐ Ⓑ Ⓒ Ⓓ Ⓔ
80. Ⓐ Ⓑ Ⓒ Ⓓ Ⓔ

SAT II:
SUBJECT TEST IN
GERMAN

ANSWER SHEET

1. Ⓐ Ⓑ Ⓒ Ⓓ Ⓔ
2. Ⓐ Ⓑ Ⓒ Ⓓ Ⓔ
3. Ⓐ Ⓑ Ⓒ Ⓓ Ⓔ
4. Ⓐ Ⓑ Ⓒ Ⓓ Ⓔ
5. Ⓐ Ⓑ Ⓒ Ⓓ Ⓔ
6. Ⓐ Ⓑ Ⓒ Ⓓ Ⓔ
7. Ⓐ Ⓑ Ⓒ Ⓓ Ⓔ
8. Ⓐ Ⓑ Ⓒ Ⓓ Ⓔ
9. Ⓐ Ⓑ Ⓒ Ⓓ Ⓔ
10. Ⓐ Ⓑ Ⓒ Ⓓ Ⓔ
11. Ⓐ Ⓑ Ⓒ Ⓓ Ⓔ
12. Ⓐ Ⓑ Ⓒ Ⓓ Ⓔ
13. Ⓐ Ⓑ Ⓒ Ⓓ Ⓔ
14. Ⓐ Ⓑ Ⓒ Ⓓ Ⓔ
15. Ⓐ Ⓑ Ⓒ Ⓓ Ⓔ
16. Ⓐ Ⓑ Ⓒ Ⓓ Ⓔ
17. Ⓐ Ⓑ Ⓒ Ⓓ Ⓔ
18. Ⓐ Ⓑ Ⓒ Ⓓ Ⓔ
19. Ⓐ Ⓑ Ⓒ Ⓓ Ⓔ
20. Ⓐ Ⓑ Ⓒ Ⓓ Ⓔ
21. Ⓐ Ⓑ Ⓒ Ⓓ Ⓔ
22. Ⓐ Ⓑ Ⓒ Ⓓ Ⓔ
23. Ⓐ Ⓑ Ⓒ Ⓓ Ⓔ
24. Ⓐ Ⓑ Ⓒ Ⓓ Ⓔ
25. Ⓐ Ⓑ Ⓒ Ⓓ Ⓔ
26. Ⓐ Ⓑ Ⓒ Ⓓ Ⓔ
27. Ⓐ Ⓑ Ⓒ Ⓓ Ⓔ

28. Ⓐ Ⓑ Ⓒ Ⓓ Ⓔ
29. Ⓐ Ⓑ Ⓒ Ⓓ Ⓔ
30. Ⓐ Ⓑ Ⓒ Ⓓ Ⓔ
31. Ⓐ Ⓑ Ⓒ Ⓓ Ⓔ
32. Ⓐ Ⓑ Ⓒ Ⓓ Ⓔ
33. Ⓐ Ⓑ Ⓒ Ⓓ Ⓔ
34. Ⓐ Ⓑ Ⓒ Ⓓ Ⓔ
35. Ⓐ Ⓑ Ⓒ Ⓓ Ⓔ
36. Ⓐ Ⓑ Ⓒ Ⓓ Ⓔ
37. Ⓐ Ⓑ Ⓒ Ⓓ Ⓔ
38. Ⓐ Ⓑ Ⓒ Ⓓ Ⓔ
39. Ⓐ Ⓑ Ⓒ Ⓓ Ⓔ
40. Ⓐ Ⓑ Ⓒ Ⓓ Ⓔ
41. Ⓐ Ⓑ Ⓒ Ⓓ Ⓔ
42. Ⓐ Ⓑ Ⓒ Ⓓ Ⓔ
43. Ⓐ Ⓑ Ⓒ Ⓓ Ⓔ
44. Ⓐ Ⓑ Ⓒ Ⓓ Ⓔ
45. Ⓐ Ⓑ Ⓒ Ⓓ Ⓔ
46. Ⓐ Ⓑ Ⓒ Ⓓ Ⓔ
47. Ⓐ Ⓑ Ⓒ Ⓓ Ⓔ
48. Ⓐ Ⓑ Ⓒ Ⓓ Ⓔ
49. Ⓐ Ⓑ Ⓒ Ⓓ Ⓔ
50. Ⓐ Ⓑ Ⓒ Ⓓ Ⓔ
51. Ⓐ Ⓑ Ⓒ Ⓓ Ⓔ
52. Ⓐ Ⓑ Ⓒ Ⓓ Ⓔ
53. Ⓐ Ⓑ Ⓒ Ⓓ Ⓔ
54. Ⓐ Ⓑ Ⓒ Ⓓ Ⓔ

55. Ⓐ Ⓑ Ⓒ Ⓓ Ⓔ
56. Ⓐ Ⓑ Ⓒ Ⓓ Ⓔ
57. Ⓐ Ⓑ Ⓒ Ⓓ Ⓔ
58. Ⓐ Ⓑ Ⓒ Ⓓ Ⓔ
59. Ⓐ Ⓑ Ⓒ Ⓓ Ⓔ
60. Ⓐ Ⓑ Ⓒ Ⓓ Ⓔ
61. Ⓐ Ⓑ Ⓒ Ⓓ Ⓔ
62. Ⓐ Ⓑ Ⓒ Ⓓ Ⓔ
63. Ⓐ Ⓑ Ⓒ Ⓓ Ⓔ
64. Ⓐ Ⓑ Ⓒ Ⓓ Ⓔ
65. Ⓐ Ⓑ Ⓒ Ⓓ Ⓔ
66. Ⓐ Ⓑ Ⓒ Ⓓ Ⓔ
67. Ⓐ Ⓑ Ⓒ Ⓓ Ⓔ
68. Ⓐ Ⓑ Ⓒ Ⓓ Ⓔ
69. Ⓐ Ⓑ Ⓒ Ⓓ Ⓔ
70. Ⓐ Ⓑ Ⓒ Ⓓ Ⓔ
71. Ⓐ Ⓑ Ⓒ Ⓓ Ⓔ
72. Ⓐ Ⓑ Ⓒ Ⓓ Ⓔ
73. Ⓐ Ⓑ Ⓒ Ⓓ Ⓔ
74. Ⓐ Ⓑ Ⓒ Ⓓ Ⓔ
75. Ⓐ Ⓑ Ⓒ Ⓓ Ⓔ
76. Ⓐ Ⓑ Ⓒ Ⓓ Ⓔ
77. Ⓐ Ⓑ Ⓒ Ⓓ Ⓔ
78. Ⓐ Ⓑ Ⓒ Ⓓ Ⓔ
79. Ⓐ Ⓑ Ⓒ Ⓓ Ⓔ
80. Ⓐ Ⓑ Ⓒ Ⓓ Ⓔ

SAT II:
SUBJECT TEST IN
GERMAN

ANSWER SHEET

1. Ⓐ Ⓑ Ⓒ Ⓓ Ⓔ
2. Ⓐ Ⓑ Ⓒ Ⓓ Ⓔ
3. Ⓐ Ⓑ Ⓒ Ⓓ Ⓔ
4. Ⓐ Ⓑ Ⓒ Ⓓ Ⓔ
5. Ⓐ Ⓑ Ⓒ Ⓓ Ⓔ
6. Ⓐ Ⓑ Ⓒ Ⓓ Ⓔ
7. Ⓐ Ⓑ Ⓒ Ⓓ Ⓔ
8. Ⓐ Ⓑ Ⓒ Ⓓ Ⓔ
9. Ⓐ Ⓑ Ⓒ Ⓓ Ⓔ
10. Ⓐ Ⓑ Ⓒ Ⓓ Ⓔ
11. Ⓐ Ⓑ Ⓒ Ⓓ Ⓔ
12. Ⓐ Ⓑ Ⓒ Ⓓ Ⓔ
13. Ⓐ Ⓑ Ⓒ Ⓓ Ⓔ
14. Ⓐ Ⓑ Ⓒ Ⓓ Ⓔ
15. Ⓐ Ⓑ Ⓒ Ⓓ Ⓔ
16. Ⓐ Ⓑ Ⓒ Ⓓ Ⓔ
17. Ⓐ Ⓑ Ⓒ Ⓓ Ⓔ
18. Ⓐ Ⓑ Ⓒ Ⓓ Ⓔ
19. Ⓐ Ⓑ Ⓒ Ⓓ Ⓔ
20. Ⓐ Ⓑ Ⓒ Ⓓ Ⓔ
21. Ⓐ Ⓑ Ⓒ Ⓓ Ⓔ
22. Ⓐ Ⓑ Ⓒ Ⓓ Ⓔ
23. Ⓐ Ⓑ Ⓒ Ⓓ Ⓔ
24. Ⓐ Ⓑ Ⓒ Ⓓ Ⓔ
25. Ⓐ Ⓑ Ⓒ Ⓓ Ⓔ
26. Ⓐ Ⓑ Ⓒ Ⓓ Ⓔ
27. Ⓐ Ⓑ Ⓒ Ⓓ Ⓔ

28. Ⓐ Ⓑ Ⓒ Ⓓ Ⓔ
29. Ⓐ Ⓑ Ⓒ Ⓓ Ⓔ
30. Ⓐ Ⓑ Ⓒ Ⓓ Ⓔ
31. Ⓐ Ⓑ Ⓒ Ⓓ Ⓔ
32. Ⓐ Ⓑ Ⓒ Ⓓ Ⓔ
33. Ⓐ Ⓑ Ⓒ Ⓓ Ⓔ
34. Ⓐ Ⓑ Ⓒ Ⓓ Ⓔ
35. Ⓐ Ⓑ Ⓒ Ⓓ Ⓔ
36. Ⓐ Ⓑ Ⓒ Ⓓ Ⓔ
37. Ⓐ Ⓑ Ⓒ Ⓓ Ⓔ
38. Ⓐ Ⓑ Ⓒ Ⓓ Ⓔ
39. Ⓐ Ⓑ Ⓒ Ⓓ Ⓔ
40. Ⓐ Ⓑ Ⓒ Ⓓ Ⓔ
41. Ⓐ Ⓑ Ⓒ Ⓓ Ⓔ
42. Ⓐ Ⓑ Ⓒ Ⓓ Ⓔ
43. Ⓐ Ⓑ Ⓒ Ⓓ Ⓔ
44. Ⓐ Ⓑ Ⓒ Ⓓ Ⓔ
45. Ⓐ Ⓑ Ⓒ Ⓓ Ⓔ
46. Ⓐ Ⓑ Ⓒ Ⓓ Ⓔ
47. Ⓐ Ⓑ Ⓒ Ⓓ Ⓔ
48. Ⓐ Ⓑ Ⓒ Ⓓ Ⓔ
49. Ⓐ Ⓑ Ⓒ Ⓓ Ⓔ
50. Ⓐ Ⓑ Ⓒ Ⓓ Ⓔ
51. Ⓐ Ⓑ Ⓒ Ⓓ Ⓔ
52. Ⓐ Ⓑ Ⓒ Ⓓ Ⓔ
53. Ⓐ Ⓑ Ⓒ Ⓓ Ⓔ
54. Ⓐ Ⓑ Ⓒ Ⓓ Ⓔ

55. Ⓐ Ⓑ Ⓒ Ⓓ Ⓔ
56. Ⓐ Ⓑ Ⓒ Ⓓ Ⓔ
57. Ⓐ Ⓑ Ⓒ Ⓓ Ⓔ
58. Ⓐ Ⓑ Ⓒ Ⓓ Ⓔ
59. Ⓐ Ⓑ Ⓒ Ⓓ Ⓔ
60. Ⓐ Ⓑ Ⓒ Ⓓ Ⓔ
61. Ⓐ Ⓑ Ⓒ Ⓓ Ⓔ
62. Ⓐ Ⓑ Ⓒ Ⓓ Ⓔ
63. Ⓐ Ⓑ Ⓒ Ⓓ Ⓔ
64. Ⓐ Ⓑ Ⓒ Ⓓ Ⓔ
65. Ⓐ Ⓑ Ⓒ Ⓓ Ⓔ
66. Ⓐ Ⓑ Ⓒ Ⓓ Ⓔ
67. Ⓐ Ⓑ Ⓒ Ⓓ Ⓔ
68. Ⓐ Ⓑ Ⓒ Ⓓ Ⓔ
69. Ⓐ Ⓑ Ⓒ Ⓓ Ⓔ
70. Ⓐ Ⓑ Ⓒ Ⓓ Ⓔ
71. Ⓐ Ⓑ Ⓒ Ⓓ Ⓔ
72. Ⓐ Ⓑ Ⓒ Ⓓ Ⓔ
73. Ⓐ Ⓑ Ⓒ Ⓓ Ⓔ
74. Ⓐ Ⓑ Ⓒ Ⓓ Ⓔ
75. Ⓐ Ⓑ Ⓒ Ⓓ Ⓔ
76. Ⓐ Ⓑ Ⓒ Ⓓ Ⓔ
77. Ⓐ Ⓑ Ⓒ Ⓓ Ⓔ
78. Ⓐ Ⓑ Ⓒ Ⓓ Ⓔ
79. Ⓐ Ⓑ Ⓒ Ⓓ Ⓔ
80. Ⓐ Ⓑ Ⓒ Ⓓ Ⓔ

SAT II:
SUBJECT TEST IN
GERMAN

ANSWER SHEET

1. Ⓐ Ⓑ Ⓒ Ⓓ Ⓔ
2. Ⓐ Ⓑ Ⓒ Ⓓ Ⓔ
3. Ⓐ Ⓑ Ⓒ Ⓓ Ⓔ
4. Ⓐ Ⓑ Ⓒ Ⓓ Ⓔ
5. Ⓐ Ⓑ Ⓒ Ⓓ Ⓔ
6. Ⓐ Ⓑ Ⓒ Ⓓ Ⓔ
7. Ⓐ Ⓑ Ⓒ Ⓓ Ⓔ
8. Ⓐ Ⓑ Ⓒ Ⓓ Ⓔ
9. Ⓐ Ⓑ Ⓒ Ⓓ Ⓔ
10. Ⓐ Ⓑ Ⓒ Ⓓ Ⓔ
11. Ⓐ Ⓑ Ⓒ Ⓓ Ⓔ
12. Ⓐ Ⓑ Ⓒ Ⓓ Ⓔ
13. Ⓐ Ⓑ Ⓒ Ⓓ Ⓔ
14. Ⓐ Ⓑ Ⓒ Ⓓ Ⓔ
15. Ⓐ Ⓑ Ⓒ Ⓓ Ⓔ
16. Ⓐ Ⓑ Ⓒ Ⓓ Ⓔ
17. Ⓐ Ⓑ Ⓒ Ⓓ Ⓔ
18. Ⓐ Ⓑ Ⓒ Ⓓ Ⓔ
19. Ⓐ Ⓑ Ⓒ Ⓓ Ⓔ
20. Ⓐ Ⓑ Ⓒ Ⓓ Ⓔ
21. Ⓐ Ⓑ Ⓒ Ⓓ Ⓔ
22. Ⓐ Ⓑ Ⓒ Ⓓ Ⓔ
23. Ⓐ Ⓑ Ⓒ Ⓓ Ⓔ
24. Ⓐ Ⓑ Ⓒ Ⓓ Ⓔ
25. Ⓐ Ⓑ Ⓒ Ⓓ Ⓔ
26. Ⓐ Ⓑ Ⓒ Ⓓ Ⓔ
27. Ⓐ Ⓑ Ⓒ Ⓓ Ⓔ

28. Ⓐ Ⓑ Ⓒ Ⓓ Ⓔ
29. Ⓐ Ⓑ Ⓒ Ⓓ Ⓔ
30. Ⓐ Ⓑ Ⓒ Ⓓ Ⓔ
31. Ⓐ Ⓑ Ⓒ Ⓓ Ⓔ
32. Ⓐ Ⓑ Ⓒ Ⓓ Ⓔ
33. Ⓐ Ⓑ Ⓒ Ⓓ Ⓔ
34. Ⓐ Ⓑ Ⓒ Ⓓ Ⓔ
35. Ⓐ Ⓑ Ⓒ Ⓓ Ⓔ
36. Ⓐ Ⓑ Ⓒ Ⓓ Ⓔ
37. Ⓐ Ⓑ Ⓒ Ⓓ Ⓔ
38. Ⓐ Ⓑ Ⓒ Ⓓ Ⓔ
39. Ⓐ Ⓑ Ⓒ Ⓓ Ⓔ
40. Ⓐ Ⓑ Ⓒ Ⓓ Ⓔ
41. Ⓐ Ⓑ Ⓒ Ⓓ Ⓔ
42. Ⓐ Ⓑ Ⓒ Ⓓ Ⓔ
43. Ⓐ Ⓑ Ⓒ Ⓓ Ⓔ
44. Ⓐ Ⓑ Ⓒ Ⓓ Ⓔ
45. Ⓐ Ⓑ Ⓒ Ⓓ Ⓔ
46. Ⓐ Ⓑ Ⓒ Ⓓ Ⓔ
47. Ⓐ Ⓑ Ⓒ Ⓓ Ⓔ
48. Ⓐ Ⓑ Ⓒ Ⓓ Ⓔ
49. Ⓐ Ⓑ Ⓒ Ⓓ Ⓔ
50. Ⓐ Ⓑ Ⓒ Ⓓ Ⓔ
51. Ⓐ Ⓑ Ⓒ Ⓓ Ⓔ
52. Ⓐ Ⓑ Ⓒ Ⓓ Ⓔ
53. Ⓐ Ⓑ Ⓒ Ⓓ Ⓔ
54. Ⓐ Ⓑ Ⓒ Ⓓ Ⓔ

55. Ⓐ Ⓑ Ⓒ Ⓓ Ⓔ
56. Ⓐ Ⓑ Ⓒ Ⓓ Ⓔ
57. Ⓐ Ⓑ Ⓒ Ⓓ Ⓔ
58. Ⓐ Ⓑ Ⓒ Ⓓ Ⓔ
59. Ⓐ Ⓑ Ⓒ Ⓓ Ⓔ
60. Ⓐ Ⓑ Ⓒ Ⓓ Ⓔ
61. Ⓐ Ⓑ Ⓒ Ⓓ Ⓔ
62. Ⓐ Ⓑ Ⓒ Ⓓ Ⓔ
63. Ⓐ Ⓑ Ⓒ Ⓓ Ⓔ
64. Ⓐ Ⓑ Ⓒ Ⓓ Ⓔ
65. Ⓐ Ⓑ Ⓒ Ⓓ Ⓔ
66. Ⓐ Ⓑ Ⓒ Ⓓ Ⓔ
67. Ⓐ Ⓑ Ⓒ Ⓓ Ⓔ
68. Ⓐ Ⓑ Ⓒ Ⓓ Ⓔ
69. Ⓐ Ⓑ Ⓒ Ⓓ Ⓔ
70. Ⓐ Ⓑ Ⓒ Ⓓ Ⓔ
71. Ⓐ Ⓑ Ⓒ Ⓓ Ⓔ
72. Ⓐ Ⓑ Ⓒ Ⓓ Ⓔ
73. Ⓐ Ⓑ Ⓒ Ⓓ Ⓔ
74. Ⓐ Ⓑ Ⓒ Ⓓ Ⓔ
75. Ⓐ Ⓑ Ⓒ Ⓓ Ⓔ
76. Ⓐ Ⓑ Ⓒ Ⓓ Ⓔ
77. Ⓐ Ⓑ Ⓒ Ⓓ Ⓔ
78. Ⓐ Ⓑ Ⓒ Ⓓ Ⓔ
79. Ⓐ Ⓑ Ⓒ Ⓓ Ⓔ
80. Ⓐ Ⓑ Ⓒ Ⓓ Ⓔ

SAT II:
SUBJECT TEST IN
GERMAN

ANSWER SHEET

1. Ⓐ Ⓑ Ⓒ Ⓓ Ⓔ
2. Ⓐ Ⓑ Ⓒ Ⓓ Ⓔ
3. Ⓐ Ⓑ Ⓒ Ⓓ Ⓔ
4. Ⓐ Ⓑ Ⓒ Ⓓ Ⓔ
5. Ⓐ Ⓑ Ⓒ Ⓓ Ⓔ
6. Ⓐ Ⓑ Ⓒ Ⓓ Ⓔ
7. Ⓐ Ⓑ Ⓒ Ⓓ Ⓔ
8. Ⓐ Ⓑ Ⓒ Ⓓ Ⓔ
9. Ⓐ Ⓑ Ⓒ Ⓓ Ⓔ
10. Ⓐ Ⓑ Ⓒ Ⓓ Ⓔ
11. Ⓐ Ⓑ Ⓒ Ⓓ Ⓔ
12. Ⓐ Ⓑ Ⓒ Ⓓ Ⓔ
13. Ⓐ Ⓑ Ⓒ Ⓓ Ⓔ
14. Ⓐ Ⓑ Ⓒ Ⓓ Ⓔ
15. Ⓐ Ⓑ Ⓒ Ⓓ Ⓔ
16. Ⓐ Ⓑ Ⓒ Ⓓ Ⓔ
17. Ⓐ Ⓑ Ⓒ Ⓓ Ⓔ
18. Ⓐ Ⓑ Ⓒ Ⓓ Ⓔ
19. Ⓐ Ⓑ Ⓒ Ⓓ Ⓔ
20. Ⓐ Ⓑ Ⓒ Ⓓ Ⓔ
21. Ⓐ Ⓑ Ⓒ Ⓓ Ⓔ
22. Ⓐ Ⓑ Ⓒ Ⓓ Ⓔ
23. Ⓐ Ⓑ Ⓒ Ⓓ Ⓔ
24. Ⓐ Ⓑ Ⓒ Ⓓ Ⓔ
25. Ⓐ Ⓑ Ⓒ Ⓓ Ⓔ
26. Ⓐ Ⓑ Ⓒ Ⓓ Ⓔ
27. Ⓐ Ⓑ Ⓒ Ⓓ Ⓔ

28. Ⓐ Ⓑ Ⓒ Ⓓ Ⓔ
29. Ⓐ Ⓑ Ⓒ Ⓓ Ⓔ
30. Ⓐ Ⓑ Ⓒ Ⓓ Ⓔ
31. Ⓐ Ⓑ Ⓒ Ⓓ Ⓔ
32. Ⓐ Ⓑ Ⓒ Ⓓ Ⓔ
33. Ⓐ Ⓑ Ⓒ Ⓓ Ⓔ
34. Ⓐ Ⓑ Ⓒ Ⓓ Ⓔ
35. Ⓐ Ⓑ Ⓒ Ⓓ Ⓔ
36. Ⓐ Ⓑ Ⓒ Ⓓ Ⓔ
37. Ⓐ Ⓑ Ⓒ Ⓓ Ⓔ
38. Ⓐ Ⓑ Ⓒ Ⓓ Ⓔ
39. Ⓐ Ⓑ Ⓒ Ⓓ Ⓔ
40. Ⓐ Ⓑ Ⓒ Ⓓ Ⓔ
41. Ⓐ Ⓑ Ⓒ Ⓓ Ⓔ
42. Ⓐ Ⓑ Ⓒ Ⓓ Ⓔ
43. Ⓐ Ⓑ Ⓒ Ⓓ Ⓔ
44. Ⓐ Ⓑ Ⓒ Ⓓ Ⓔ
45. Ⓐ Ⓑ Ⓒ Ⓓ Ⓔ
46. Ⓐ Ⓑ Ⓒ Ⓓ Ⓔ
47. Ⓐ Ⓑ Ⓒ Ⓓ Ⓔ
48. Ⓐ Ⓑ Ⓒ Ⓓ Ⓔ
49. Ⓐ Ⓑ Ⓒ Ⓓ Ⓔ
50. Ⓐ Ⓑ Ⓒ Ⓓ Ⓔ
51. Ⓐ Ⓑ Ⓒ Ⓓ Ⓔ
52. Ⓐ Ⓑ Ⓒ Ⓓ Ⓔ
53. Ⓐ Ⓑ Ⓒ Ⓓ Ⓔ
54. Ⓐ Ⓑ Ⓒ Ⓓ Ⓔ

55. Ⓐ Ⓑ Ⓒ Ⓓ Ⓔ
56. Ⓐ Ⓑ Ⓒ Ⓓ Ⓔ
57. Ⓐ Ⓑ Ⓒ Ⓓ Ⓔ
58. Ⓐ Ⓑ Ⓒ Ⓓ Ⓔ
59. Ⓐ Ⓑ Ⓒ Ⓓ Ⓔ
60. Ⓐ Ⓑ Ⓒ Ⓓ Ⓔ
61. Ⓐ Ⓑ Ⓒ Ⓓ Ⓔ
62. Ⓐ Ⓑ Ⓒ Ⓓ Ⓔ
63. Ⓐ Ⓑ Ⓒ Ⓓ Ⓔ
64. Ⓐ Ⓑ Ⓒ Ⓓ Ⓔ
65. Ⓐ Ⓑ Ⓒ Ⓓ Ⓔ
66. Ⓐ Ⓑ Ⓒ Ⓓ Ⓔ
67. Ⓐ Ⓑ Ⓒ Ⓓ Ⓔ
68. Ⓐ Ⓑ Ⓒ Ⓓ Ⓔ
69. Ⓐ Ⓑ Ⓒ Ⓓ Ⓔ
70. Ⓐ Ⓑ Ⓒ Ⓓ Ⓔ
71. Ⓐ Ⓑ Ⓒ Ⓓ Ⓔ
72. Ⓐ Ⓑ Ⓒ Ⓓ Ⓔ
73. Ⓐ Ⓑ Ⓒ Ⓓ Ⓔ
74. Ⓐ Ⓑ Ⓒ Ⓓ Ⓔ
75. Ⓐ Ⓑ Ⓒ Ⓓ Ⓔ
76. Ⓐ Ⓑ Ⓒ Ⓓ Ⓔ
77. Ⓐ Ⓑ Ⓒ Ⓓ Ⓔ
78. Ⓐ Ⓑ Ⓒ Ⓓ Ⓔ
79. Ⓐ Ⓑ Ⓒ Ⓓ Ⓔ
80. Ⓐ Ⓑ Ⓒ Ⓓ Ⓔ

SAT II:
SUBJECT TEST IN
GERMAN

ANSWER SHEET

1. Ⓐ Ⓑ Ⓒ Ⓓ Ⓔ
2. Ⓐ Ⓑ Ⓒ Ⓓ Ⓔ
3. Ⓐ Ⓑ Ⓒ Ⓓ Ⓔ
4. Ⓐ Ⓑ Ⓒ Ⓓ Ⓔ
5. Ⓐ Ⓑ Ⓒ Ⓓ Ⓔ
6. Ⓐ Ⓑ Ⓒ Ⓓ Ⓔ
7. Ⓐ Ⓑ Ⓒ Ⓓ Ⓔ
8. Ⓐ Ⓑ Ⓒ Ⓓ Ⓔ
9. Ⓐ Ⓑ Ⓒ Ⓓ Ⓔ
10. Ⓐ Ⓑ Ⓒ Ⓓ Ⓔ
11. Ⓐ Ⓑ Ⓒ Ⓓ Ⓔ
12. Ⓐ Ⓑ Ⓒ Ⓓ Ⓔ
13. Ⓐ Ⓑ Ⓒ Ⓓ Ⓔ
14. Ⓐ Ⓑ Ⓒ Ⓓ Ⓔ
15. Ⓐ Ⓑ Ⓒ Ⓓ Ⓔ
16. Ⓐ Ⓑ Ⓒ Ⓓ Ⓔ
17. Ⓐ Ⓑ Ⓒ Ⓓ Ⓔ
18. Ⓐ Ⓑ Ⓒ Ⓓ Ⓔ
19. Ⓐ Ⓑ Ⓒ Ⓓ Ⓔ
20. Ⓐ Ⓑ Ⓒ Ⓓ Ⓔ
21. Ⓐ Ⓑ Ⓒ Ⓓ Ⓔ
22. Ⓐ Ⓑ Ⓒ Ⓓ Ⓔ
23. Ⓐ Ⓑ Ⓒ Ⓓ Ⓔ
24. Ⓐ Ⓑ Ⓒ Ⓓ Ⓔ
25. Ⓐ Ⓑ Ⓒ Ⓓ Ⓔ
26. Ⓐ Ⓑ Ⓒ Ⓓ Ⓔ
27. Ⓐ Ⓑ Ⓒ Ⓓ Ⓔ

28. Ⓐ Ⓑ Ⓒ Ⓓ Ⓔ
29. Ⓐ Ⓑ Ⓒ Ⓓ Ⓔ
30. Ⓐ Ⓑ Ⓒ Ⓓ Ⓔ
31. Ⓐ Ⓑ Ⓒ Ⓓ Ⓔ
32. Ⓐ Ⓑ Ⓒ Ⓓ Ⓔ
33. Ⓐ Ⓑ Ⓒ Ⓓ Ⓔ
34. Ⓐ Ⓑ Ⓒ Ⓓ Ⓔ
35. Ⓐ Ⓑ Ⓒ Ⓓ Ⓔ
36. Ⓐ Ⓑ Ⓒ Ⓓ Ⓔ
37. Ⓐ Ⓑ Ⓒ Ⓓ Ⓔ
38. Ⓐ Ⓑ Ⓒ Ⓓ Ⓔ
39. Ⓐ Ⓑ Ⓒ Ⓓ Ⓔ
40. Ⓐ Ⓑ Ⓒ Ⓓ Ⓔ
41. Ⓐ Ⓑ Ⓒ Ⓓ Ⓔ
42. Ⓐ Ⓑ Ⓒ Ⓓ Ⓔ
43. Ⓐ Ⓑ Ⓒ Ⓓ Ⓔ
44. Ⓐ Ⓑ Ⓒ Ⓓ Ⓔ
45. Ⓐ Ⓑ Ⓒ Ⓓ Ⓔ
46. Ⓐ Ⓑ Ⓒ Ⓓ Ⓔ
47. Ⓐ Ⓑ Ⓒ Ⓓ Ⓔ
48. Ⓐ Ⓑ Ⓒ Ⓓ Ⓔ
49. Ⓐ Ⓑ Ⓒ Ⓓ Ⓔ
50. Ⓐ Ⓑ Ⓒ Ⓓ Ⓔ
51. Ⓐ Ⓑ Ⓒ Ⓓ Ⓔ
52. Ⓐ Ⓑ Ⓒ Ⓓ Ⓔ
53. Ⓐ Ⓑ Ⓒ Ⓓ Ⓔ
54. Ⓐ Ⓑ Ⓒ Ⓓ Ⓔ

55. Ⓐ Ⓑ Ⓒ Ⓓ Ⓔ
56. Ⓐ Ⓑ Ⓒ Ⓓ Ⓔ
57. Ⓐ Ⓑ Ⓒ Ⓓ Ⓔ
58. Ⓐ Ⓑ Ⓒ Ⓓ Ⓔ
59. Ⓐ Ⓑ Ⓒ Ⓓ Ⓔ
60. Ⓐ Ⓑ Ⓒ Ⓓ Ⓔ
61. Ⓐ Ⓑ Ⓒ Ⓓ Ⓔ
62. Ⓐ Ⓑ Ⓒ Ⓓ Ⓔ
63. Ⓐ Ⓑ Ⓒ Ⓓ Ⓔ
64. Ⓐ Ⓑ Ⓒ Ⓓ Ⓔ
65. Ⓐ Ⓑ Ⓒ Ⓓ Ⓔ
66. Ⓐ Ⓑ Ⓒ Ⓓ Ⓔ
67. Ⓐ Ⓑ Ⓒ Ⓓ Ⓔ
68. Ⓐ Ⓑ Ⓒ Ⓓ Ⓔ
69. Ⓐ Ⓑ Ⓒ Ⓓ Ⓔ
70. Ⓐ Ⓑ Ⓒ Ⓓ Ⓔ
71. Ⓐ Ⓑ Ⓒ Ⓓ Ⓔ
72. Ⓐ Ⓑ Ⓒ Ⓓ Ⓔ
73. Ⓐ Ⓑ Ⓒ Ⓓ Ⓔ
74. Ⓐ Ⓑ Ⓒ Ⓓ Ⓔ
75. Ⓐ Ⓑ Ⓒ Ⓓ Ⓔ
76. Ⓐ Ⓑ Ⓒ Ⓓ Ⓔ
77. Ⓐ Ⓑ Ⓒ Ⓓ Ⓔ
78. Ⓐ Ⓑ Ⓒ Ⓓ Ⓔ
79. Ⓐ Ⓑ Ⓒ Ⓓ Ⓔ
80. Ⓐ Ⓑ Ⓒ Ⓓ Ⓔ

REA's Test Prep Books Are The Best!

(a sample of the <u>hundreds of letters</u> REA receives each year)

" I am writing to congratulate you on preparing an exceptional study guide. In five years of teaching this course I have never encountered a more thorough, comprehensive, concise and realistic preparation for this examination. "
Teacher, Davie, FL

" I have found your publications, *The Best Test Preparation...*, to be exactly that. "
Teacher, Aptos, CA

" I used your *CLEP Introductory Sociology* book and rank it 99% — thank you! "
Student, Jerusalem, Israel

" Your *GMAT* book greatly helped me on the test. Thank you. "
Student, Oxford, OH

" I recently got the *French SAT II* Exam book from REA. I congratulate you on first-rate French practice tests."
Instructor, Los Angeles, CA

" Your *AP English Literature and Composition* book is most impressive."
Student, Montgomery, AL

" The REA *LSAT* Test Preparation guide is a winner! "
Instructor, Spartanburg, SC

(more on front page)